THE *BHAGAVAD-GĪTĀ*

This volume is a systematic and comprehensive introduction to one of the most read texts in South Asia, the *Bhagavad-gītā*. The *Bhagavad-gītā* is at its core a religious text, a philosophical treatise and a literary work, which has occupied an authoritative position within Hinduism for the past millennium.

This book brings together themes central to the study of the Gītā, as it is popularly known – such as the *Bhagavad-gītā*'s structure, the history of its exegesis, its acceptance by different traditions within Hinduism and its national and global relevance. It highlights the richness of the Gītā's interpretations, examines its great interpretive flexibility and at the same time offers a conceptual structure based on a traditional commentarial tradition.

With contributions from major scholars across the world, this book will be indispensable for scholars and researchers of religious studies, especially Hinduism, Indian philosophy, Asian philosophy, Indian history, literature and South Asian studies.

Ithamar Theodor is an associate professor of Hindu studies at Zefat Academic College, Safed, Israel, and the director of the Hindu-Jewish studies programme at Bar-Ilan University, Israel. His publications include *Exploring the Bhagavad-gītā: Philosophy, Structure and Meaning* (2010), *The Fifth Veda in Hinduism: Philosophy, Poetry and Devotion in the Bhāgavata Purāṇa* (2016) and *Dharma and Halacha: Comparative Studies in Hindu-Jewish Philosophy and Religion* (2018).

THE *BHAGAVAD-GĪTĀ*

A Critical Introduction

Edited by Ithamar Theodor

Routledge
Taylor & Francis Group
LONDON AND NEW YORK

First published 2021
by Routledge
2 Park Square, Milton Park, Abingdon, Oxon OX14 4RN

and by Routledge
52 Vanderbilt Avenue, New York, NY 10017

Routledge is an imprint of the Taylor & Francis Group, an informa business

British Library Cataloguing-in-Publication Data
A catalogue record for this book is available from the British Library

Library of Congress Cataloging-in-Publication Data
A catalog record for this book has been requested

ISBN: 978-0-367-07692-4 (hbk)
ISBN: 978-0-367-55637-2 (pbk)
ISBN: 978-1-003-09445-6 (ebk)

Typeset in Times New Roman
by Apex CoVantage, LLC

In memory of
Joseph T. O'Connell and Mudumby N. Narasimhachary:
revered scholars and beloved teachers

CONTENTS

CONTRIBUTORS

Raj Balkaran is a scholar of Sanskrit narrative texts. His recent book, *The Goddess and The King in Indian Myth* (2019), provides an in-depth literary analysis of the myths of Durgā, demonstrating their significance for royal ideology. He teaches religion and mythology courses at the University of Toronto School of Continuing Studies and was Ryerson University's first ever religious studies professor. Alongside his academic training, he has privately studied the *Bhagavad-gītā* for over a decade as part of an oral Indian wisdom tradition.

Richard H. Davis is a professor in the Religion and Asian Studies Programs at Bard College, Annandale-on-Hudson, New York, USA. His most recent publication is *The Bhagavad-gītā: A Biography* (2014). He is the author of four books and has edited two volumes. He has also written the text for a catalogue of Indian religious prints, *Gods in Print: Masterpieces of India's Mythological Art* (2012). Currently, he is working on the reception history of the *Bhagavad-gītā* and on a history of religions in early South Asia.

J.E. Llewellyn is a professor in the Department of Religious Studies at Missouri State University in the United States. He is the author of two books about the Arya Samaj and is the editor of a third book about the problem of defining Hinduism. His recent research has been on Hindu devotionalism.

Joseph T. O'Connell was a professor emeritus of Hinduism at the University of Toronto, Canada. He served as the academic director at the Oxford Centre for Hindu Studies in 1999–2000 and since then was also a senior associate fellow of the centre. He was a visiting professor at the University of Dhaka, Bangladesh, where he was instrumental in the development of the Department of World Religions. He has done much for the study of Gaudiya Vaishnavism since his PhD in the 1950s on the social aspects of the Caitanya movement. He has published widely on the history of Vaiṣṇavism in Bengal and on the social and ethical issues in the tradition.

Carl Olson is a professor emeritus at Allegheny College, USA. He has published extensively on Hinduism, Buddhism, comparative philosophy and method and theory in the study of religion. His most recent books include *The Allure of Decadent Thinking: Religious Studies and the Challenge of Postmodernism* (2013) and *Indian Asceticism: Power, Violence, and Play* (2015). He held the national endowment for the humanities chair, 1991–1994; the teacher-scholar chair in the humanities, 2000–2003; and visiting fellowship at Clare Hall, University of Cambridge, UK, 2002.

James D. Ryan is a professor emeritus and distinguished adjunct faculty at the California Institute of Integral Studies, San Francisco, USA, where he was a professor of Sanskrit and Indian philosophy, 1986–2016. His publications include a full translation of the Tamil Jain epic: *Cīvakacintāmaṇi: The Hero Cīvakaṉ, the Gem that Fulfills All Wishes* by Tiruttakkatēvar (Verses 1-1165, 2005); *Cīvakacintāmaṇi* (Verses 1166-1888, 2011) and *Cīvakacintāmaṇi* (Verses 1889-3145, 2018).

Arvind Sharma is the Birks professor of comparative religion at McGill University, Canada. His works focus on comparative religion, Hinduism and the role of women in religion. He has published extensively in the area of Hindu studies and is an authority on the Bhagavad-gīta.

Ithamar Theodor is Associate Professor of Hindu studies at Zefat Academic College, Safed, Israel, a graduate of the Theology Faculty, University of Oxford, and a Life Member of Clare Hall, University of Cambridge. His publications include *Exploring the Bhagavad Gıta: Philosophy, Structure and Meaning* (2010), *Brahman and Dao: Comparative Studies in Indian and Chinese Philosophy and Religion* (2014), *The Fifth Veda in Hinduism: Philosophy, Poetry and Devotion in the Bhagavata Purana* (2016) and *Dharma and Halacha: Comparative Studies in Hindu and Jewish Philosophy and Religion* (2018).

Aleksandar Uskokov is a lector in South Asian Studies at Yale University, USA, where he teaches Sanskrit, Indian philosophy and Hinduism. He holds a PhD from the Department of South Asian Languages and Civilizations at the University of Chicago and has published Macedonian translations of select Upaniṣads, Kālidāsa's *Abhijñāna-Śākuntalam*, the *Nalopākhyāna* and the *Hitopadeśa*.

PREFACE

The *Bhagavad-gītā* is no doubt an extraordinary treatise and a Hindu, Indian, Asian and world classic. Its richness allows diverse interpretations and categorizations, and thus, it appeals to thinkers representing various points of view, at times even opposing, who substantiate their views and doctrines on that same text. Thus, the Gītā is deeply grounded in the six *darśanas* or orthodox schools of Indian philosophy, and at the same time, it appeals to the various world religions, echoing ideas similar to theirs.

The *Bhagavad-gītā* is one of the three foundations of the *Vedānta* school known as the *prasthāna-trayī*, and the liberation of the *ātman* from *saṁṣāra* is indeed a major topic with which the Gītā engages. It is also deeply grounded in the *mīmāṁsā* school in that its philosophy of action is grounded in Vedic sacrificial concepts such as the idea of the relation of action and its fruits. It is similarly grounded in the teachings of the *Yoga* school, and one of its main messages is that of devotional *yoga* or *bhakti-yoga*. It accepts *Sāṅkhya* metaphysics, and thus, the deconstruction of the universe into 24 elements activated by the three *guṇas* occupies a central place. It also echoes *Vaiśeṣika* in that it highlights the position of the five elements, i.e. earth, water, fire, air and ether as composing the world, and it echoes *Nyāya* in considering false knowledge to be a major source of suffering.

The *Bhagavad-gītā* is also compatible with world religions as it contains similar ideas and modes of religious experiences. It resembles the Jain idea of *anekāntavāda*, according to which reality is not objective but rather can be seen from different point of views, and similar Jain concepts of *jīva*, *karma* and *ahiṁsā*, or the soul, action and nonviolence. It expresses ideas similar to Buddhism in that it accepts the reality of the four noble truths, thus considering existence to represent suffering, the source of suffering being lust or desire, the existence of a liberated state without suffering and promoting a path based on a life of ethical and spiritual practice leading to the cessation of suffering. It is similar to Sikh tradition in that it accepts the transcendence of a monotheistic supreme God, the central position of the guru, and the practice of chanting divine names. The *Bhagavad-gītā* has also much in common with the three Abrahamic traditions and thus shares the idea of *dharma*, i.e. of a life based on duty with the Jewish tradition, which is based on the similar idea of the law or Halacha. It is similar to Christianity in that it holds that divinity has descended in a human form to deliver humanity and in that it was rejected by some and accepted by others. Also, the Christian idea of living a life of humility as a preparation for entering into the kingdom of God has its counterpart as a central idea in the *Gītā*. As far as Islam, the meaning of the word "Islam" itself is "submission" or "surrender", and surrender to the supreme is indeed one of the central teachings of the *Bhagavad-gītā*. The god of the Quran is a transcendent, powerful and all-merciful being; his transcendence ensures his uniqueness and infinitude over and against all other creatures, and the *Bhagavad-gītā* holds a similar view regarding the transcendence of the one single and supreme God. The *Bhagavad-gītā* also shares much with the Iranian religions; the Zoroastrian message is delivered in 17 Gathas or songs; this is close to the Sanskrit term '*Gītā*', which also represents the term "song", and indeed, a common translation of *Bhagavad-gītā* is "The Song of the Blessed Lord". Zoroastrianism is close to the *Gītā*'s *Vedism* in several ways; the word for sacrifice, *yaz*, is close to the *Vedic* word *yajña*, and the word for the heavenly elixir is *haoma* and is close to the Sanskrit *soma*

All in all, there are wide connections between the ancient Indian and Iranian worlds echoed in the *Gītā*. According to the Baha'i™ tradition, there is a unity of religion, according to which the founders of the great world religions are considered messengers of a monotheistic God, delivering the divine message according to time and place with the aim of re-establishing justice and morality. This is similar to the *Gītā*'s *avatāra* doctrine, according to which the supreme descends into this world time and again in various ages and forms, to re-establish *dharma*.

The *Bhagavad-gītā* also has similarities to Chinese religions: Confucianism furthers a notion of immanent spirituality that is deeply related to ethics; it furthers religious or spiritual humanism, and therefore, it identifies the moral or virtuous with the religious or transcendental. A central Confucian term refers to a person of virtue called *junzi,* a term that has been translated as "a person of virtue" or "a gentleman"; the *Gītā* maintains a similar concept of the ideal person who follows *dharma* out of duty and without regard to the fruits of action. In regard to Daoism, it seems that the words *yin* and *yang* are close in many ways to the *guṇa*s, a concept that plays a major role in the *Gītā*. *Yin* and *yang* are explanatory categories characterizing the relationships and interactions between immediate concrete and particular phenomena and things of the world; they describe the relationships that are constitutive of unique particulars and provide a vocabulary for capturing various subtleties, and in that way, they are quite similar to the *guṇas* as described in the *Bhagavad-gītā*.

This volume aspires to offer a critical introduction to the *Bhagavad-gītā*. It opens with the volume's editor's general survey of the *Gītā*'s contents, which looks into the various topics discussed in the *Gītā*, such as *dharma*, comprising and defining human society; *Mokṣa* and relinquishment of the world of birth and death altogether; the tension between *dharma* and *Mokṣa* and its reconciliation; the Vedic sacrifices and their humanistic worldview; the embodied soul, the problem of transmigration and the *yogic* view of existence; mental restraint as the focus of the various *Yoga* systems; human nature as comprised of the three *guṇas*; action and the principle of *karma*; the *Bhagavad-gītā*'s educational doctrine; the vision of the supreme; and, of course, *Bhakti*, or devotion.

After the introductory chapter comes the second chapter, by Ithamar Theodor, engaged with the *Bhagavad-gītā*'s structure. The discussion of the *Gītā*'s structure is perhaps the central thread of this volume and is grounded in at least two more chapters: Arvind Sharma's chapter "The *Bhagavad-gītā*; its philosophy and interpretation" and Joseph T. O'Connell's chapter "*Karma* in the *Bhagavad-gītā*: *Caitanya Vaiṣṇava* views". All three chapters have a common thread, and this is the ladder approach to the interpretation of the *Bhagavad-gītā*. In this regard, Arvind Sharma writes,

> According to the ladder approach, although the *Gītā* initially approves of several approaches, it ultimately settles for only one – whether it be a matter of theory or practice. The natural conclusion which the ladder approach points to is that either the *Gītā* itself ultimately espouses only one philosophy, and only one *Yoga*, or as a whole the *Gītā* itself constitutes the only way. *(Chapter 3)*

Joseph T. O'Connell does not engage directly with idea of the ladder; however, his chapter offers a thorough study of Viśvanātha Cakravartin's commentary on the *Bhagavad-gītā*, based on which Theodor articulates and develops the idea of considering the *Bhagavad-gītā*'s structure to be ladder-like, leading from *karma-yoga* to *bhakti*, or from *dharma* to *mokṣa*. Theodor adds another component to the ladder: the idea of considering the *Gītā* in terms of three layers or tiers. The outcome of the combination of these two elements, i.e. the ladder and the three tiers, is the model of the "three-storey house" offered as a metaphor with which the structure of the *Bhagavad-gītā* could be simplified.

In the third chapter, Arvind Sharma first focuses on the exegesis of the *Bhagavad-gītā* in the Hindu tradition, showing that it was understood as both a philosophical text and a religious text. He shows the richness of the commentarial tradition since it was first commented on by Śaṅkara, although he mentions that Śaṅkara refers to previous commentators. Sharma mentions various famous commentaries by Bhāskara, Rāmānuja, Madhva, Keśavakāśmīrin, Abhinavagupta and Viśvanātha Cakravartin. However, the *Bhagavad-gītā* was considered to be not just a philosophical text in the tradition but also a religious classic as well and as such served as a source text for devotional movements. In its role as a source text of the devotional movements, it has played a particularly significant role in the rise of the *Varkari* movement in Maharashtra, through its rendering into Marathi by Jñāneśvara and in the devotional movement in Orissa through its translation into Oriya by Achyutānanda Dās and Jasovanta Dās. Similarly, it was translated into Telugu by Annamācārya and is cited by Gopāldās, a Dādūpanthī from Rajasthan. Sharma points that during the period from the 14th to the 17th century, which was marked by Hindu–Muslim interaction, a large number of Sanskrit works were translated into Persian by Muslim scholars. Thus, 'Abdur Rahman Chishti syncretized Hindu theories of cosmogony and offered an Islamizing explanation of the *Bhagavad-gītā*. Dārā Shukoh translated, apparently with the help of pandits, *Bhagavad-gītā* under the misleading title of "Battle between Arjuna and Duryodhan"; the fact that he should choose to translate the *Gītā* seems to attest to its influence and popularity.

Sharma raises the question whether the *Bhagavad-gītā* has a philosophy and an interpretation of its own. He points at how two presuppositions begin to mediate our understanding of the *Bhagavad-gītā* imperceptibly the moment it enters the exegetical circle of *Vedānta*: first, the *Bhagavad-gītā* possesses a *single* correct philosophical interpretation in keeping with the implication of *Brahma-sūtra* 1.1.4. and, second, this correct philosophical interpretation accords with that of the particular school of *Vedānta* involved, be it *Advaita, Viśiṣṭādvaita, Dvaita, Śuddhādvaita, Dvaitādvaita, Acintya-bhedābheda* or something else. Apparently, various commentators have put as many interpretations on the book, and there has not been a commentator of the *Gītā* who did not put forward a pet theory of their own and has not tried to support the same by showing that the *Bhagavad-gītā* lent them support. Sharma concludes his chapter by stating that although the *Bhagavad-gītā* has been largely studied with the hope to arrive at its one correct meaning or determine its one correct interpretation, the *Gītā*'s own approach to itself seems to indicate that it might be studied to raise our awareness of its interpretive possibilities, consistently with its belief that reality is multilayered and the approaches to it multisided.

In the fourth chapter, Carl Olson looks into Śaṅkara's *Bhagavad-gītā*'s commentary and asserts that because of the profoundly theistic nature of the *Gītā*, Śaṅkara's hermeneutical convictions and metaphysical certainties motivate him to deconstruct the theistic features of the *Gītā* by adhering to his beliefs about the role of revelation, his method of sublation and his philosophical preunderstanding. By using these instruments to deconstruct the text, Śaṅkara also reconstructs the *Gītā* into a document that more accurately reflects his philosophy. Olson argues that since, according to Śaṅkara, the revealed nature of the *Upaniṣads* embodies the absolute truth, the correct interpretation of a text such as the *Bhagavad-gītā* must be made to reflect the revealed and preordained truth in the *Upaniṣads*, as suggested by his philosophical preunderstanding – *Advaita Vedānta*. A reader of Śaṅkara's commentary on the *Bhagavad-gītā* will notice that he not only brings his non-dual philosophy with him to his task but also often cites texts from the *Upaniṣads* and *dharma* literature, such as the *Manusmṛti*, to support his interpretation of a passage. With his overall approach in mind, it is possible to grasp how Śaṅkara interprets the *Gītā*, by examining his metaphysical stance, aspects of his epistemology and his understanding of the proper path to liberation. Accordingly, it becomes evident that Śaṅkara's interpretive commentary of the *Gītā* is not concerned with determining the authorship of the text or its sociohistorical context, because he is more concerned with religio-philosophical truth. For Śaṅkara, the *Gītā* represents the essence of the meaning of the *Veda*s. Since the word *Vedānta* means the end of the *Veda*s in the sense of their completion as embodied by the *Upaniṣads*, it appears reasonable also to conclude that the *Bhagavad-gītā* is included in the literature that represents the completion of the *Veda*s.

In the fifth chapter, Aleksandar Uskokov looks into the *Bhagavad-gītā* of the *Śrīvaiṣṇava* tradition. Rāmānuja, like his predecessor Yāmuna, had a dual agenda: establishing the respectability of *Śrīvaiṣṇava* doctrine in the wider *brāhmaṇical* world and incorporating major *Āḻvār* themes in normative *Vedāntic* discourse. While his *Vedāntic* works were more about the first task, he accomplished the second in the *Bhagavad-gītā* (*Bhg*) commentary. Uskokov focuses on Yāmuna's *Gītārtha-saṅgraha*, on Rāmānuja's *Bhagavad-gītā-bhāṣya* and on Vedāntadeśika's *Gītārtha-saṅgraha-rakṣā* and *Tātparya-candrikā*. Yāmuna's thesis is that the *Bhg* is all about Nārāyaṇa, the supreme *Brahman*, who can be attained solely by devotion, *bhakti*; accordingly, devotion must be brought about by the performance of duties, knowledge and dispassion. According to Rāmānuja and Deśika, chapters two through five should bring one to the level of knowing oneself as *Brahman*, or rather the knowing of the self as identical with *Brahman in kind* within the corresponding vision of sameness; consequently, a meditation on the self as described in the *Gītā*'s sixth chapter can begin. The practice of meditation on oneself as *Brahman* in kind, on the other hand, brings one to the direct experience of the nature of the self, perfect *jñāna*, and only then is one ready to engage in *bhakti*, or meditation on the Lord. Uskokov devotes special attention to the *Śrīvaiṣṇava* commentaries of the Ultimate Verse (*carama-śloka*, *Bhg* 18.66); in this way, the renunciation of the sense of personal agency and the consideration of the Lord as the agent and the object of worship are discussed. He also discusses the idea of *prapatti* as an independent soteriological practice and the idea that post-Rāmānuja doctrine was the centre of major disagreements that split the *Śrīvaiṣṇava* tradition into *Tĕṉkalai* and *Vaṭakalai*, or Southern and Northern brands.

In the sixth chapter, Joseph T. O'Connell addresses the relations between the *Caitanya Vaiṣṇava* tradition and the *Bhagavad-gītā*. The question of the scope of religious piety has also been raised by Bankimcandra Chatterji, who in his novel Ānandamaṭh raises the question whether Caitanya *Vaiṣṇavas* are indeed committed to follow *dharma*. In this way, the following question is raised by Mahendra: "How can the children be *Vaiṣṇavas*? For *Vaiṣṇavas* non-violence is the highest code of practice". In reply, Satyānanda says,

> Yes, for the *Vaiṣṇavas* who follow Lord Caitanya . . . the mark of authentic Vaiṣṇava practice is subduing the evildoer and rescuing the world. For is it not Viṣṇu himself the protector of our world! On no fewer than ten occasions did He take on a body to rescue the earth!
>
> *(Lipner 2005, 179)*

The topic is raised in the *Gītā* itself: "But for one who is delighted in the self alone, and is thus self-satisfied and self-content indeed, for him – no *dharmic* duty exists" (*Bhg* 3.17, my translation). Apparently, the devotional tradition has been somewhat unclear as to its commitment to *dharma*, which in this chapter O'Connell refers to as *Karma*. He points out that it is a bit surprising to find that not until the end of the 17th century, more than a century and a half after the passing away of Caitanya, did any *Caitanya Vaiṣṇava* produce a commentary on the *Gītā* that is extant today.

O'Connell confines his attention to two influential theologians, who may be presumed to represent mainline *Caitanya Vaiṣṇava* views: Kṛṣṇadāsa Kavirāja and Viśvanātha Cakravartin. Referring to the latter, he concludes that what Viśvanātha does say about work seems to exclude two extreme positions: *varṇāśrma-dharma* is wrong in itself and must be opposed, and *varṇāśrma-dharma* is necessary to the ultimate religious quest, devotion to Kṛṣṇa. Between these extremes seems to be an open field for situationally appropriate resolutions of the tension between devotion to Kṛṣṇa and everything else in the world. Consequently, his commentary aspires to reconcile these two seemingly opposing positions.

In the seventh chapter, Richard H. Davis looks into the topic of the *Gītā-māhātmyas*. In general, the *māhātmya* is a common genre of medieval literature concerned with the exaltation of the greatness of a particular place, ritual or implement charged with religious power. Most often the *māhātmya* centres on a *tīrtha* or holy pilgrimage place, but in some special cases, a verbal text can also be the subject of a *māhātmaya*. The best known of the *māhātmyas* that was focused on texts, evidently, was the *Bhāgavata-māhātmya*, exalting the greatness of the *Bhāgavata Purāṇa*. So too with the *Gītā-māhātmyas*, which are texts glorifying and exalting the *Bhagavad-gītā* itself. These are often considered to have been spoken by gods or seers or may even be an integral part of the *Gītā*. Davis discusses the term "verbal icon" as a self-standing unit or repository of meaning. Adopted from the Greek *eikōn*, the word "icon" denotes a physical representation or symbolic object that partakes in some way in the sacred reality it represents. As the physical location for the actual presence of a god, it is necessary therefore to treat the enlivened icon with veneration or worship. The recited words of the *Gītā*, Viṣṇu proclaims, can serve as just such a physical icon.

Davis shows that in the *Bhagavad-gītā*, Kṛṣṇa promises his teachings will be efficacious for future readers and listeners: "One who promulgates this ultimate secret to my devotees," he says, "shows the highest devotion to me and will undoubtedly come to me" (*Bhg* 18.68). The dissemination of Kṛṣṇa's teachings in the *Gītā* is a form of *bhakti* and a way of reinforcing the mutual relationship between devotee and God: "Among all humanity, no one shows greater love to me than such a person, and no one on earth shall be dearer to me" (*Bhg* 18.69). Benefits are not confined to those who transmit the dialogue; those who recite it to themselves and those who simply listen to it also share in them.

In the eighth chapter, James D. Ryan looks into the *Bhagavad-gītā* and the Indian nationalist movement, specifically the interpretations of Tilak, Gandhi and Aurobindo. He emphasizes how important of a text it is for India and thus surveys various translations and commentaries made by Hindus and Muslims alike. Ryan emphasizes that no religious text has been as frequently invoked or as passionately deployed by the Indian nationalists as the *Bhagavad-gītā*. In a certain sense, *mokṣa*, the release from the cycle of birth and rebirth, took on a dual meaning, implying that "release" from the British was as much a spiritual as it was a political project. Ryan considers the most influential term in the nationalists' reinterpretation of the *Gītā* to be *lokasaṅgraha*, "holding or keeping the world together". Tilak insisted that the "duty", or *dharma*, of maintaining the world was not just for an enlightened elite but rather for all. Moreover, he believed that the *Gītā* was not merely charting individual, liberatory goals but also offering guidance towards the public and the universal. Aurobindo disagreed with his fellow nationalist interpreters of the *Gītā* on the meaning of the crucial word *lokasaṅgraha*; he was adamant that this "maintaining of the world" is not to be understood in purely modern terms as a call to social humanitarian motives, principals and ideals; rather, he believed that one should extract the living truth that it contains, and he insisted on a more integral reading of it. He saw that the text could guide to a "new age of development" in which humanity would look to its "perfection and highest spiritual welfare". Aurobindo, from the beginning, saw the three *yogas* of the *Gītā*, *jñāna* and *bhakti* and the *karma yogas* as being a map to the development of "integral" being. *Jñāna yoga* was to be developed to refine the cognitive aspect of being, *bhakti* was needed to divinize, as it were, the emotional aspect of being, and *karma yoga* was there to develop the more physical aspects of being to, in the end, produce the integral person, who, in their apotheosis, would be fully divine. Mohandas Karamchand Gandhi particularly opposed interpretations of the *Gītā*, like those of Tilak and Aurobindo, that sought to justify violence in the name of politics. He believed that the spiritual and *yogic* elements of *Gītā* were paramount, and thus, for him, justifying warfare by appeal to the text was a serious misreading. Gandhi understood that the *Gītā*'s central message of non-attachment (*anāsakti*) would naturally culminate in *ahiṃsā* and truth. Accordingly, developing a notion of nonviolence from the *Gītā* is not farfetched under the understanding that the *Gītā* leads to a perfection of *yoga* with a constant reference to God.

Not only did the national leaders extract various and at times even opposing meanings out of the *Bhagavad-gītā*, but also the spiritual leaders, the gurus, also read the *Gītā* in different ways. The ninth chapter, by J.E. Llewellyn, engages with the interpretations of five prominent gurus. Maharishi Mahesh Yogi was the founder of the transcendental meditation (TM) movement; he taught TM to a Western audience and sought to strip away those aspects that US-Americans felt uncomfortable with. He promised that the individual could experience absolute being in cosmic consciousness without all the Indian or Hindu cultural aspects; consequently, he formulated his interpretation of the *Gītā* according to four levels of consciousness: the waking state, transcendental consciousness, cosmic consciousness and God consciousness.

A.C. Bhaktivedanta Swami Prabhupada was a devotee of Kṛṣṇa in the *Gauḍīya Vaiṣṇava* tradition founded by Kṛṣṇa Caitanya in the 16th century, and he founded the International Society of Kṛṣṇa Consciousness. His approach was different from other Indian teachers in the United States; his followers practised an altogether Indian way of life, rising by 4:30 in the morning, wearing flowing saffron robes and adhering to a diet of vegetarian food ritually offered first to Kṛṣṇa. His English translation and commentary are named *The Bhagavad-gītā As It Is*, and the distinctive emphasis in his commentary on the *Gītā* is devotion to Kṛṣṇa as "the Supreme Personality of Godhead". Swami Chinmayananda, founder of the Chinmaya Mission, called his public lectures *Jñāna Yajñas*, literally "knowledge sacrifices". His religious teaching was based on *Advaita Vedānta*, although he presented himself as non-sectarian and claimed to speak for all Hindus. In *The Holy Geeta*, Chinmayananda says, "for self-development, each type of seeker, according to the vehicle available, chooses either the path-of-Devotion or the path-of-Action or the path-of-Knowledge". Swami Rama founded the Himalayan International Institute of Yoga Science and Philosophy in the United States and began sharing his teachings on *yoga* and *tantra* with his contemporary Western audience. Among the many books that Swami Rama wrote, *Perennial Psychology of the Bhagavad-gītā* combines his South Asian roots with his modern aspirations and desire to make *yoga* accessible to all. He offered advice to modern psychologists and aspiring students of yoga while critiquing the methods of contemporary gurus. Anandamurti Gurumaa was initiated as a renouncer and developed a reputation as a religious teacher, not only in India but also in the Indian diaspora, especially in the US and the UK. Her teaching is distinct in three ways. First is her pluralism and her syncretic identity, drawing on various religious sources in her teaching. Second is her commitment to gender activism, which includes not only speaking out strongly against sexism but also founding a nongovernmental organization, called Shakti, to provide financial support for girls' education. And, finally, there is her embrace of new media.

The tenth and final chapter, by Raj Balkaran, looks into the various epithets in the *Bhagavad-gītā*. Following Bhargava, he divides Kṛṣṇa's epithets into three categories: first, his patronymics, i.e. Mādhava (descendent of Madhu), Vārṣṇeya (descendent of Vṛṣṇi) and Vāsudeva (descendent of Vasudeva); second, epithets invoking his martial prowess, i.e. Keśiṇisūdana (slayer of Keśin), Janārdarna (destroyer of evil people) and Madhusūdana (slayer of Madhu); and, third, epithets referring to his "moral qualities," i.e. Hṛṣīkeśa (controller of the senses) and Acyuta (one not deviating from righteousness or not yielding to passions). Balkaran argues that the symbolism of the epithet Acyuta is most elegant: not only is Kṛṣṇa unfallen in a spiritual sense (in being undisturbed, permanently unshaken and unshakable, indeed imperishable), but he also reveals his imperishable nature in order to compel Arjuna to become physically unfallen, commanding him throughout to stand and fight. The dilemma that frames the *Gītā* consist of an Arjuna who upon standing erect and summoning the onset of war by blowing his conch alongside his brethren falls hopelessly into despair, sinking into his chariot. Only his unfallen charioteer, Acyuta, can succeed in inspiring him to stand up and fight and, in short, to return to his own upstanding, unfallen state. In summary, looking into the various epithets applied by Kṛṣṇa, one can see why he calls Arjuna to return to his original nature in a spiritual sense: for the protection of *dharma* and the welfare of the world.

Bibliography

Lipner, Julius. 2005. *Ānandamaṭh or the Sacred Brotherhood.* New York: Oxford University Press.

ACKNOWLEDGEMENTS

I acknowledge and thank all the individuals and institutions that have helped, encouraged and supported the publication of this volume. My gratitude goes to Aakash Chakrabarty and the Routledge editorial team for supporting and bringing this project to fruition. I am thankful to Daniella Gurevitch and the Hindu-Jewish Studies Division at the Dangoor Center, Bar-Ilan University, who supported this publication in many ways. I am grateful to Ella Teltsch for all her editorial work and similarly to Alexander Cherniack for his Sanskrit editing. I am especially grateful and indebted to Darshan and Kalpa Bhagat for their many years of friendship and constant support, for supporting the Hindu-Jewish Studies Program at Bar-Ilan University and for their enthusiasm in furthering *Bhagavad-gītā* studies. My profound thanks go to the scholars who contributed their research to this volume with great diligence and to my family, who is a constant source of inspiration. Finally, I acknowledge the inspiration I received years ago from two distinguished scholars who among many other things were my mentors at the Oxford Centre for Hindu Studies: Prof. Joseph T. O'Connell (1940–2012) and Prof. Mudumby N. Narasimhachary (1939–2013). It is to them that this book is dedicated.

Ithamar Theodor
Zefat Academic College, Safed
26 December 2019

PRONUNCIATION GUIDE

For readers unfamiliar with the subtleties of the Sanskrit alphabet and the commonly accepted transliteration system, a brief guide is offered, roughly exemplifying the pronunciation of the main transliterated characters:

ā, ī: *gītā* – geetaa
ū: sūtra – sootra
ai, ś: *vaiśya* – vayshya
au, ī: Draupadī – Drowpadee
ṣ, ṭ, ā: aṣṭāṅga – ashtaanga
ṇ, ḍ: *pāṇḍava* – paandava
ṛ, ṣ, ṇ: Kṛṣṇa – Krishna
c, ā: Cekitāna – Chekitaana
jñ: *jñāna* – gyaana
ṇ: *Karṇa* – Karna
ś: Aśvins – Ashvins
ṁ: *ahaṁkāra* – ahankaara (the *ṁ* may be in most cases translated into *n* but before *p*, *ph*, *b* and *bh* into *m*)

1

THE *BHAGAVAD-GĪTĀ* AND ITS CONTENTS

Ithamar Theodor

The *Bhagavad-gītā* is a literary and theological treatise and a foremost world classic; it has occupied both an authoritative position and a popular position in Hinduism for the past 1000 years or so. Due to its major influence, it is sometimes called the Hindu Bible or even the Indian Bible; moreover, innumerable people worldwide are able to quote it – whether in their mother language or in the original Sanskrit – as an expression of their faith or worldview. The treatise itself appears as part of the *Mahābhārata*,[1] the great Indian epic, and comprises a dialogue conducted between two of its heroes – the warrior Arjuna and his cousin, charioteer and friend Kṛṣṇa. Although the dialogue is rather short and does not exceed 700 verses, it is engaged with subject matters of the highest theological and philosophical order; thus, it concerns everyone who faces human existence, namely each and every human being. The epical circumstances are rather dramatic; due to a long family strife, all the world's armies gather at the battlefield of *Kurukṣetra*, some supporting one family branch, the *Pāṇḍavas*, or the sons of Pāṇḍu, and the others supporting the Kauravas, or the sons of Dhṛtarāṣṭra. Arjuna foresees the massacre about to take place and is reluctant to direct his weapons toward his family members, friends and teachers; he desires to relinquish the war altogether and avoid fighting in these terrible circumstances. Out of his deep distress, Arjuna turns to his friend Kṛṣṇa and asks for directions that may rescue him from this severe crisis. Answering Arjuna, Kṛṣṇa speaks the *Bhagavad-gītā*, that might be translated somewhat roughly as the 'Song of God', or perhaps more precisely as the 'Supreme Person's Sacred Poetical Treatise'. It is likely that the *Bhagavad-gītā* was composed around the 4th–2nd century BCE and thus belongs roughly to the same period as that of the great Greek philosophers Plato and Aristotle. From a religious point of view, the *Bhagavad-gītā* is a *Vaiṣṇava* text, because it considers Viṣṇu or Kṛṣṇa to be the supreme lord, whereas from the philosophical point of view, the *Bhagavad-gītā* comprises one of the triple foundations of the *Vedānta* tradition,[2] along with the *Brahmasūtras* and the *Upaniṣads*. From the cultural and social point of view, the *Bhagavad-gītā* represents orthodox and mainstream Hinduism, in that it accepts the authority of the *Veda* and accepts the socio-religious order of four social groups called *Varṇāśrama*, which is at the heart of *dharma*.

Dharma as comprising and defining human society

The word *dharma* is central to Indian thought and may be translated as religion, duty, morality, justice, law and order. *Dharma* is not only external to the human being, but rather, it is perceived as comprising the essence or nature of everything. It aspires to place everything – not only the human being but the whole of phenomena – in its proper place. Thus, for example, the *dharma* of the teacher is to teach, and the *dharma* of the sun is to shine. *Dharma* aspires to establish human society on a solid moral foundation, and in this way, it defines the human being through two parameters: the personal and professional statuses. The personal status is defined through one's relation to family life, and it is composed by dividing human life into four stages. Accordingly, one spends one's childhood and youth as a celibate student, a *brahmacārī*, practicing austerity and discipline while living devoid of possessions under the direction of the *guru*. Along with the character building that one undergoes, one studies the spiritual traditions and develops awareness of the highest truth, named *Brahman*. Having concluded his training period, one enters the stage of married life, called *gṛhastha*, and fulfils the four aims of life: one follows *dharma* and contributes to the maintenance of the social order; one accumulates wealth; one satisfies one's desires; and one eventually turns one's attention toward *mokṣa*, the ideal of liberation from the cycle of birth and death. Once one's children have grown up, one gradually returns to the more renounced mode of life practiced during youth and enters into the *vānaprastha* stage along with one's spouse. Gradually, the couple becomes detached from family, social, economic and political matters and turns their attention toward more-spiritual subject matters. At the last stage of one's life, one becomes a *sannyāsī* and renounces the world altogether, both internally and externally. In this stage, one meets death, and being enlightened and detached, one is able to get freed from the vicious cycle of rebirth.

The second parameter defining the human being is the professional one; here *dharma* defines four occupational groups that cover the entire range of occupations supporting a proper human society. The first group is that of the *brāhmaṇas*, who, according to the ancient *Vedic* metaphor, comprise the head of the social body. This is the intellectual class, comprised of teachers, priests, philosophers and intellectuals, and they are characterized by qualities such as tranquillity, self-restraint, austerity, purity, tolerance, honesty, knowledge, wisdom and religious piety. They guide and advise human society, and they do this from a distant position, without assuming political or governmental authority. The second group is that of the *kṣatriyas*, who, according to the *Vedic* metaphor, comprise the arms of the social body. This is the ruling class comprising kings, nobles, generals and administrators, and they are characterized by heroism, ardor, determination, expertise, fighting spirit, generosity and leadership. The third group is that of the *vaiṣyas*, or the agriculture and mercantile class; they comprise the hips of the social body and support society through establishing a firm economic foundation that is based on agriculture and trade. The fourth group, the *śūdras*, comprise the legs or feet of the social body, and this is the working and serving class, which includes artisans. The system itself is considered to be of a divine origin and, moreover, not be artificially enforced on human society but rather to spring from natural categories and human nature. Kṛṣṇa says that 'the four social classes were created by me according to the divisions of the *guṇas*[3] and modes of work'.[4] *Dharma* is upheld through adhering to one's duties, and the *Bhagavad-gītā* supports this principle, by advising or requesting each and every one to adhere to their duty. On this, it says, 'Better to be deficient in following one's own *dharmic* duty than to perform another's duty well; even death while performing one's own duty is better, for following another's duty invites danger'.[5] Apparently, this idea of the four *varṇas*, or classes, is philosophical rather than empirical.[6]

Mokṣa – the call for relinquishing the world of birth and death altogether

The ideal moral world that is aimed at by *dharma* is doomed to confront human reality, which is naturally less ideal, because human existence, which is full of weaknesses and faults, is somewhat different from the ideal *dharmic* world, which is somewhat utopian. This gap occupies a major part of the *Mahābhārata*, where, on the one hand, a description of people who were able to adhere to *dharma* despite various obstacles is given and, on the other hand, various human weaknesses that prevent one from adherence to duty are delineated. This more pessimistic view of the world leads to the understanding that human existence is ultimately doomed to suffering and that the only real solution to this problem is the relinquishment of the world altogether. This call, characterizing the *Upaniṣadic* literature and the *Vedāntin* tradition, calls on the human being to undergo a process of self-correction or self-realization and altogether relinquish the vicious cycle of birth and death called *saṁsāra*. Accordingly, this world, which is temporary and transient, is never to be considered one's highest goal, as it is of lesser value than the principle or person from whom the world has emanated. Accordingly, the *Bhagavad-gītā* states,

> Having come to me, these great souls do not again undergo rebirth into that transient abode of misery, as they have attained the highest perfection. All the worlds, up to Brahmā's world, are subject to repeated births, but having once reached me, there is no further rebirth.[7]

This well exemplifies the *Upaniṣadic* idea according to which one should relinquish this world in favor of a higher, imperishable perfect and eternal state, which is the state of liberation, or *mokṣa*.

The tension between *Dharma* and *Mokṣa* and its reconciliation

Whereas *dharma* aspires for the moral upliftment of the world and the establishment of a proper and prosperous human society, the *Upaniṣadic* ideal is entirely different and even contradictory, in that it calls for a total relinquishment of this world, along with the helpless transmigration from one body to another that characterizes it. Moreover, the *Upaniṣadic* tradition calls one to transcend *dharma*, to go beyond morality and the quest for social order, in favor of a state of introspection and a constant thrust toward self-realization and liberation from the cycle of birth and death. The *Bhagavad-gītā* states that 'for one who is delighted in the self alone and is thus self-satisfied and self-content indeed, for him – no *dharmic* duty exists'.[8] It seems that the *Upaniṣadic* tradition is not that concerned with morality and social order; rather, it is concerned mainly with the relinquishment of this world and with self-realization. The idea that one who is established in the path of liberation is free from *dharmic* and moral obligations is rather extreme and no doubt exemplifies the deep gap between these two systems of thought.

The *Dharma* and *Upaniṣadic* traditions are opposed to each other on yet another cardinal question: the question of action versus knowledge. The *dharma* tradition carries a notable performative flavor, which may have its origins traced back to the ancient *Vedic Mīmāṁsā* school, whereas the *Upaniṣadic* tradition is different in that it emphasizes knowledge over action. *Dharma* aspires to organize the world through action: the *brāhmaṇa* teaches and sacrifices; the *kṣatriya* rules and protects; the *vaiṣya* farms and trades; and the *śūdra* works manually. The *Upaniṣadic* tradition aspires to reach the understanding or knowing of the essence of all things, which is ultimately spiritual. Moreover, it encourages the renunciation of action and of worldly involvement in favor of the attainment of real knowledge and enlightenment. Arjuna asks for clear direction on which path is to be followed: the path of action and adherence to duty or the path of renunciation of duty in favor of enlightenment. He asks,

> O Janārdana, if you consider enlightenment to be better than action, why then do you enjoin me to perform this terrible act? Your equivocal like words confuse my mind; I beg you, make me certain of one thing, by which I may attain the best.[9]

The *Bhagavad-gītā* occupies a unique place in the history of Indian literature and thought in that it reconciles this deep tension and gap. On the one hand, the *Bhagavad-gītā* adheres to *dharma* by enjoining the following of one's duty in accordance with the *varṇāśrama* system, thereby supporting the moral and social order. At the same time, it supports the *Upaniṣadic* ideal of renouncing the world altogether in favor of self-realization and the attainment of liberation, but propounds the unique and groundbreaking idea of an internal relinquishment rather than an external one. In other words, as opposed to an external relinquishment, where ones leaves home and social responsibility in favor of becoming a wandering mendicant or a forest dweller, the *Bhagavad-gītā* furthers an internal relinquishment, by which one adheres to *dharma* but makes an internal progress along the path of renunciation, by gradually learning to renounce the fruits of action and then devote them to the supreme. This interesting reconciliation of the two otherwise-contradictory ideals offers a system that intertwines social responsibility and action in the world, with a deep sense of spirituality and relinquishment of worldly attachments. A famous verse propounding this internal renunciation says, 'Your sole entitlement is to perform *dharmic* activity, not ever to possess its fruits; never shall the fruit of action motivate your deed, and never cleave to inaction'.[10]

The *Vedic* sacrifices and their humanistic worldview

Vedic ritualistic sacrifices were common in ancient India; some sacrifices were domestic, whereas others were public; some were simple, whereas others were sophisticated and expensive. Underlying all the various sacrifices was a deep faith in the perfection of the *Veda* and the conviction that sacrifice is the way for the attainment of prosperity, both in this life and the next.

A major purpose or fruit to be achieved by the performance of the *Vedic* sacrifice was the attainment of heaven. It is not entirely clear where exactly heaven is situated; it may be taken geographically, as a particular higher planet, but also as a higher state of existence. It is apparent, however, that heavenly life was considered to be a more pleasurable existential state and that normally one would aspire to achieve this state in the next life. Heaven's opposite was considered to exist too, and that is hell; whether this refers to a geographical place, apparently located at the bottom of the universe, or whether this refers to a lower state of existence, it is apparent that according to *Vedic* thought, hellish life is a state of suffering and should be avoided.

The *Vedas* are considered eternal and perfect – hence the somewhat problematic position of the *Vedic* sacrifices and rituals. On the one hand, some claim that as the *Vedas* are of a divine origin: it is one's sacred duty to perform *Vedic* sacrifice and attain prosperity, both in this life and the next. On the other hand, others, who further the path of liberation, agree that the *Vedas* are of a divine origin but consider the ultimate goal to be the renunciation of worldly pleasures and prosperity in favor of liberation. Consequently, they consider worldly prosperity a blessing that should be accepted moderately but certainly not as the ultimate goal; accordingly, worldly prosperity should be considered as a healthy condition of a society that is gradually progressing toward liberation.

Given the foregoing points, it seems that the *Vedic* worldview represents a humanistic worldview; it is optimistic in that it aspires for healthy, moral, proper and prosperous human life. In this way, it aspires to avoid that which is immoral and unjust and further that which is healthy and righteous. It is humanistic in that it perceives reality in complete and unbroken terms centered on the human being;

its worldview is constructed by the human being, the family, society and, above all, *dharma*, which constantly thrives to uplift human society.

The embodied soul, the problem of transmigration and *yogic* view of existence

The main problem characterizing this world, and even the next or the heavenly world, is the constant repetition of birth and death. The constant change, the inherent instability, the caging of an otherwise free spiritual soul in a body destined to die and the constant struggle with the senses and their unsatiated desires all make the worldly and embodied state undesirable. Moreover, seen from the *Bhagavad-gītā*'s *yogic* point of view, even the state of heavenly life, which can be attained through the performance of *Vedic* sacrifices, is flawed by this vicious cycle of birth and death. In other words, having spent prolonged periods of time in the enjoyable heavenly state, one falls down again into the lower worlds and into lower states of existence. This vision naturally leads to an attempt to get free from this embodied state, by taking to the process of self-realization, which includes a different set of categories. Progressing along the path of self-realization, one begins to think of oneself in different terms; instead of considering oneself to be a human being, one starts thinking of oneself as an eternal spiritual soul, rather different from the gross and subtle coverings, i.e. the body and the mind, which cover and encage: 'As childhood, youth and old age befall the soul within this body, so it comes to acquire another body; the wise is not swayed by illusion in this matter'.[11]

This point of view is what we may call '*yogic*' or 'spiritualistic'; from this point of view, one sees one's body and mind as external, considers one's deep entanglement with matter to be circumstantial, nonessential and an obstacle on the path of liberation, and in this state, one tries not only to severe one's deep relations with matter and mind but also to get hold of the spiritual reality of *Brahman*, in either its personal form or its impersonal form. This worldview or the vision of the soul, does not really aim at constructing a prosperous and moral human society; rather, it furthers the relinquishment of this world altogether. It is not really humanistic, because the term 'human being' does not play a significant role in it; rather the term 'spiritual soul' seems to construct the individual identities in this view, and thus, it may be considered 'spiritualistic'. The fundamental individual element is the spiritual soul, covered by various bodies that are not necessarily human; these may be bodies of plants, trees, reptiles, fish, animals, humans, gods or something else. This worldview, which is based on the vision of spiritual souls encaged in gross and subtle bodies, has an ethical implication too; as it envisions souls encaged in bodies, it naturally furthers the release of those embodied souls. Thus, it furthers a different set of values: instead of furthering human prosperity, it propounds equanimity toward both the good and the bad, toward both happiness and distress, toward both prosperity and poverty and toward both the moral and the immoral. This equanimity serves as a foundation based on which one can look beyond this world and search after the spiritual reality, which is utterly different and is designated as eternal, conscious and blissful.

There are two components characterizing the *yogic* point of view: on the one hand the attempt to release oneself from the embodied state and on the other hand the attempt to establish or yoke oneself within the supreme, absolute and spiritual reality. These two principles, i.e. attempting to detach oneself from this world and attempting to yoke oneself to a higher state or reality, underlie the various *yoga* systems.

Mental restraint as the focus of the various *yoga* systems

The various *yoga* systems all aspire to transfer the practitioner from the state of worldly existence into the enlightened and liberated state. The practice focuses on the mind (in Sanskrit, *manas*), which in the unrestrained state binds the soul to embodiment and in the restrained and transparent state leads the soul to liberation. The mind unites the physical body, the senses and the soul and is considered to have an immense capability of leading the soul toward enlightenment. However, being unrestrained, disturbed and obscure due to its close relation with the senses and the various worldly desires aroused by them, it fails to realize its potential. The *yoga* systems, therefore, aspire to restrain and clean the mind, just like one cleans a mirror or a lens for the purpose of seeing clearly. In its obscure state, the mind is disturbed by the working of nature represented by the three *guṇas* such as agitation aroused by attraction, repulsion aroused by sense objects, misconceptions of the self and various memories and the urge of self-perseverance and the fear of death. A clear consciousness may be compared to a clear and peaceful lake, which is transparent, and as such, its bottom may be viewed, whereas an obscure consciousness may be compared to a stormy lake of muddy water, which is naturally opaque, and as such, its bottom remains imperceptible. The two core principles of the *yoga* system are practice and detachment; while practice aims at the gradual restraint of the turbulent mind, detachment aims at disconnecting the mind from the various sense objects to which it is attached. The sixth chapter engages with this topic and advises the practitioner of *yoga* that

> Casting aside all desires arising from worldly intentions, he should subdue completely the combined senses through the mind. Little by little should he bring his mind to rest, while firmly controlling his consciousness; he should fix his mind on the self, contemplating nothing else. From whatever and wherever the flickering and unsteady mind wanders, it is to be restrained and led back into the control of the self.[12]

The *yoga* system is not merely theoretical, but rather, it furthers a psycho-physical practice. The classical text *Yogasūtra*, traditionally attributed to Patañjali (2nd–3rd century CE), articulates an eight-stage ladder-like structure that in a sense serves as an archetype for the various *yoga* systems; the eight stages commence with practices that may be considered ethical and that may culminate with the stage of *samādhi*, a liberated state of *enstasy*, or enlightenment. The first stage is called *yama* or restraint, and it includes the practice of nonviolence, adherence to truthfulness, not stealing, *brahmacarya* (which includes sexual abstinence) and non-accumulation. The second stage is *niyama*, and it comprises cleanliness or purity, satisfaction, austerity, self-study and scriptural study and devotion to the supreme. The third stage, *āsana* includes an elaborate practice of bodily postures, and this is followed by *prāṇāyāma*, the stage of breath control. Following that one practices *pratyāhāra* or the withdrawal of the senses from their objects, and this is followed by *dhāraṇā* or concentration in which one strives to maintain this sense of withdrawal over an extended period of time. The seventh stage is that of *dhyāna* and its essence is meditation on the supreme, while the peak of the system is the eighth stage called *samādhi*, in which the yogi enters a state of an introspective enlightenment beyond worldly existence. This state is described in the sixth chapter of the *Bhagavad-gītā*:

> When the consciousness rests peacefully, restrained by practice of *yoga*, then can the self see itself directly, and be thus satisfied within itself. At that time he knows infinite bliss, experienced by an internal consciousness beyond the senses; firmly established, he deviates not from the truth. Having attained this, he holds no other acquisition greater, and thus situated, even grievous misery does not shake him. Let it be known that dissolution of the deep union with misery is called *yoga*, and it should be practiced with whole-hearted determination.[13]

Human nature as composed of the three *guṇas*

The theory underlying the *Yoga* and *Sāṅkhya* schools considers nature to consist of three qualities or strands, called *guṇas*; the three qualities are named *sattva*, representing goodness and transparency; *rajas*, representing passion and desire; and *tamas*, representing ignorance, indolence and darkness. The three *guṇas* comprise human nature, and they bind the soul to mind and matter, or to the subtle and gross bodies. As opposed to the soul, which remains steady and unchanging, the *guṇas* constantly interact with each other and unite in various combinations; consequently, sometimes goodness prevails, sometimes passion and sometimes darkness. Because the *guṇas* are so dominant and govern every aspect of life, this world is sometimes called the world of the *guṇas*. Because the three *guṇas* comprise human nature, they are reflected through each and every thought, word or deed. So the way one thinks, speaks and acts reflects the combination of the conditioning *guṇas*. This concept offers a unique division of human and even nonhuman existence that groups together various aspects of life, such as various psychological components, activity and adherence to duty, social grouping, eating habits and cosmological divisions. The *guṇa* of goodness is characterized by knowledge and happiness and by adherence to duty for the sake of duty; it represents the intellectual social group, or the *brāhmaṇas*; is associated with fresh vegetarian food; and cosmologically leads to the higher planets. The *guṇa* of passion is characterized by desire and attachment and by adherence to duty for the sake of its fruits or for some ulterior gain; when mixed with a larger amount of goodness, it represents the ruling class, and when mixed with a somewhat lesser amount of goodness, it represents the mercantile and farming class. It is associated with vegetarian food that agitates the senses, such as spicy or salty food, and cosmologically, it leads to the middle planets. The *guṇa* of ignorance is characterized by darkness, indolence and madness, and it involves the negligence of duty; it is more dominant among the productive social class; it is associated with non-vegetarian food and intoxicating drinks, and cosmologically, it leads to the lower planets.

The *guṇas* may also be thought of as universal paths on which the soul travels during its journey through *saṁsāra*. The path of goodness seems at first to be somewhat pale, but as one adheres to it, one gradually begins to experience happiness, stability and illumination. The path of passion is contrary in that it seems attractive and exciting at first, but as one adheres to it, one begins to experience distress and exhaustion. The lowest path, that of darkness, represents the lowest human condition; it is characterized by indolence, foolishness and even madness, and it leads to self-destruction. Despite the possibility of rationalizing these three paths, it may be rather difficult for the embodied to escape the influence or even bondage of the particular *guṇas* binding them. For the *Bhagavad-gītā*, the idea of the *guṇas* is fundamental, and elaborate discussions on the nature of the *guṇas* take place, especially in chapters 14, 17 and 18. The *Bhagavad-gītā* suggests a gradual elevation, by which one raises oneself from a lower *guṇa* to a higher one; here various characteristics of the *guṇas*' bondage are delineated, and these enable a process of self-examination or self-study and a consequence practice of changing one's habits for the purpose of raising oneself in this ladder of the *guṇas*. This idea of the *guṇas* is firmly tied to the ladder-like structure of the *Bhagavad-gīta*, so, for example, in being established in the *guṇa* of goodness, one finds oneself adhering to *dharma*. In other words, when one adheres to *dharma* by being motivated by some ulterior motives, one is considered to be governed by the two lower *guṇas*, but when one is able to rise to the *guṇa* of goodness, one practices following *dharma* for its own sake, in a disinterested manner, with no desire for its fruits. This is the highest position one may reach within what we consider to be the humanistic realm; hence, one continues to progress toward the position 'beyond the *guṇas*'.

Action and beyond – the principle of *karma*

The *Yogic-Upaniṣadic* point of view[14] is somewhat complex in its perception of human action. While soul is considered eternal, given that the *guṇas* act and influence the soul beyond this life, similarly is the concept of action taken to have implications beyond the present life, having its roots in previous lives and its consequences in future lives. In essence, every action is considered to bear not only on immediate consequences but on long-term ones as well. Consequently, one may give charity to the needy and as a result be born in one's next life in a rich family, consequently living an opulent life. Alternatively, one may commit some evil and as a result be born in a poor family and consequently live in difficult conditions. This may also reinforce the vision of the *guṇas* as universal paths; for example, a person influenced by the *guṇa* of goodness gives charity, and this elevates them in their next life to a pious environment where they are well educated and, as such, continue to do good for others and be subsequently further elevated. Alternatively, a person influenced by the lower *guṇas* causes distress to others and is consequently born in lower conditions or bodies, where a bad nature is enforced upon them and drags them further down the existential root. Although no doubt this concept may suggest the lack of free will and a somewhat fatalistic worldview, the *Bhagavad-gītā* firmly propounds the idea of free will, and underlying the entire conversation is the understanding that Arjuna can choose his own way or path. In other words, this suggests that despite the seemingly fatalism sentenced by the *guṇas*, one still has a fair amount of free will and is able to change one's course of life and existence.

The fourth chapter of the *Bhagavad-gītā* deals extensively with the subject matter of action and states:

> What is action? What is inaction? Even the wise are confused in this matter. Now I shall explain to you this subject matter of action; having known this you shall be free from evil. One must know what action (*karma*) is, one must know what improper action (*vikarma*) is, and one must know what inaction (*akarma*) is, as profound indeed is the course of action.[15]

Proper action is performed in accordance with one's duty or *dharma* and bears good results, whereas improper action is contrary to one's *dharmic* duties and thus bears some distressful results. Seen from this point of view, good acts and bad acts ultimately bind one to continuous existence, as one will have to be born again to enjoy or suffer the results or the fruits of their actions. Alternatively, one is encouraged to perform a 'clean' or 'pure' action, which is considered to be inaction: the reason is that when this is done in the appropriate way, i.e. without regard to the fruits, accompanied by knowledge and as an offering to the supreme, it does not bear consequential fruits in future lives but instead leads to liberation. As such, it doesn't have the normal binding characteristics of action. The following is the highest mode of action proposed at the end of the *Bhagavad-gītā*, in a statement that is sometimes considered to be the text's culmination and peak: 'Abandon all sorts of *dharmas* and take refuge in me alone, and I shall release you from all evils; do not fear'.[16] This raises a question in regard to the relinquishment of duty or the external abstention from action; it seems that this is taken as a sort of improper action and as such is liable to bear a bad result. The *Bhagavad-gītā* emphasizes the path of *karma yoga*, which is a *yoga* of action; accordingly, one undergoes the same *yogic* transformation through the performance of action – or, more specifically, action according to *dharma*. Thus, one examines one's own mode of action and constantly endeavors to sublimate it; in this way, by adhering to one's duty, by constantly sublimating it and by refining one's inner motivations, one attains enlightenment through action. In the *Bhagavad-gītā*, Arjuna is presented with various motivations for performing his duty and fighting: he may fight out of some utilitarian purposes, he may fight for the sake of duty, his fighting may be taken as a practice of *yoga* and he may fight out of devotion to the supreme.

The *Bhagavad-gītā's* educational doctrine

Having surveyed the two armies about to fight, Arjuna becomes despondent in his attempt to resolve the seemingly impossible moral dilemma facing him. At that time, he turns to Kṛṣṇa, his friend and charioteer in a new way; he approaches Kṛṣṇa as a student approaches his *guru*, teacher or master, and declares 'I am now your disciple and I fall at your feet; please instruct me!'[17] The *guru* teaches his student through personal tutorship, while the student not only learns from the *guru* theoretical knowledge but also serves their *guru* and aspires to please the *guru*. The fourth chapter refers to the *guru*–disciple relationship in the following way: 'Know this by falling at the feet of the master, asking him questions and offering him service; in so doing, men of wisdom and vision of the truth will impart knowledge unto you'.[18] This seems to be a personal mode of knowledge transmission, and it entails character building and a transfer of values. The *Bhagavad-gītā* is highly transformational; the training process offered by the *guru* aspires to further a moral and spiritual transformation, and a gradual elevation and sublimation of values that may be considered ladder-like, i.e. each component leading to a higher one. The *Bhagavad-gītā* begins with the lowest stage of the ladder, represented by Arjuna's lamentation, which appears in the first chapter; it follows a gradual ascendance throughout the entire text; and this ascendance reaches its peak at the end of the last chapter, where Arjuna surrenders himself entirely to Kṛṣṇa. The following question may be raised at this point: what is considered to represent proper knowledge, according to the *Bhagavad-gītā*, or what does the *guru* teach? Also, are the various components of knowledge organized hierarchically too? The sixteenth chapter the *Bhagavad-gītā* offers a list of the divine qualities and opposes this with the demonic ones:

> Fearlessness, purification of one's whole being, firmness in spiritual knowledge, generosity, self control and sacrifice, studying the *Veda*, austerity, righteousness, nonviolence, truthfulness, absence of anger, renunciation, tranquility, avoiding vilification, compassion for all beings, absence of greed, gentleness, modesty, reliability, vigor, tolerance, fortitude, purity, absence of envy and pride – these are the qualities of one born to divine destiny, O Bhārata. Hypocrisy, arrogance, conceit, anger, harshness and ignorance – these are the qualities of one who is born to a demonic destiny.[19]

From analyzing this list, it seems that these are humanistic educational ideals. In other words, these are ideal qualities to be pursued while living in accordance with *dharma*, and their counterparts, the demonic qualities, are to be avoided. The thirteenth chapter offers a somewhat similar list of qualities, which represent knowledge:

> Absence of pride and arrogance, nonviolence, forbearance, honesty, attendance upon the *guru*, purity, firmness, self control, lack of attraction to sense objects, absence of ego-notion, visioning the distress and evil of birth, death, old age and disease, detachment, aloofness from sons, wife, home and the like, constant equanimity toward desired and undesired events, single-minded devotion to me supported by *yoga*, preferring of solitary places and avoiding the crowds, constant contemplation of knowledge of the self, envisioning the purpose of knowledge concerned with the truth – all these are declared knowledge, whereas all else is ignorance.[20]

This list seems to be aiming at a somewhat higher position along the ladder and might be more compatible with the *yogic* point of view. It is more introspective and emphasizes *yoga*, detachment, absence of ego and the vision of equality. Although it is not as explicit as these two lists, one may find the following verse to supply values that may be considered even higher in the sense of expressing deep absorption and devotion to the supreme:

> Those whose consciousness is absorbed in me, for whom I am everything, enlighten one another about me, constantly speaking of me; thus absorbed, they are delighted and content.[21]

This is a description of devotees immersed in the supreme; they are entirely absorbed in the supreme; they have no other object of interest; and they not only enlighten each other about the supreme but also take great pleasure in doing so. It may well be that implicit in this statement is the idea that this stage of being deeply immersed in the supreme represents not only the highest devotion but also the highest degree of knowledge

Bhakti

Bhakti, or devotion, is one of the *Bhagavad-gītā*'s major components; it represents a loving attitude toward the supreme, who is generally thought of in the context of *bhakti* in personal terms. Looking deeper into the emotional state characterizing *bhakti*, one may discern love, devotion, a desire to please the supreme person, a sense of dependence upon him, a desire to glorify him and share this glorification with other devoted people or *bhaktas*, a desire to serve the supreme lord through one's profession, a sense of loyalty to him, a desire to worship him and a desire to please him by offering various articles such as flowers or fruits. Kṛṣṇa, who according to the *Bhagavad-gītā* is the supreme lord in person and who is the object of devotion, is not indifferent to his devotees but rather is affectionate toward and protective of them. As opposed to the general masculine voice dominating the *Bhagavad-gītā*, when it comes to devotion, the text specifically refers to female devotees, in a declaration that could be taken as groundbreaking for its time: 'Those who take refuge in me, be they of lowly origin, women, merchants and even servants; even they may attain the highest destination'.[22]

Looking into the structure of the *Bhagavad-gītā*, it becomes evident that *bhakti* serves as a major or maybe even *the* major elevating force, which 'pulls', so to speak, or raises one in his transformational journey toward self-transcendence. Although there are other motivations for elevation along the transformational ladder, such as the desire to attain true knowledge, the desire to get free from the implications of *karma* and the desire for a *yogic* perfection, *bhakti* is perhaps the central source of inspiration for one to leave this world altogether.

The idea of *bhakti* first appears explicitly toward the end of the third chapter, where Kṛṣṇa urges Arjuna to fight in the mood of surrender unto him: 'Surrendering all your activities unto me with mind fixed on the highest self, without desire and avoiding possessiveness, cast lethargy aside and fight!'[23] Arjuna's reaction follows soon after, and at the beginning of the fourth chapter, he asks of Kṛṣṇa's identity,[24] to which Kṛṣṇa answers that he is the lord of all beings, descending to uphold *dharma*. Following that, Kṛṣṇa encourages Arjuna in numerous places throughout the *Bhagavad-gītā*, to take refuge in him in a devotional mood. In general, Kṛṣṇa urges Arjuna to become his devotee in three basic ways, or rather stages: Kṛṣṇa encourages Arjuna to adhere to his work and duty according to *dharma* and to offer this work and its results unto him. An example of this kind of devotion is found at the end of the ninth chapter: 'Whatever you do, whatever you eat, whatever you offer in sacrifice, whatever you give away and whatever austerity you may practice, O Kaunteya, do it as an offering unto me'.[25] Underlying this statement is the understanding that Arjuna is thinking in humanistic terms, and thus, he is encouraged to maintain his sense of human individuality and offer Kṛṣṇa the fruits of his work.

A higher state of *bhakti* is that of *yogic* devotion exemplified by Kṛṣṇa's conclusion of the fourth chapter: 'Therefore, O Bharata, you should cut the doubt residing in your heart which springs from nothing but ignorance, with your own sword of knowledge, resort to *yoga* and rise up to battle!'[26] This represents a *yogic* position, where Arjuna is attempting to rise above his own worldly attachments, represented by the doubts residing in his heart, and obstructing him from hearing Kṛṣṇa clearly and from following his instructions. Kṛṣṇa urges him to cut his doubts, which represent ignorance with the sword of knowledge and to do so by resorting to *yoga*.

A verse that seems to carry a similar import, though with a slightly more personal emphasis, can be found in the eighth chapter: 'Therefore, at all times remember me and fight; with your mind and intelligence absorbed in me, you will come to me without doubt'.[27] This verse also relates the external fighting to the internal one; the fighting here is considered to be a kind of a *yogic* practice, involving sense restraint, mental control and an inner meditation of Kṛṣṇa. It well exemplifies the two main components of the *yogic* point of view: on the one hand attempting to cut the bonds that hold one in embodied existence and on the other hand attempting to connect or yoke oneself to the higher, supreme and spiritual reality, here represented by Kṛṣṇa himself. The highest *bhakti* may be exemplified by two of the *Bhagavad-gītā*'s concluding verses:

> Always think of me, become my devotee, worship me and pay your homage to me, and thus you shall undoubtedly come to me; I promise you this as you are dear to me. Abandon all *dharmas* and take refuge in me alone, and I shall release you from all evils; do not fear.[28]

These two verses represent a higher and more peaceful state of devotion to Kṛṣṇa; this is the state beyond both *dharma* and the internal *yogic* struggle, a state of intense but peaceful absorption in the mood of devotion, in which one always thinks of Kṛṣṇa in loving devotion, and is very dear to Kṛṣṇa. A more structured and condensed description of a descending 'ladder of devotion' appears in chapter 12:

> Fix your mind on me alone, and absorb your consciousness in me; thus you shall surely abide in me. If you cannot fix your consciousness steadily upon me, then aspire to reach me through repeated *yoga* practice, O Dhanañjaya. If you are incapable even of that, embrace the path of action, for which I am the highest goal, since by acting for me you shall attain perfection. But if you are even unable to follow this path of refuge in me through acts devoted to me, then give up the fruits of all your actions, thus restraining yourself. Knowledge is superior to practice, meditation is superior to knowledge, and relinquishing the fruits of actions is higher than meditation, as tranquility soon follows such relinquishment.[29]

The ladder begins with a complete absorption of one's consciousness in Kṛṣṇa, which represents the highest position. The next and lower stage is a direct *yogic* practice, and the next stage after that is working for Kṛṣṇa and offering him the fruits of labor; both of these stages represent a *yogic* position. Lower than that is the humanistic position of relinquishing the fruits of labor; following that come meditation, knowledge and practice.

The vision of the supreme

The *Bhagavad-gītā* reaches its theological climax in the seventh and ninth chapters, where the vision of divinity is articulated. Having led Arjuna from lower to higher visions, Kṛṣṇa at last relinquishes the various logical arguments and turns to a description of the spiritual reality. Kṛṣṇa speaks of his complex relationships with the spiritual souls and the world, moving between transcendence and immanence. In this way, he describes two natures, the lower and the higher:

> Earth, water, fire, air, ether, mind, intellect and ego – these eight comprise my separated lower nature; but you should know that beside this lower nature, O mighty-armed one, there is another higher nature of mine, comprised of spirit souls, by which this world is sustained.[30]

Both of these natures are Kṛṣṇa's natures, but the first, which is composed of matter and mind, is lower and separated, whereas the second, which is composed of spiritual souls, is higher and apparently connected or deeply related to Kṛṣṇa, who himself supports the entire creation, as everything rests on him just like pearls that are strung on a thread.[31] The relationships between the supreme person and the creation are complex, and much has been said and written in this regard by later *Vedāntin* commentators, who articulated systematic theologies engaged with the dualism and the non-dualism of the world. The text continues to impart a vision:

> I pervade the entire world in my unmanifest form; all beings rest in me, but I do not rest in them, and yet all beings do not rest in me. See my mystic splendor! I sustain beings but rely not on them; my very self is the cause of their being. As the great wind that goes everywhere is eternally contained within space, know that similarly all beings are contained in me.[32]

This description is free from argumentative language, and it may be difficult to articulate it according to common theological categories such as transcendence, immanence and pantheism. These statements do not seem to adhere to simple logic; rather, all beings rest in Kṛṣṇa, but at the same time all beings do not rest in him. The reason is that this description comprises a *darśana*, or vision. This vision is not open to all, but rather, one must become a surrendered devotee of Kṛṣṇa to overcome his deluding power and maintain such a vision: 'Divine indeed and difficult to penetrate is my deluding power, consisting of the three *guṇas*; but those who have surrendered unto me alone, they can transcend it'.[33] Accordingly, one must overcome desires and become a surrendered devotee of Kṛṣṇa to absorb and maintain such a vision. The ninth chapter concludes with a statement that seems to represent the epitome of the entire *Bhagavad-gītā*, which is a call for pure devotion: 'Always think of me and become my devotee, worship me and pay homage unto me; thus yoked to me and intent on me as your highest goal, you shall come to me'.[34]

Notes

1 Chs. 23–40 of the *Bhīṣmaparvan*.
2 *Prasthāna trayī*.
3 Quality, constituent; for a more elaborate explanation of the term, see p. 15.
4 *Bhg* 4.13. This and all other *Bhg* translations in this chapter are my own.
5 *Bhg* 3.35.
6 As a philosophical treatise, the *Bhagavad-gītā* furthers the idea of four classes or *varṇas*, whereas the present-day Indian empirical reality, which may be historically derived from the *Vedic* ideal of four classes, is characterized by *jātis*, or hundreds of social subdivisions.

7 *Bhg* 8.15–16.
8 *Bhg* 3.17.
9 *Bhg* 3.1–2.
10 *Bhg* 2.47.
11 *Bhg* 2.13.
12 *Bhg* 6.24–6.
13 *Bhg* 6.20–3.
14 Apparently the *Upaniṣads* contain also humanistic or *pravṛttic* sections furthering the ideal of *dharma*, and similarly, the *Yoga* traditions also contain ideals furthering humanistic ethics such as the stages of *yama* and *niyama*. Still, these traditions emphasize and further an attitude of renunciation or *nivṛtti*, as opposed to, say, traditions such as the *mīmāṁsā*, which is far more humanistic.
15 *Bhg* 4.16–17.
16 *Bhg* 18.66.
17 *Bhg* 2.7.
18 *Bhg* 4.34.
19 *Bhg* 16.1–4.
20 *Bhg* 13.7–11.
21 *Bhg* 10.9.
22 *Bhg* 9.32.
23 *Bhg* 3.30.
24 *Bhg* 4.4.
25 *Bhg* 9.27.
26 *Bhg* 4.42.
27 *Bhg* 8.7.
28 *Bhg* 18.65–6.
29 *Bhg* 12.8–12.
30 *Bhg* 7.4–5.
31 *Bhg* 7.7.
32 *Bhg* 9.4–6.
33 *Bhg* 7.14.
34 *Bhg* 9.34.

2

THE STRUCTURE OF THE *BHAGAVAD-GĪTĀ*

Ithamar Theodor

The *Bhagavad-gītā* is no doubt a unique literary creation, but at the same time, deciphering its meaning and philosophy is not easy or simple. Klaus Klostermaier refers to the challenge facing the reader in understanding the *Bhagavad-gītā*:

> Whoever reads it for the first time will be struck by its beauty and depth; countless Hindus know it by heart and quote it in many occasions as an expression of their faith and their insights. All over India, and also in many places in the Western hemisphere, *Gītā* lectures attract large numbers of people. Many are convinced that the *Bhagavad-gītā* is the key book for the re-spiritualization of humankind in our age. A careful study of the *Gītā*, however, will very soon reveal the need for a key to this key-book. Simple as the tale may seem and popular as the work has become, it is by no means an easy book and some of the greatest scholars have grappled with the historical and philosophical problems it presents.
>
> *(Klostermaier 2007, 74)*

Klaus Klostermaier's words no doubt touch upon one of the main challenges in understanding this treatise; can it be tied together by a relatively simple and unifying theme or structure? The *Bhagavad-gītā* is a rich treatise containing numerous ideas fundamental to Hinduism; however, are these ideas consistent and coherent? This chapter argues that seen from a theological-philosophical perspective, the *Bhagavad-gītā* indeed possesses a coherent and consistent theme, which could be followed from the beginning of the treatise to its end. In this way, this chapter aims at looking deeper into the *Bhagavad-gītā*'s structure which is founded on a three-tier concept of reality intertwined with a transformational ethical ladder.

The three-story house metaphor

To lay out the *Bhagavad-gītā*'s structure and main theme, this chapter uses the metaphor of a three-story house. This house not only has three floors, stories or tiers but also has a staircase or ladder leading the residents from the first floor to the second and from the second to the third. This staircase is grounded in *dharmic* action and may also be described as a ladder grounded in *karma-yoga* gradually ascending to *bhakti* or *mokṣa*. The lower floor is humanistic and represents human life in this world; the second floor is spiritualistic and is an intermediate floor, whereby one relinquishes worldly life and seeks the state of liberation; and the third floor represents full absorption in the liberated state. The stages of the staircase or the ladder are comprised of various states of *dharmic* action categorized according to their underlying motivation: at the lower stage, one acts as motivated by some utilitarian principle or gain; one stage higher is when one seeks gain beyond this life into the heavenly world; a stage higher than that is the stage of relinquishment of action's fruits, thus acting for the sake of duty, or *dharma*, alone; and a state still higher is the performance of one's *dharmic* duty as a practice of *yoga*, i.e. considering the performance of duty to be the means by which the mind may be subdued. The highest state is the state of performing one's *dharmic* duty while being liberated and entirely immersed in the supreme. In this way, the *Bhagavad-gītā* adheres to both ideals: it supports social responsibility, morality and *dharma*, and at the same time, it endorses the *Upaniṣadic* path of self-realization, which leads one from the depth of material existence all the way up to liberation.

The idea of the ladder is grounded in the writings of Viśvanātha Cakravartī, a *Vaiṣṇava* author who lived around the years 1640–1730;[1] he grew up in present-day West Bengal at the Nadia district and later moved to Rādhā Kuṇḍa at the Mathurā district, which was an important center for *Vaiṣṇava* scholarship. He wrote about 20 books on *Vaiṣṇava* theology, and the idea of the ladder may be found in his book *Sārārtha-Varṣiṇī-Ṭīkā*, which is his commentary on the *Bhagavad-gītā*. Viśvanātha's ethical ladder is somewhat implicit; however, reading through his commentary reveals that such a ladder indeed explicitly exists. His ladder consists of three main stages: *sakāma-karma*, *niṣkāma karma* and *bhakti*. *Sakāma-karma* means following the *Vedic* rules with a desire for some gain; *niṣkāma karma* means following the *Vedic* rules without a desire for gain; and *bhakti* means devotion to or love of God. Viśvanātha's ethical ladder contains also mixed stages, such as a state of devotion mixed with some desire for gain, devotion mixed with knowledge or scholasticism and devotion confined to the realm of one's nature.[2] The idea of dividing reality into levels is grounded in the *Vedānta* tradition, although the hierarchy is generally depicted in two levels; an example of this is Śaṅkara's two levels of reality (Hamilton 2001, 130).

The idea of hierarchical reality suggests that reality is not unified but rather it contains differing tiers or levels.[3] There is a higher reality as well as a lower reality, and one must distinguish between the two. Moreover, each tier has its own unique language, terms and underlying assumptions. The ethical ladder is composed of various stages, and these enable one to rise from the lower tier of reality to the intermediate tier and then to the higher one. Each of the ladder's stages is defined by its underlying motivation; the more one undergoes transformation through the sublimation of one's motives for action, the more one transcends this ethical ladder. The ethical ladder is rooted at the lower stage of reality, which represents worldly life, and as one gradually rises up the ladder, one makes progress toward the state of *mokṣa*. This structure highlights the *Bhagavad-gītā*'s *jñāna* and *karma* aspects; the *jñāna* aspect is represented by the three-tier metaphysical concept, whereas the *karma* aspect is represented by the ladder of action's various grades. The three metaphysical tiers and the ladder of ethical stages are complementary; the division of reality into these three tiers highlights one's present condition in the lower tier and one's goal, which is the highest tier, whereas the ladder of action provides the practical means of gradually overcoming this gap step by step, by a process of self-transformation.

Hierarchical reality in the *Bhagavad-gītā*

The *Bhagavad-gītā* is one of the triple foundations of *Vedānta* and as such shares qualities characterizing a *Vedāntin* text, such as hierarchical grades of reality. In general, one can find two principal metaphysical positions in Indian philosophy: the realistic or direct position and the hierarchical position. The direct-realistic position assumes that reality is unified – that is, does not contain divisions or layers; consequently, it is subject to direct human recognition and should not be submitted to different interpretations. The hierarchical position assumes that reality is not unified but rather contains different levels or tiers. There is a higher or superior reality and a lower or inferior reality, and one must distinguish between absolute reality and relative reality (Biderman 1980, 61). The two-leveled reality concept, the first empirical and conventional and the second absolute, the first changing and finite and the second permanent and infinite, may be treated by applying *dharma* and *mokṣa*; the level of *dharma* is representative of the human or worldly condition, whereas the level of *mokṣa* is representative of the real or absolute condition.

Dharma's opposite term, *adharma*, deserves consideration as well. Ordinarily, *dharma* and *adharma* are considered opposite terms; however, seen from the point of view of *mokṣa*, both *dharma* and *adharma* are in an entirely different category. According to our terminology, both *dharma* and *adharma* represent the finite level, whereas *mokṣa* represents the infinite level. Simplifying terms, the embodied state representing both *dharma* and *adharma* is the world of *saṁsāra*, whereas the liberated state is of an entirely different nature, called *mokṣa*. These two kinds of dichotomies – between *dharma* and *adharma* and between *dharma* and *mokṣa* – can be understood through a somewhat graphic description: the dichotomy between *dharma* and *adharma* may be taken to be horizontal, as both exist within the same realm, whereas the dichotomy between both *dharma* and *adharma* on one hand and *mokṣa* on the other may be taken to be vertical. This is so because both *dharma* and *adharma* are situated in the worldly or finite level, whereas *mokṣa* is situated in a completely different and higher level, which is infinite and absolute. Besides the two tiers underlying the *Bhagavad-gītā* – which could be considered the finite and the infinite, or alternatively, *dharma* and *mokṣa* – there is a third tier, serving as an intermediate one that connects the two tiers, which would otherwise be unrelated to each other due to an insurmountable gap separating the two, and this is the tier of *yoga*. Moreover, the first tier represents *dharma* and furthers proper human life; the second tier represents *yoga* and furthers attempts to escape the viscous state of *saṁsāra* while gradually seeking hold of the state of *mokṣa*, and the third tier represents the state of *mokṣa* itself.

But how can these tiers be studied or distinguished? I suggest that to distinguish the tiers from each other, their underlying assumptions of values and being may be examined.[4] Thus, in the first tier, that of *dharma*, the general rule in terms of value is to prosper; accordingly, worldly happiness and prosperity are desired and are good. In terms of being, the individual is defined in this tier as a human being or any other living being, such as an animal, plant or other. In the second tier, the value of worldly prosperity is rejected in favor of non-attachment to the world and indifference to both worldly happiness and worldly distress, along with yoking oneself to a higher reality, that of *mokṣa*. In terms of being, the individual person does not consider himself any longer a human (or other) being but rather as an eternal spiritual soul bound by the laws of *saṁsāra*. Thus, the individual's subjective identity is no longer a human being but rather that of an eternal spiritual soul. In the third tier, the ideal value is the experience of *brahmānanda*, or the bliss of *Brahman*; this realization takes place in the wider context of the supreme person, who is the foundation underlying the immortal and imperishable *Brahman*. Thus, the indifference and the non-attachment of the second tier are replaced by a deep attachment to the supreme person and deep love expressed by loving feelings toward him. As far as being is concerned, the spiritual soul of the second tier not only becomes pure existence and one with *Brahman* but also assumes the identity of a pure servant and a lover of the supreme person.

The three tiers represent internal mental states or attitudes. Thus, those who see the world from the point of view of the first tier are convinced that they are human beings and that their aim is to prosper. Similarly, those who see the world. From the point of view of the second tier are convinced that they are embodied spiritual selves and that their aim is to get released from that condition. Those who reside in the third tier may realize their oneness with *Brahman*, see the supreme in person everywhere and aspire to serve and love him. I suggest the usage of a three-story house as a metaphor, with each tier representing a story or floor and the ethical ladder serving as a staircase. Each such story or tier contains unlimited existential opportunities and paths; moreover, the residents of each floor have their own language, terms and underlying assumptions, which are different from those of the other story's residents. In a sense, the *Bhagavad-gītā* speaks in three languages and constantly moves between the three tiers. Once recognizing the story or tier from which the text is speaking, that section becomes intelligible and consistent with the rest of the treatise. On a more practical level, once recognizing one's ethical stage, it becomes apparent what the next stage of progress is. These distinctions may appear to be somewhat sharp, whereas in the text itself, there are connecting links between the stories or tiers. However, this could possibly be compared to the study of grammar, where tables of roots and stems are articulated and discussed; although these linguistic forms are merely theoretical or structural and do not appear in actual spoken language, they actually underlie it. Similarly, the distinction between the tiers underlies the text, though in the text itself, these distinctions may not always be easy to inspect.

A textual reference for the three-tier metaphor

These ideas may be better demonstrated by a textual reference. The following example demonstrates how the text shifts from the first tier to the second; when Arjuna argues against fighting the war, he does so from the position of the first tier:

> When *adharma* overpowers the family its ladies become corrupt, O Kṛṣṇa, and when the women become corrupt there is miscegenation of classes. Surely miscegenation among classes leads both the clan's destroyers and the family itself to hell. The family ancestors fall too, deprived of their due offerings of sanctified food and water. As such, the evil deeds of the destroyers which lead to miscegenation among classes, wipe out eternal caste and family *dharma*. O Janārdana, we have heard that hell awaits those whose family *dharma* has been obliterated. Alas, resolved are we on committing a great evil, if we intend to kill our own people out of greed for royal pleasure. Better had I been killed on the battlefield, unarmed and unresisting, by Dhṛtarāṣṭra's sons with weapons in their hands.[5]

This passage may now be examined according to the two parameters mentioned: values and being. As far as values, it is clear that underlying Arjuna's speech is a desire for worldly prosperity; he believes that prosperity is good and objects to the war, which would cause the decline of *dharma*, the rise of *adharma* and the infliction of suffering on all involved and beyond. As far as being is concerned, Arjuna thinks of himself and the others as human beings. In answering Arjuna, Kṛṣṇa doesn't address his concerns directly but raises the conversation to the second tier:

> While speaking words of wisdom, you lament for that which is not to be grieved for; wise are those who do not lament either for the living or for the dead. Never was there a time when I did not exist, nor you, nor all

> these kings, nor in the future shall any of us cease to exist. As childhood, youth and old age befall the soul within this body, so it comes to acquire another body; the wise is not swayed by illusion in this matter. Heat, cold, happiness and distress – sensual perception alone produces them all, and it is impermanent, coming and going; you should seek to endure them, O Bhārata. The wise one whom these do not disturb, who thus remains even tempered in both happiness and distress, is fit for immortality, O bull among men.[6]

The values propounded here are utterly different from the values underlying Arjuna's speech. Kṛṣṇa does not accept the idea that prosperity in the world is good but instead calls for indifference and endurance of both worldly happiness and worldly distress. These are taken to be impermanent and to be produced by sensual perception alone.

As far as being is concerned, Kṛṣṇa does not refer to the individuals present as human beings; rather, he refers to them as spiritual souls or selves. In a sense, Kṛṣṇa doesn't directly answer Arjuna's doubts in regard to fighting but instead performs a kind of a 'Copernican revolution' by changing the conversation's underlying assumptions. Arjuna, for his part, argues that killing his relatives is bad; this is an obvious first-tier statement that assumes that people are subjected to death and that death is to be avoided as much as possible for the sake of prosperous life. Kṛṣṇa doesn't answer Arjuna's arguments; rather, he shifts the conversation to a different tier or level altogether and speaks from different assumptions. From this higher point of view, Kṛṣṇa says that death doesn't exist at all; from his second-tier point of view, he doesn't see human beings subjected to death but rather sees eternal spiritual souls and thus doesn't see much logic in Arjuna's arguments. As far as values, Kṛṣṇa challenges Arjuna's idea that worldly prosperity and happiness is good and to be desired, by propounding the idea that indifference to both happiness and distress is good and to be desired. Thus, Kṛṣṇa speaks here from a second-tier position.

We may now examine a different passage, one that represents the ascension from the second to the third tier; this is the opening section of the seventh chapter. The section begins with Kṛṣṇa's inviting Arjuna to attach his mind to him and thus ascend to the third tier and gain a vision of divinity:

> The Blessed Lord said: O Pārtha, with your mind attached to me, being fixed in *yoga* and finding refuge in me, you can know me entirely and beyond doubt; hear now. I shall now reveal to you fully knowledge accompanied by realization; having acquired this knowledge, nothing further in this world will remain to be known. Among thousands of men, hardly anyone strives for perfection, and even among those who have striven and achieved perfection, hardly anyone knows me in truth. Earth, water, fire, air, ether, mind, intellect and ego – these eight comprise my separated lower nature. But you should know that beside this lower nature, O

> mighty-armed one, there is another higher nature of mine, comprised of spirit souls, by which this world is sustained. Realize that all entities have their source in these two natures. I am the origin of this entire universe and of its dissolution too. O Dhanañjaya, there exists nothing higher than me; everything rests upon me as pearls are strung on a thread. I am the taste of water, O Kaunteya, and I am the light of the sun and the moon; I am the sacred syllable OṀ in all the *Vedas*, the sound in ether, and the humanity in man. The pure fragrance of the earth am I, and the brilliance in fire; I am the life of all living beings and the austerity of the ascetics.[7]

In this section, Kṛṣṇa describes his divinity in detail and prepares the ground for emphasizing *bhakti* or devotion unto him. The opening statement consisting of three verses is significant and sets the agenda for the discussion about to start. Kṛṣṇa begins by defining the state of mind required of Arjuna, a state of mind that is a requirement for understanding the knowledge about to be revealed. The salient step taken in this brief section is the discussion's ascension from the second to the third tier; this level no longer propounds knowledge of sensual restraint but instead knowledge of the supreme person and devotion unto him. The first characteristic of this new and higher state is *mayy āsakta manāḥ*, literally meaning 'with your mind absorbed or attached to me'. The word *āsakta* is significant and means attachment; in Zaehner's commentary on the first verse, he refers to this:

> 'Attach your mind to me': this is utterly new and apparently at variance with the whole content of the last two chapters. There we had been told almost *ad nauseam* that we had to *detach* ourselves from everything: only by total detachment could liberation be won. Meditate on God certainly as a means of concentrating your mind, as the *Yoga-sūtras* recommend, but do not *attach* yourself to him or anything else because 'liberation' is clearly incompatible with attachment of any kind. Here, however, Arjuna is told most bluntly that this is not so: the true athlete of the spirit who has succeeded in integrating his personality and in becoming *Brahman* must now not only continue his spiritual exercise unremittingly, he must also attach his whole personality in all its newfound fullness and freedom to Kṛṣṇa who is God and, being God, transcends the immortal *Brahman* as much as he transcends the phenomenal world. Continued spiritual exercise preserving the integrated personality intact, attachment to God, and total trust in him are what Kṛṣṇa demands in this stanza.
>
> *(Zaehner 1969, 244)*

Zaehner points at the change occurring here: instead of practicing detachment from the world, as has been recommended so far, Arjuna is now encouraged to practice attachment to the supreme person. In other words, the phase of struggle with both attraction and repulsion toward sense objects ends with the sixth chapter, and a new phase now begins, by which Arjuna is to view the world from a newer and higher point of view; accordingly, the world is no longer perceived as a threat but rather as a manifestation of divine abundance.

The *Bhagavad-gītā's* transformational aspects

Besides the *Bhagavad-gītā*'s theoretical aspects, which may be considered in the category of *jñāna*, there are practical aspects that may be considered to be in the realm of *karma*. The *Upaniṣads* and the *Brahmasūtras* are rather theoretical and thus do not offer much scope for developing a philosophy of conduct and spiritual self-culture; however, the *Bhagavad-gītā* is the work in the realm of *Vedānta* that lays down the plan of life for realizing the ultimate good. This practical emphasis is not so fully present in the other two texts and thus without the *Bhagavad-gītā*, *Advaita*, *Viśiṣṭādvaita* and *Dvaita* would be substantially impoverished and would lack the doctrine of the way of life (Raghavacar 1991, vii). As a practical scripture, the *Bhagavad-gītā* offers the means of crossing over the gap between the first tier, that of *dharma*, and the third tier, that of *mokṣa*. Merely following *dharma* while avoiding *adharma* is not sufficient to attain the stage of *mokṣa*; a different type of endeavor or path is needed. This process or enterprise is sometimes called self-realization, and it involves a transformational path by which one progresses step by step, thus making advancement from the lower tiers to the higher ones. The question may now be raised regarding what means the *Bhagavad-gītā* offers the practitioner who desires to make progress in the process of self-realization. In other words, if the gap between *dharma* and *mokṣa* is insurmountable, how is one expected to cross it, leaving behind the world of *saṁsāra* and attaining the liberated realm of *mokṣa*? What practical means or system does the *Bhagavad-gītā* offer the individual or the community that aspires to ascend this transformative path?

A major question raised in the *Bhagavad-gītā* is whether one should choose the path of action or that of contemplation. This question is clearly raised twice, at the beginning of the third and fifth chapters, and is further discussed elsewhere.[8] The *Bhagavad-gītā* clearly recommends the path of action, which offers the means by which the performer is to be elevated all the way from the level of *dharma* to the state of *mokṣa*. This uplifting action is performed according to one's *dharma* and continues to be carried out all along the way. Thus, Arjuna is encouraged all along his conversation with Kṛṣṇa to follow his *dharma* and fight. However, as the text progresses, he is encouraged to refine his motives for fighting; in this way, the act of fighting is carried out in higher and higher inner states of consciousness. Thus, although externally one continues to carry out one's prescribed duty, one undergoes an internal transformation through the sublimation or purification of one's motives for performing *dharmic* action. In this way, a kind of ladder is formed, the climbing of which raises one higher and higher, from *dharma* to *mokṣa* – along the path of self-transcendence or self-realization.

At the lowest stage, one's actions are motivated by simple utilitarianism,[9] and one in this stage acts for the purpose of directly achieving something for oneself. Underlying the following reference is the notion of simple utilitarianism:

> Beside that, people will be speaking of you as eternally infamous, and for one who has been honoured, dishonour is worse than death. The generals will assume that you have withdrawn from the battle out of fear, and thus, those who have once esteemed you highly will think little of you. Your ill wishers will speak many unspeakable words, thus ridiculing your capacity; what could be more distressful than this?[10]

Here Kṛṣṇa attempts to convince Arjuna to take arms, based on an argument underlain by simple utilitarianism. He assumes that Arjuna aspires to accumulate gain such as fame and argues that by withdrawing from the battle Arjuna will lose his fame. The next argument is also utilitarian, but it is somewhat higher in that it accepts scriptural authority; it accepts the idea that warriors who die in battle attain heaven. Thus, it can be called the stage of religious utilitarianism or *dharmic* utilitarianism. In other words, Arjuna is advised to follow *dharma* to achieve some end in this life or the next:

> Happy are the *kṣatriyas* to whom such an opportunity to fight comes by good luck, as it opens heaven's gates for them.[11]

A stage still higher is following *dharma* for its own sake, or performing one's duty for the sake of duty:

> Fight for the sake of fighting, regarding alike happiness and distress, gain and loss, victory and defeat; thus, you shall not incur evil.[12]

The stage of performing one's duty for the sake of duty represents a pure mode of action, free from a desire for its fruits, and is one of the central teachings of the *Bhagavad-gītā*. The same idea appears again soon in a slightly different version:

> Your sole entitlement is to perform *dharmic* activity, not ever to possess its fruits; never shall the fruit of an action motivate your deed, and never cleave to inaction.[13]

Despite the centrality of this idea, it is still within the first story as it doesn't include an awareness of the ultimate good, which is, according to the *Bhagavad-gītā*, release from *saṁsāra*. Those who embody this attitude reach the top of the first tier and can progress further into the next stage, which is already in the second tier.

The next stage rejects the value of the *Vedas*, which are considered to be engaged with worldly gains, in favor of a higher ideal – the attainment of *Brahman*:

> As much value as there is in a well, when there is a flood of water on all sides, such is the value of all the *Vedas* for he who is a knower of *Brahman*.[14]

This stage may be called action for the sake of the highest good, or *Brahman*, and one who thus acts is situated in the second tier, which is characterized by various *yoga* processes. One may act now in *karma yoga*, disinterested from the fruits of one's actions, and may offer those fruits to the supreme or may practice *jñāna yoga*, *aṣṭāṅga yoga* or *bhakti-yoga*. However, these various *yoga* practices have the common goal of detaching oneself from worldly existence and attachments and of attaching oneself to the supreme. The stage of *yoga* is thus characterized by enlightenment and renunciation:

> The enlightened renounces both good and evil deeds here in this world. Therefore, perform *yoga* for the sake of *yoga*, as *yoga* is the skill in action.[15]

Having perfected the stage of *yoga*, one finally elevates oneself to the third tier, that of *mokṣa*, and becomes absorbed in *Brahman*, either in an impersonal way, such as in Śaṅkara's system, or through love of the supreme person, such as in Rāmānuja's system. This is the impersonal version of 'becoming one with *Brahman*', following Śaṅkara:

> He whose happiness is within, whose pleasure is within, and his enlightenment too is within is actually a *yogī*; with his whole being absorbed in *Brahman*, he attains to extinction in *Brahman*.[16]

However, the *Bhagavad-gītā* has dominant devotional characteristics, and the loving relations to be exchanged with the personal deity serve as a stimulus for elevation in the ethical ladder of values or motives. Pure devotion to the supreme person is indeed the highest achievement attainable for the devoted *bhakta*. Kṛṣṇa writes,

> Always think of me and become my devotee, worship me and pay homage unto me; thus yoked to me and intent on me as your highest goal, you shall come to me.[17]

The stages may be summarized as simple utilitarianism, *dharmic* utilitarianism, duty for its own sake, acting for the sake of the highest good (or *Brahman*), the stage of *yoga* and the state of *mokṣa* in its personal or impersonal version. Thus, an ethical ladder of motives is formed, where the higher one's motive for action is, the higher one is situated in the *Bhagavad-gītā*'s metaphysical structure. In this way, the *Bhagavad-gītā* aspires to encompass the entire realm of existence while encouraging all to ascend the ladder of motives, thus distancing oneself from *saṁsāra* and absorbing oneself in *Brahman*, either personally or impersonally. Following this structure, I believe that the *Bhagavad-gītā* can be seen as a coherent theological-philosophical treatise, firmly tied together as a single and unified text.

Notes

1 For a thorough discussion of his life period, see Burton (2000, 13–22).

2 For a further development of this idea, see "The Yoga Ladder" in Bhūrijana Dāsa (1997, 59–68).
3 Sharma also discusses the idea of reality containing different tiers or being multilayered in the next chapter, p. 43.
4 Corresponding to the categories of ethics and ontology.
5 *Bhg* 1.41–6. This and all other *Bhg* translations in this chapter are my own.
6 *Bhg* 2.10–15.
7 *Bhg* 7.1–9.
8 *Bhg* 3.1–3, 5.1–2, 6.1.
9 The term 'utilitarianism' is applied here in its simple rendering, and not as a philosophical school associated with thinkers such as Bentham or Mill.
10 *Bhg* 2.34–6.
11 *Bhg* 2.32.
12 *Bhg* 2.38.
13 *Bhg* 2.47.
14 *Bhg* 2.46.
15 *Bhg* 2.50.
16 *Bhg* 5.24.
17 *Bhg* 9.34.

Bibliography

Bhānu, Svāmī (trs.). 2003. *Sārārtha-varṣinī-ṭīkā. The Bhagavad gītā commentary of Śrīla Viśvanātha Cakravartī Ṭhākura*. 2nd ed. Chennai: Sri Vaikuntha Enterprises.

Bhūrijana, Dāsa. 1997. *Surrender Unto Me*. New Delhi: VIHE Publications.

Biderman, Shlomo. 1980. *Indian Philosophy – The Foundations*, p. 61. Tel Aviv: Ministry of Defense Publications.

Burton, Adrian. 2000. *Temples, Texts and Taxes: The Bhagavad-gītā and the Politico – Religious Identity of the Caitanya Sect*. PhD dissertation, Canberra: The Australian National University.

Hamilton, Sue. 2001. *Indian Philosophy: A Very Short Introduction*. New York: Oxford University Press.

Klostermaier, Klaus. 2007. *A Survey of Hinduism*. 3rd ed. Albany: SUNY Press.

Raghavacar, Singra. 1991. *Rāmānuja on the Gītā*. Calcutta: Advaita Ashrama – Rāmakṛṇṣa Vedānta Centre.

Zaehner, Robert C. 1969. *The Bhagavad-gītā*. Oxford: Oxford University Press.

3

BHAGAVAD-GĪTĀ

Its philosophy and interpretation[1]

Arvind Sharma

The exegetical history of the *Bhagavad-gītā*

The *Bhagavad-gītā* has given rise to a vast body of literature, both in the Hindu tradition and beyond.[2] In this chapter, I will first focus on the exegesis of the *Bhagavad-gītā* in the Hindu tradition, in preparation to narrowing the focus gradually on the text itself.

The exegetical history of the *Bhagavad-gītā* in the Hindu tradition has remained almost entirely uninterrupted since it was first commented on by Śaṅkara,[3] who is usually thought to have lived during the 8th century[4] and whose life is sometimes specified, perhaps overconfidently, as extending from 788 to 820 CE.[5] Śaṅkara, however, refers to previous commentators,[6] and another commentary by Bhāskara from this early period is also available on nine chapters of the *Bhagavad-gītā*.[7] The commentaries by Rāmānuja (1017–1037) and Madhva (1199–1278) are too well known to require comment.[8] However, leading figures from other schools of *Vedānta* have also commented on the *Bhagavad-gītā*, such as Keśavakāśmīrin from the *Vaiṣṇava Dvaitādvaita* school,[9] Abhinavagupta from the school of Kashmir *Śaivism*,[10] and Viṣvanātha Cakravartin from the *Acintya-Bhedābheda* school of Caitanya.[11]

This tradition of scholarly philosophical exegesis of the *Bhagavad-gītā* within the broader framework of the history of Hindu philosophy is common knowledge and by now fairly well documented. However, although it is well known that from 'early in its history, the *Bhagavad-gītā* was an important focus for commentators', it is less widely known that 'later it became a source text for devotional movements'.[12] In other words, it is not just a philosophical text in the tradition but a religious classic as well.

In its role as a source text of the devotional movements, it has played a particularly significant role in the rise of the *Varkari* movement in Maharashtra through its rendering into Marathi by Jñāneśvara (c. 1300)[13] and in the devotional movement in Orissa through its translation into Oriya by Achyutānanda Dās and

Jasovanta Dās (two of the traditional 'five stalwarts' of Oriya devotional literature).[14] Similarly, during the medieval period, it was translated into Telugu by Annamācārya.[15] Closer to the end of the medieval period, it is cited by Gopāldās, a Dādūpanthī from Rajasthan, in his *Sarvāṅgī* (1627), which is otherwise in Rajasthani, in Sanskrit,[16] and an abridged version of the *Bhagavad-gītā* written in Hindi verse, also belonging to the 17th century, is now available in print.[17]

This oversight regarding the continuing significance of the *Bhagavad-gītā*, in its dual role as a philosophical text and as a religious text in medieval India, may be partly responsible for the claim that the *Bhagavad-gītā* has been artificially projected as a major text of Hinduism in modern times by the spokespeople of the Hindu renaissance. This is a major claim to make from the point of view of the *Bhagavad-gītā* and must be closely examined.

This argument is fairly widespread, although it is stated with different degrees of vigour and vehemence by various scholars. For example, A.C. Bouquet remarks, somewhat straightforwardly, that

> there was a period when the *Gītā* was largely forgotten, but for many years now it has recovered its favour, and national enthusiasts have tended to enthrone it in the hearts of Hindus as a worthy rival of the New Testament.[18]

L.S.S. O'Malley packs more punch into his statement when he says, while citing C.F. Andrews about the *Bhagavad-gītā*, that

> this work, which was scarcely known outside the learned circle of the pandits a century ago, can now be bought for a very small amount by any Hindu student, and commentaries, versions and translations abound. Within the memory of educational missionaries still living, it has been elevated from a position of comparative obscurity to that of a common and well-read scripture for the whole of educated India.[19]

Agehananda Bharati makes an even stronger statement:

> Indians and sympathetic occidentals alike have come to regard the *Bhagavad-gītā* as the Hindu Bible. No challenge against this notion has ever emerged from the spokesmen of the Renaissance, yet this claim is not part of an informed view about Hindu lore. The people who might challenge it are the ones that won't: The grass-root scholars, the orthodox pandits, cannot participate in the give-and-take of the Indian Renaissance with its English language premises, due to lack of social and economic access to a strictly urban milieu. But the informed Hindu must contest the *Bhagavad-gītā*'s Renaissance status. . . . Historically seen, the suzerain status ascribed to it is another paradigm of the pizza effect.[20] It was Annie Besant's impressionistic English translation of the text which impressed Gandhi when he read it in London; no doubt he must have heard about the *Gītā* in the orthodox setting of his *Vaiṣṇava* childhood, but the conversion

> that made him espouse this text as the *vademecum* of his political creed, happened at about the time when he read Besant's translation. By that time, B.G. Tilak (1856–1920) had published his *Gitā-rahasyā* in Marathi, and again, this might suggest to the unwary that the text must have had focal importance. Yet even Tilak chose the *Gītā*, not only because it was a text into which political action might be fitted with impunity-there are dozens of other epic texts which prompt their audience towards activism. There is no doubt in my mind that Tilak knew one or all of the several English translations which had been published by this time.[21]

One may now proceed to examine these arguments. One may begin by pointing out that some scholars do not seem to see a period of obscurity immediately preceding the attention that the *Gītā* received during the Hindu renaissance. For example, A.L. Basham observes that 'the inspiration of the *Bhagavad-gītā* has been widely felt in India from the time of the Guptas to the present day'.[22] It is clear, however, that those who ascribe its recent popularity to the period following Charles Wilkins's translation of the poem into English in 1785 imply that is was not an influential work in the preceding few centuries – that is, from the 14th century to the 17th century. It is difficult to contend that even in the 13th century, the *Bhagavad-gītā* had come upon an age of obscurity when Madhva (1199–1276 CE) 'wrote two works on the *Bhagavad-gītā*: the *Gītābhāṣya* and *Gītātātparya*'.[23]

The period of the alleged obscurity of the *Gītā* also happens to be the period of Hindu–Muslim interaction, first under the Delhi Sultanate and then under the Moghul Empire. If the *Gītā* continued to be a text of any significance, then one would expect it to figure in the Hindu–Muslim encounter. One would also expect the exponents of various schools of Hindu thought to continue commenting on it. Such indeed seems to be the case. As is well known, during these centuries, the regional languages of India started coming into their own. The *Jñāneśvarī*, 'a commentary in Marathi verse' on the *Gītā*, written by Jñāneśvara, a revered saint of the *Bhāgavata* sect,[24] has already been alluded to. During the 14th century, the tradition of commenting on the *Gītā* in the classical fashion was maintained. For example, Vedāntadeśika (1268–1369)[25] wrote a commentary on Rāmānuja's commentary on the *Gītā* in Tamilnadu, called the *Tātparyacandrikā*.[26] Then, at the beginning of the 15th century, Śrīdhara Svāmin of Benaras commented on the *Bhagavad-gītā*, his commentary being 'best known' among numerous commentaries written by Śaṅkara's disciples.[27] Similarly Nīlakaṇṭha, 'the best known commentator of the *Mahābhārata*', 'who lived at Kurpara, to the west of Godavari, in Maharashtra, and according to Burnell, belongs to the 16th century',[28] wrote a commentary on the *Bhagavad-gītā* as a part of his larger commentarial effort. Madhusūdana Sarasvatī, 'a 16th-century *Advdaitin*' and 'the author of many works on *Advaita* philosophy',[29] commented on the *Bhagavad-gītā*,[30] and although Vijñānabhikṣu, 'who lived about the beginning of the 17th century',[31] did not write a commentary on the *Bhagavad-gītā*, he composed the *Īśvara-gītā* and thought 'that since the *Īśvara-gītā* contains the main purport of the *Bhagavad-gītā* it was unnecessary for him to write any commentary on the latter'.[32] Baladeva, who 'is said to have lived about the beginning of the 18th century',[33] he also wrote a commentary on the *Gītā*, called *Gītā-bhūṣaṇa*.[34]

This period from the 14th century to the 17th century, as pointed out earlier, was also marked by Hindu–Muslim interaction, the high point of which was reached during and following the reign of Akbar, who died in 1605.[35] 'In Akbar's reign a large number of Sanskrit works were translated into Persian under his patronage, and after his death such translations continued to be made by Muslim scholars working on their own initiative'.[36] The *Bhagavad-gītā* attracted the attention of some of these scholars. For example, 'Abdur Rahman Chishti syncretized Hindu theories of cosmogony in his *Mir'atu'l-Makhluqāt* and offered an Islamizing explanation of the *Bhagavad-gītā*'.[37] It also attracted the notice of Dārā Shukoh. It is well known that he translated the *Upaniṣads* into Persian; it is not equally well known that 'he translated (apparently with the help of pandits) *Bhagavad-gītā* under the misleading title of "Battle between Arjuna and Duryodhan," divided into 18 chapters, as we learn from a marginal note in the India Office Library MS. of this work'.[38] Dara Shukoh lived in the 17th century, and the fact that he should choose to translate the *Gītā* seems to attest to its influence and popularity.

Thus, it does not seem correct to say that the *Gītā* had fallen on bad days from the 14th century to the 17th century. It is true that during this period, the *Bhāgavata Purāṇa* and the *Rāmāyaṇa* gained immense popularity under the influence of the *Bhakti* movement, but that does not mean that the *Gītā* was forgotten, and at no time can it be said to have suffered obscurity. That it continued to be philosophically important is obvious. And on the issue of its 'comparative obscurity', the preface of Charles Wilkins to his translation is particularly enlightening. Some scholars, as was seen earlier, seemed to suggest that the *Bhagavad-gītā* became important because Charles Wilkins chose to translate it; the real state of affairs seems to have been that Charles Wilkins chose to translate it because the work enjoyed great influence and popularity among the Hindus. The advertisement of the book, dated 30 May 1785, states that 'The antiquity of the original, and the veneration in which it hath been held for many ages, by a very considerable portion of the human race, must render it one of the greatest curiosities ever presented to the literary world'.[39] More pertinently, in the translator's preface, Charles Wilkins refers to the fact that

> The *brāhmaṇas* esteem this work to contain all the grand mysteries of their religion; and so careful are they to conceal it from the knowledge of those of a different persuasion, and even the vulgar of their own, that the Translator might have sought in vain for assistance, had not the liberal treatment that they have experienced from the boldness of our government . . . at length created in their breasts a confidence in his countrymen sufficient to remove every jealous prejudice from their minds.[40]

The recognition of the importance of the *Gītā* is further attested to by the remarks that Warren Hastings presented on the work to Nathaniel Smith. One of the ways that Warren Hastings tries to justify the literary undertaking on the part of the East India Company, which had become a political power in India by this time, was in the favourable impact it would have on the Hindus.[41] If one is out to achieve such a goal, then in all likelihood, one would promote the translation of a work *already* popular among the Hindus rather than select an obscure work.[42]

One may next turn to an examination of the arguments adduced by Agehananda Bharati. In this connection, the following points need to be noted. First, Bharati states that the *Bhagavad-gītā* has come to be regarded as the Hindu Bible and that 'no challenge against this notion has ever emerged from the spokesmen of the Renaissance'.[43] One wonders whether he regards Dayānanda Sarasvatī as one of these spokespeople[44] – probably not if he is concerned only with the English-speaking spokespeople. But Dayānanda Sarasvatī, founder of the militant *Ārya Samāj*, 'refused to recognize the authority of the *Gītā* and limited the scriptural sources of his movement to the *Vedas*',[45] so the 'grassroots pandit' did have his say. But to what effect? 'He thereby weakened the theoretical appeal of his dynamic reform programme',[46] a further testimony to the importance of the *Gītā*. So the challenge did emerge but did not go far. Second, Bharati states that although Mohandas Gandhi 'must have heard about the *Gītā* in the orthodox setting of his *Vaiṣṇava* childhood', it was when he read it in London that he began to 'espouse the text as the *vademecum* of his political creed'.[47] This last statement does not seem to fully correspond to facts. The political creed of Mohandas Gandhi emerged quite some time *after* his stay in London. It is well known that *ahimsā* was a key element in this creed. But Gandhi wrote in 1925 that

> My first acquaintance with the *Gītā* was in 1889, when I was almost twenty, I had not then much of an inkling of the principle of *ahimsa*. . . . I believed in those days for preparing ourselves for a fight with the English.[48]

Here again the pizza effect seems to have been overdone.[49]

From a consideration of the various facts which attest to the continued importance of the *Bhagavad-gītā* in the Hindu tradition, it is clear that the scholars who attribute its recent importance to the Hindu renaissance have overstated their point. What they perceive correctly is that the *Gītā* seems tailormade to suit the ideological orientation of the Hindu renaissance – hence its fascination for it.[50] But to go beyond this perception, and especially to perceive an artificial inflation of the importance of the *Bhagavad-gītā*, is to go beyond the evidence. The following comment by Madeleine Biardeau is more judicious:

> Interesting statistics might also be generated-but we are lacking in sufficient data for relatively early times-on variations on the number of commentaries written on the *Gītā* in each period of history. It would be a rather safe bet here to say that their numbers have increased markedly over the past decades, and that this renewal of interest is more than a mere effect of advances in publishing techniques. The *Gītā* is the sole widely accessible text that is able to preach to today's Hindu an ideal of action compatible

> with its deepest held beliefs. India thus possesses, in its most ancient and most authorized tradition, all that it needs to renew its vision of the world and to edify a theology capable of giving spiritual nourishment to a 'modern' society.[51]

This makes it all the more imperative that we now ask the following crucial question: what does the text think of itself?

Does the *Bhagavad*-gītā then have a philosophy and an interpretation of its own?

Does the *Bhagavad-gītā* then have a philosophy and an interpretation of its own? Let us begin by asking, does the *Bhagavad-gītā* possess a philosophy of its own? For the moment, the *Bhagavad-gītā* is studied as a part of the *prasthāna-traya*, so it loses its integrity in this respect and gets subsumed in a system. Such a subsumption has a subtle effect on how we approach the *Bhagavad-gītā*. Two presuppositions begin to mediate our understanding of the *Bhagavad-gītā* imperceptibly the moment it enters the exegetical circle of *Vedānta*: first, the *Bhagavad-gītā* possesses a *single* correct philosophical interpretation in keeping with the implication of *Brahma-sūtra* 1.1.4., and, second, this correct philosophical interpretation accords with that of the particular school of *Vedānta* involved, be it *Advaita*, *Viśiṣṭādvaita*, *Dvaita*, *Śuddhādvaita*, *Dvaitādvaita*, *Acintya-bhedābheda*, or another.

These presuppositions are *not* confined to the traditional interpretations of the *Bhagavad-gītā*. In essence, though not in form, the situation remains unchanged when we begin to consider the modern interpretations of the *Bhagavad-gītā*. When a modern scholar offers a philosophical interpretation of the *Bhagavad-gītā*, the exercise is usually carried out with the same presuppositions underlying it: there is only one correct philosophical interpretation of the *Bhagavad-gītā*, and the scholar in question has disclosed it to us. What is being claimed here, though slightly unusual, is not at all revolutionary. It only makes explicit what has been implicit in the hermeneutical discourse around the *Bhagavad-gītā*. Although it is true that when the implicit is made explicit, a fresh vision seems to emerge, it is by no means clear that it also constitutes a new vision. Nevertheless, the situation seems to involve sufficient novelty to require evidentiary support.

In the case of the traditional position, the doctrine of *ekavākyatā* ensures that the univocality of the *Bhagavad-gītā* is assumed. The assumption may not be as arbitrary as it might appear at first sight, because two pieces of evidence can he adduced in support, though not strong enough to clinch the issue. The first rests on the assumption that both the *Bhagavad-gītā* and the *Brahma-sūtra* may have a common author, and the second rests on the claim that the *Bhagavad-gītā* and the *Brahma-sūtra* refer to each other. On the basis of these pieces of evidence, it could be claimed that, according to tradition, univocality in relation to the *Bhagavad-gītā* should be assumed.

Let us then turn to an examination of these two points. First, according to tradition, the *Bhagavad-gītā* is the 'work' of Vyāsa. The doctrine of *ekavākyatā* can be traced to the *Brahma-sūtra*. The authorship of the *Brahma-sūtra* has been attributed to Bādarāyaṇa, who, and this is the important point, has also been identified by tradition as Vyāsa.[52] If both of the texts are the work of a single author, then it becomes all the more credible to suggest that two texts should be read in the light of each other. There is a paradox one often plays with in comparative religion: what if two traditions are locked boxes, each containing the other's key? We are saved from this predicament in studying a single tradition – the Hindu in this case – by the possibility that the key found in one text may help unlock the other. It must, however, be added that some scholars regard this identification of the two as 'recent tradition'.[53]

Second, the expression *smaryate* and related expressions often occur in the *Brahma-sūtra*, i.e., as stated in the *Smṛtis*. In several contexts, the Hindu hermeneutical tradition exhibits impressive unity in identifying the *Bhagavad-gītā* as the referent[54] – substantiating the claim that '*Bhagavad-gītā* is referred to in the *Brahma-sūtra*'.[55] From the other side, *Bhagavad-gītā* 13.4 employs the word brahmasūtra, which, significantly, Śaṅkara does *not* read[56] specifically as a reference to the *Brahma-sūtra*. However, some scholars accept the identification without hesitation, while others regard it as an open question. R.C. Zaehner remarks, '*Brahma-sūtra-padaiś*, aphoristic verses concerning *Brahman*. Some commentators take this to refer to the *Brahma-sūtras* of Bādarāyaṇa, the basic classic of *Vedānta* philosophy on which all the great ancient commentators have written commentaries. That, however, is anyone's guess'.[57]

In the case of modern interpretations of the *Bhagavad-gītā*, we are fortunate in possessing an explicit statement on the univocality of the *Bhagavad-gītā*. It emanates from no less a figure than B.G. Tilak:

> In my boyhood I was told that *Bhagavad-gītā* was universally acknowledged to be a book containing all the principles and philosophy of the Hindu religion, and I thought if this be so I should find an answer in this book to my query; and thus began my study of the *Bhagavad-gītā*. I approached the book with a mind prepossessed by no previous ideas about any philosophy, and had no theory of my own for which I sought any support in the *Gītā* . . . When you want to read and understand a book, especially a great work like the *Gītā*-you must approach it with an unprejudiced and unprepossessed mind. To do this, I know, is one of the most difficult things. Those who profess to do it may have a lurking thought or prejudice in their minds which vitiates the reading of the book to some extent. However, I am describing to you the frame of mind one must get into if one wants to get at the truth and, however difficult it be, it has to be done. The next thing one has to do is to take into consideration the time and the circumstances in which the book was written and the purpose for which the book was written. In short the book must not be read devoid of its context. This is especially true about a book like the *Bhagavad-gītā*. Various commentators have put as

> many interpretations on the book, and surely the writer or composer could not have written or composed the book for so many interpretations being put on it. He must have but one meaning and one purpose running through the book and that I have tried to find out, I believe I have succeeded in it, because having no theory of mine for which I sought any support from the book so universally respected, I had no reason to twist the text to suit my theory. There has not been a commentator of the *Gītā* who did not advocate a pet theory of his own and has not tried to support the same by showing that the *Bhagavad-gītā* lent him support.[58]

The two theatres of modern scholarship around the *Gītā* have been India and the West. In the case of India, a host of scholars have tried to interpret the *Bhagavad-gītā*, and the underlying impulse seems to have been to arrive at the *one* underlying meaning of the text or, better still, the one meaning underlying the text. These modern thinkers believe that in a variety of ways they are in touch with truth or truths which provide an esoteric understanding of the text.

Theosophy, with its occult ties from the time of H.P. Blavatsky, had a truth which functioned as a controlling orthodoxy in its interpretation of the *Gītā* at least implicitly. Although Tilak's interpretation is a combination of traditional interpretations and modern scholarship, Tilak titled his result *Gītā Rahasya*, 'the Esoteric Import of the *Gītā*'. For Gandhi, the esoteric interpretation was based on one's living the *Gītā* in one's own life, so that the philosophy based on his experiences, which he confidently believed were 'experiments with Truth', provided the correct interpretation. For Vinoba Bhave, the real meaning of the *Gītā* is not always evident to the average reader. It may even involve the alteration of the text itself. Aurobindo brings his experiences of higher levels of consciousness to the *Gītā* and thus claims experiences of truth which ultimately leave the *Gītā* behind, and *Bhaktivedānta* claims the insights of correct 'disciplic succession' as opposed to 'mundane scholarship'. As a *guru*, Shivananda also claims an authentic line of succession, and his own self-realization within that spiritual inheritance is the apparent basis for his interpretations. Vivekananda and Radhakrishnan are less interested in esoteric interpretations, but Radhakrishnan speaks of the 'eternal truths' of the *Gītā*, which need recognition apart from its historical teachings, and these, he believes, are based on an essential religious experience found in all traditions. Only Bankim, whose goal was to be a model of Western argument and logic, did not seem to claim a special knowledge for interpreting the *Gītā*.[59]

The same esoterism also seems to be the driving force behind Western orientalist interpretations to the *Bhagavad-gītā*. Once again, these, implicitly or explicitly, lay claim to being the one correct interpretation, as the following excerpt illustrates:

> Hopkins makes the *Gītā* a Kṛṣṇaite version of a Viṣṇuite poem, which was itself a late Upaniṣad. Keith believes that it was originally an Upaniṣad of the type of the *Śvetāśvataram* but was later adapted to the cult of Kṛṣṇa. Hollzmann looks upon it as a Viṣṇuite remodeling of a pantheistic poem.

> Barnett thinks that different strands of tradition became confused in the mind of the author. Deussen makes it a late product of the degeneration of the monistic thought of the *Upaniṣads*, belonging to a period of transition from theism to realistic atheism.[60]

These developments seem to make the following statement about Hinduism as a whole, made by B.S. Yadav, equally applicable to the *Bhagavad-gītā* as a text. He writes,

> The so-called Hinduism is a rolling conference of conceptual spaces, all of them facing all, and all of them requiring all. Each claims loyalty to the *śrutis*, each showing how its claims are decisively true, and charging the rival schools with perpetuating the confusion of tongue in the *dharmakṣetra* (the field of religion). . . . A lay Hindu . . . is a living contradiction, unsynthetic and logically incomplete to any and all. 'Synthetic unity' has never existed in Hinduism, neither in conceptual space nor in lived time. Hinduism is a moving form of life whose predicament is to be incomplete to its own logics; it is a history of contradictions in flesh, fortunately demanding that their resolution be constantly postponed.[61]

It is telling that he uses an expression in the passage which occurs at the beginning of the *Bhagavad-gītā*, namely *dharmakṣetra.*

What is the *Bhagavad-gītā*'s view regarding its philosophy and interpretation?

The questions we have to face now are as follows: What is the *Bhagavad-gītā*'s own view in this matter? Does it have a philosophy of its own or does it have philosophies of its own? And once again, does the *Bhagavad-gītā* offer *an interpretation* of itself despite its forbidding hermeneutical proximity to itself, or does it too offer *interpretations* of itself? These questions, and the answers to them, constitute the core issue of this chapter.

The answers to these questions, I will now maintain, can be obtained by degrees. As a first step, we may try to elicit it from the literature, which claims to be *directly* connected with the *Bhagavad-gītā*, and then, as a second step, we could try to elicit it from the *Bhagavad-gītā* itself.

By 'literature directly connected with the *Bhagavad-gītā*', I wish to indicate that the *Bhagavad-gītā* is *not* the only text available to us in the tradition in which Kṛṣṇa and Arjuna engage in dialogue. There are, in addition to the *Bhagavad-gītā*, at least three other texts in which Kṛṣṇa and Arjuna engage in a didactic dialogue. These have been collectively referred to by R.D. *Karma*rkar as *Kṛṣṇa Gītās*, or texts wherein 'Kṛṣṇa is the teacher and Arjuna, the pupil'.[62]

The category of the *Gītā* is 'constituted of the *Bhagavad-gītā*, the *Anu-gītā*, the *Uttara-gītā* and the *Arjunopākhyāna*'.[63] Out of these, the *Bhagavad-gītā* needs no introduction, but a word of explanation, however brief, regarding the other texts may not be out of place. The *Anu-gītā*, like the *Bhagavad-gītā* (VI:23–40), belongs to the *Mahābhārata* (XIV:16–51). Therein Arjuna requests Kṛṣṇa

> repeat the instruction . . . already conveyed to him on 'the holy field of Kurukṣetra' but which has gone out of his 'degenerate mind'. Kṛṣṇa thereupon protests that he is not equal to a verbatim recapitulation of the *Bhagavad-gītā* but agrees in lieu of that to impart to Arjuna the same instruction in other words.[64]

The textual status of *Uttara-gītā* is less certain. The word *uttara* in its title 'seems to mean "later" or "last" – a relative term – hinting at some relation between the *Uttara-gītā* and the *Bhagavad-gītā*'.[65] As a text, however,

> *The Uttara-gītā* is rather an obscure work known more or less owing to the commentary thereon of the learned Gauḍapāda, the grand preceptor of Śaṅkarācārya. It is mentioned in the colophons of some of the manuscripts that it is contained in some one or the other Parvans of *The Mahābhārata*, or in the *Bhāgavata Purāṇa*, but we do not come across the actual text of the work in any of the extant editions or manuscripts of these works.[66]

By contrast, the textual status of the *Arjunopākhyāna* is settled. It forms a part (cantos 52–8, a total of 254 *ślokas*) of the *Nirvāṇa* section (first part) of[67] the *Yogavāsiṣṭha.* The *Yogavāśiṣṭha* purports to be a dialogue between Vāsiṣṭha and Rāma, who, according to traditional Hindu chronology, *precede* Kṛṣṇa and Arjuna.

> But nothing was insurmountable to the gifted writer of the *Arjunopākhyāna* who, with amazing boldness got out of this difficulty by solemnly telling his readers that Vāsiṣṭha narrates to Rāma the *Bhagavad-gītā as it would be told by Kṛṣṇa in the future.*[68]

But does this penumbral literature around the *Bhagavad-gītā* provide us with any clue about the *Bhagavad-gītā*'s own philosophy and interpretation?

I suggest that it does. Consider, for instance, the famous theophany of Kṛṣṇa in the 11th chapter of the *Bhagavad-gītā.* If we regard Sañjaya's *own* response to the dialogue between Kṛṣṇa and Arjuna as the first comment (though not a commentary) that we possess in the tradition, then we find that this theophany is showcased as the central feature of the *Bhagavad-gītā* in these inspired verses of the eighteenth chapter.

Sañjaya says,

> 74 Thus have I heard the conversation of Vāsudeva and the great soul Pārtha, so astounding that my hair stands on end. 75 By the grace of Vyāsa I have heard this supreme secret of *yoga* directly from Kṛṣṇa, the master of *yoga*, who spoke it personally. 76 O king, reflecting again and again on this wondrous and virtuous colloquy of Keśava and Arjuna, I am thrilled and

> rejoice again and again. 77 O king, recalling again and again the astonishing form of Hari, my amazement is immense, and joy excites me again and once again. 78 Wherever there is Kṛṣṇa, the master of *yoga*, and wherever there is Pārtha, the carrier of the bow, there will surely be fortune, victory, prosperity and justice. That I verily believe.[69]

However, the *Anu-gītā* alludes to the theophany[70] only in passing, whereas in the *Uttara-gītā*, 'the manifestation of Universal nature (*Viśvarūpa*) is conspicuous by its absence'.[71] I could not trace out any explicit mention of it in the *Arjunopākhyāna*.[72] The *Anu-gītā* interprets the *Bhagavad-gītā* with a strong *Sāṅkhyan* bias, a fact in keeping with its mention in the *Sāṅkhya-sāra* of Vijñānabhikṣu. On the other hand, the *Uttara-gītā* is essentially *Yogic* in its orientation:

> It is evident from the text of the *Uttara-gītā* that it rather details out the *Yogic* way of the attainment of *Brahman*. Its *claim* to be supplementing the *Bhagavad-gītā* is justified then, as the *Bhagavad-gītā* refers to many ways for the attainment of *Brahman*, of which *Karma-yoga* and *bhakti-yoga* are described, to a certain extent, whereas *'Yoga'* though mentioned often is not described. *Uttara-gītā* supplies the lacuna and explains the *Yoga* proper.[73]

The point which should galvanize our attention here is that already, in the works in the immediate vicinity of the *Gītā* itself, the saliences in the interpretation of the text are beginning to diverge. The primary orientation is provided by *Sāṅkhya*, by *jñāna* in the *Anu-gītā*, by *Yoga* in the *Uttara-gītā*, and by *kalpanā vāda*[74] in the *Arjunopākhyāna*. This last interpretation is rendered possible, if not plausible, by the appearance of the word *māyā* in the *Bhagavad-gītā*. The author of the *Arjunopākhyāna* goes all out 'to explain the same in as detailed a manner as he possibly could, and he avails himself of the various philosophical tenets current in his own times, and does not shirk at adopting several concepts from Buddhism as well'.[75] By contrast, in the *Purārṇas*, the *Bhagavad-gītā* is primarily, but again not exclusively, associated with devotion.[76]

The historical context of the *Bhagavad-gītā*

In the previous section, the immediate textual context of the *Bhagavad-gītā* was examined for the light it might shed on its philosophy and exegesis. In this section, the discussion may be extended to include the historical context of the *Bhagavad-gītā* with the same goal in mind.

Such an exercise is not free from problems. After all, the precise date of the *Bhagvad-gītā* is still a matter of conjecture. Nevertheless, there seems to be widespread agreement that it should be placed in the centuries which immediately precede the Common Era, and whether this should be the 1st, the 2nd[77] or the 3rd century[78] BCE remains a moot point. This point is further complicated by the suggestion that the text may have assumed its present from over a period of time.[79]

At this point, then, one faces a clear choice: either one can altogether abandon the attempt to situate the text historically and proceed with the rest of the chapter, or one can look for a text which shares the *Bhagavad-gītā*'s chronological ambiguity but is sufficiently close to it in point of time to serve as a foil for understanding it as a text. I have adopted the latter course here. The *Manusmṛti*, as a text, has also been placed 'around the second century B.C.E. to the first century B.C.E.'[80] It might therefore be helpful to juxtapose the two texts in the hope that such a comparison will add to our hermeneutical understanding of the *Bhagavad-gītā*'s position on related matters.

Consider now the following verses of the *Bhagavad-gītā*.

Chapter IV:25–33

25 Some *yogīs* worship the gods alone through sacrifice, while others sacrifice through offering in the fire of *Brahman*. 26 Still others sacrifice the senses such as hearing in the fire of self-restraint, while some offer the objects of the senses such as sound, in the fire of the senses. 27 Others offer all the actions of the senses and the movements of the life air in the fire of self-control *yoga*, a fire which is kindled by the torch of knowledge. 28 Stringently self-controlled and following strict vows, some sacrifice material possessions, some sacrifice through austere practices, some through the performance of *yoga*, whereas others sacrifice through study and recitation of the *Veda*. 29 Some offer the inhalation into the exhalation, and the exhalation into the inhalation; thus restraining the process of breathing they are intent on controlling the life air. 30 Others thus restricting their food offer the life air into itself; all these know the meaning of sacrifice and all their sins are destroyed by it. 31 Having eaten the nectar of the sacrifice's remnants, they go to the eternal *Brahman*. O best of the Kurus, not even this world is for him who does not sacrifice; how then the next? 32 Thus diverse sorts of sacrifices spread out in *Brahman's* mouth; know them all to be born of action, as by knowing them thus, you shall attain liberation.[81]

These verses bear comparison with the following verses of the *Manusmṛti* (IV:21–4):

21. Let him never, if he is able (to perform them), neglect the sacrifices in the sages, to the gods, to the *Bhūtas*, to men and to the manes.
22. Some men who know the ordinances for sacrificial rites, always offer these great sacrifices in their organs (of sensation), without any (external) effort.
23. Knowing that the (performance of the) sacrifice in their speech and their breath yields imperishable (rewards), some always offer their breath in their speech, and their speech in their breath.

24. Other *brāhmaṇas*, seeing with the eye of knowledge that the performance of those rites has knowledge for its root, always perform them through knowledge alone.[82]

The significance of the comparison lies in that although the language is highly sacrificial, in a ritualistic sense, it is 'intentionally soteriological'. The following observation of K. Satchidananda Murty is helpful here: when performed selflessly, 'sacrifice ceases to be (mere) ritual, and becomes as Bharadvāja said, skill in action. *Yajñaḥ karmasu kauśalam*. The *Gītā* later adopted this by substituting *Yogaḥ* for *Yajñaḥ*'[83] famously in the lapidary utterance '*yogaḥ karmasu kauśalam*' (11.50).

A second point on the relation of the *Bhagavad-gītā* to the *Manusmṛti* requires elaboration. In the current contemporary understanding of the *Bhagavad-gītā*, its association with *Karma Yoga* plays a major role. This has led scholars to propose that the *Bhagavad-gītā* shares the rigid hierarchical conception of the caste system found in the *Manusmṛti*. A celebrated exponent of this view is the dean of Western Indologists, Professor A.L. Basham:

> A feature of the *Bhagavad-gītā* which has aroused criticism in modern times is its sturdy defense of the system of the four classes. 'It is better', says Kṛṣṇa, 'to perform one's own duty, however badly, than to do another's well. It is better to die engaged in one's own duty; the duty of other men is dangerous' (3.35). The word for duty here is *dharma*, and the poet has in mind the respective *dharmas* of the four classes. This verse is repealed with variations elsewhere in the *Bhagavad-gītā* (e.g., 18.47) and in the *Dharma Śāstra* literature of a somewhat later time. Modern interpreters of the *Bhagavad-gītā*, are inclined to ignore or reinterpret the passages dealing with the class system, but it is quite clear that the text is a defense not only of the warrior's duty to wage righteous warfare but also of the whole *brāhmaṇic* social system.[84]

The analogical reasoning employed here is plausible but misleading. The reason given in the *Manusmṛti* (X.97) for not abandoning one's *svadharma* is social and not soteriological. According to Manu, one should not abandon one's caste duty, because this leads to loss of caste. There is no such suggestion in the *Bhagavad-gītā*, where the pursuit of *svadharma* is recommended on the positive grounds that it leads to *mokṣa* and not on the negative ground that a lapse from it would lead to ostracization. Nevertheless, on the whole,[85] much is to be said for Professor Murty's suggestion that the *Manusmṛti* may be found as a good exposition of the essence of Vedic religion and that the closeness of the *Vedic karma-yoga to the karma-yoga of the Bhagavad-gītā*. It succeeds in showing a way of understanding, from a higher standpoint, the apparent ritualistic religion of the earlier part of the *Veda* and relating it to the obvious spiritual teaching of the later part. This is what is important in the *smṛti*, and not its many verses about social organization, the "do's" and "don'ts" the taboos, etc., which are irrelevant.[86]

Finally, there is a striking similarity in the catholicity of the spiritual outlook found in the *Bhagavad-gītā*, and the *Manusmṛti*. The concluding portion of the *Manusmṛti* contains the following verse (XII. 123):

> Some call him Agni (Fire), others Manu,
> the Lord of Creatures, others
> Indra, others the vital air, and
> again others eternal *Brahman*.[87]

It may interest the reader that this verse is cited by Śaṅkara in his *Aitareya-upaniṣad-bhāṣya*.[88]

The insight one gains through the two previous sections may now be succinctly stated. This insight is corrective of two popular perceptions: first, the interpretation of the *Bhagavad-gītā* as a source text of *Jñāna-yoga* (through Śaṅkara in ancient India), of *bhakti-yoga* (through Rāmānuja in medieval India), and finally of *karma-yoga* (through B.G. Tilak in modern India) succeeded each other diachronically, and, second, it was universalized in modern times as text and the alchemy of modernity transmuted the Hindu *Gītā* into a universal *Gītā*. The foregoing survey demonstrates that these elements have been present in the philosophy and interpretation of the *Bhagavad-gītā* from the beginning.

What does the *Bhagavad-gītā* say about its own philosophy and interpretation?

The exercises we have carried out so far were necessary for a proper appreciation of the *Bhagavad-gītā*, but they are not sufficient, in that we must now consult the text itself as such instead of hermeneutically hovering around it. Indeed, some readers may feel that we have taken unconscionably long to arrive at the core issue, but we are there now: what does the *Bhagavad-gītā* have to say about its own philosophy and interpretation?

The *Bhagavad-gītā* seems to offer many visions of reality. Thus, one might more properly speak not of *the* philosophy but of the *philosophies* of the *Bhagavad-gītā*. Similarly, it also seems to offer many paths to salvation. Reading it, in fact, is like walking through a pluralist bazaar. The following sections from the text itself, chosen at random, provide the needed textual evidence to support these claims.

Chapter VII:21–3

> 21 Whoever that devotee may be, and whatever divine form he may desire to worship faithfully, it is I who bestow that steady faith upon him. 22
> Endowed with such faith, he endeavours to worship that deity and thus his desires obtain fulfillment; in fact by me alone are these desires fulfilled.
> 23 In any case, ephemeral is the fruit these people of little wit obtain; those who worship the gods will go to the gods, whereas my devotees will surely come to me.[89]

Chapter IX:14–15

14 Ever striving to glorify me with fortitude, bowing down to me in devotion, they are ever absorbed in worshiping me. 15 Others, offering me the sacrifice of knowledge, worship me as unity, as diversity, or as variously manifested and facing all directions.[90]

Chapter XII:8–12

8 Fix your mind on me alone, and absorb your consciousness in me; thus you shall surely abide in me. 9 If you cannot fix your consciousness steadily upon me, then aspire to reach me through repeated *yoga* practice, O Dhanañjaya. 10 If you are incapable even of that, embrace the path of action, for which I am the highest goal, since by acting for me you shall attain perfection. 11 But if you are even unable to follow this path of refuge in me through acts devoted to me, then give up the fruits of all your actions, thus restraining yourself. 12 Knowledge is superior to practice, meditation is superior to knowledge, and relinquishing the fruits of actions is higher than meditation, as tranquility soon follows such relinquishment.[91]

Chapter XIII:24–5

24 Some see the self by themselves through meditation and inner contemplation, others through *Sāṅkhya yoga*, while others through *Karma yoga*. 25 Still others, although not knowing all this, revere it upon hearing it from others. Devoted to what they have heard, they too cross beyond death.[92]

These verses can be interpreted in two ways: along the ladder approach and along the wheel approach. According to the ladder approach, although the *Gītā* initially approves of several approaches, it ultimately settles for only one: whether it be a matter of theory (in matters of philosophical structure) or practice (in matters of soteriological structure). The natural conclusion which the ladder approach points to is that either the *Gītā* ultimately espouses only one philosophy and only one *Yoga*[93] or as a whole the *Gītā* constitutes the only way.[94] In other words, it is crucial to have one's ladder against the right wall. It would be devastating to discover when one has finally managed to climb the ladder that one had it in a place it should not be.

According to the wheel approach, all the spokes point to and lead to the hub of the wheel no matter where the nave of the wheel may be resting. According to this view, all the philosophies which can be derived from the *Gītā* are different only kaleidoscopically and not essentially, and all the paths it mentions lead to the goal. In contrast, according to the previous approach, all paths lead to the path, which leads to the goal. S. Radhakrishnan remarks that

> The differences of interpretation are held to be differences determined by the viewpoint adopted. The Hindu tradition believes that the different

> views are complementary. Even the systems of Indian philosophy are so many points of view, or *darśanas*, which are mutually complementary and not contradictory. The *Bhāgavata* says that the sages have described in various ways the essential truths. A popular verse declares: 'From the viewpoint of the body, I am Thy servant, from the view point of the ego, I am a portion of Thee; from the viewpoint of the self I am Thyself. This is my conviction'. God is experienced as Thou or I according to the plane in which consciousness centres.[95]

Which of these two approaches correctly reflect *Bhagavad-gītā*'s multivalency?

To satisfactorily answer this question, one central fact of the *Bhagavad-gītā* must be kept in mind: it never loses sight of its aim that Arjuna has to be induced to fight. Its theoretical multisidedness contrasts sharply with its pragmatic single-pointedness. As M. Hiriyanna notes,

> The teaching, when taken in its details, is full of perplexity, because the work shares the heterogeneous character, previously mentioned, of the epic to which it belongs. We have already referred by the way to one aspect of it, viz., that while it is based in some places on the *Upaniṣads*, it presupposes in others a theistic view of the type designated as *Bhāgavata* religion. But whatever these perplexities may be, there is *absolutely no doubt as regards the central point of its practical teaching.*[96]

We can thus say that while *heuristically* the *Bhagavad-gītā* is multivalent, *didactically* it is univalent.

Additional comments

The chapter concludes with a few additional comments:

1 To the extent that philosophy constitutes an investigation into the nature of reality and such an investigation may disclose a structure of reality, the *Gītā* speaks in terms of several structures of reality.[97] I prescind from presenting these various structures for fear of unduly enlarging the chapter, but attention must be drawn to a common factor in all of them – that is, reality contains several tiers, or is multilayered.

2 To the extent that these structures possess a soteriological dimension, the way of achieving that salvation is multisided. Although the *Bhagavad-gītā* has been largely studied, both in India and beyond, on the whole, to arrive at its one correct meaning, identify its one correct philosophy or determine its one correct interpretation, the *Gītā*'s own approach to itself seems to indicate that it might be studied not so much with a view to determining its one correct interpretation but rather to raise our awareness of its interpretive possibilities, consistently with its belief that reality is multilayered and the approaches to it multisided (*bahudhā viśvatomukham*).

3 However, not all interpretations of the *Gītā* are valid. Pluralism should not be confused with reckless relativism. While there are many possible approaches to the *Gītā*, there are limits as to just what is acceptable to the tradition and what is not. We leave it to our readers to research the rich resources surrounding the *Gītā*, and we leave it to them, too, to decide what is a legitimate reading of this special text.

Notes

1 This chapter was originally written for the Project of History of Indian Science, Philosophy and Culture, Volume I, Part II, and then published by the *Journal of Vaishnava Studies*.

2 For bibliographic surveys, see Jagdish Chander Kapoor. 1983. *Bhagavad-gītā: An International Bibliography from 1785–1979 Imprints*. New York: Garland Publishers; W.M. Callewaert and S. Hemrai. 1983. *Bhagavadgītānuvāda*: *A Study in Transcultural Translation*. Ranchi: Sathya Bharati Publication. For Buddhist and Jaina perspectives on the *Bhagavad-gīta*, see D. Lopez (ed.). 1995. *Buddhism in Practice*, pp. 391–2. Princeton: Princeton University Press; P.S. Jaini. 1979. *The Jaina Path of Purification*, pp. 313–14 Berkeley: University of California Press.

3 See G.S. Sadhale (ed.). 1935. *The Bhagavad-gītā with Eleven Commentaries*. Bombay: The "Gujarati" Printing Press; W.L.S. Pansikar (ed.). 1967. *Śrīmadbhagavadgītā*. Bombay: Nimayasagara Press.

4 However, also see Govind Chandra Pande. 1944. *Life and Thought of Śaṅkarācārya*, Chapter 2. Delhi: Motilal Banarsidass.

5 T.M.P. Mahadevan. 1971. *Outlines of Hinduism*, p. 141. Bombay: Chetana Ltd.

6 See A. Mahadeva Sastri. 1979. *The Bhagavad-gītā with the Commentar of Śri Śaṅkarācārya*, p. 4. Madras: Smata Books.

7 See Arvind Sharma. 1986. *The Hindu Gītā*, Chapter 3. London: Duckworth.

8 Ibid., Chapters 5 and 6.

9 T.M.P. Mahadevan. *op. cit*., p. 159–60.

10 Arvind Sharma. 1983. *Abhinavagupta Gītārthasaṅgraha*. Leiden: E.J. Brill.

11 See Joseph T. O'Connell. 1995–1996. "Karma in the *Bhagavad-gītā:* Caitanya Vaiṣṇava Views," *Journal of Studies in the Bhagavad-gītā*, Vol. 25–6, p. 91.

12 W.J. Johnson. 1994. *The Bhagavad Gītā*, p. i. New York: Oxford University Press.

13 See Swami Kripananda. 1989. *Jñāneśvarī*. Albany, NY: State University of New York Press.

14 I owe this information to Dr. Jogesh Chandra Pandya of the Department of Sanskrit and Indian Studies, Harvard University.

15 Personal communication, Prof. V.N. Rao of the University of Wisconsin, Madison.

16 Personal communication, Prof. Winand M. Callewaert, University of Luvain.

17 Navaranga Svāmi Sri Mukundadāsa. 1983. *Gītā Rahasya*. Delhi: Sri Prananatha Mission.

18 A.C. Bouquet. 1948. *Hinduism*, p. 84. New York: Hutchinsons University Library.

19 L.S.S. O'Malley, ed. 1968. *Modern India and the West*, p. 230. Oxford: Oxford University Press.

20 The original pizza was a simple, hot-baked bread without any trimmings, the staple of the Calabrian and Sicilian *contadini* from whom well over 90% of all Italo-Americans descend. After World War I, a highly celebrated dish, the US pizza of many sizes, flavours, and hues, made its way back to Italy with visiting kinfolk from America. The term and the object have acquired a new meaning and a new status, as well as many new tastes in the land of its origin, not only in the south, but throughout Italy (Agehananda Bharati. 1970. "The Hindu Renaissance and Its Apologetic Patterns," *The Journal of Asian Studies*, Vol. XXIX, No. 2, February, p. 273)

21 Ibid., p. 274. So also Gerald James Larson, who after stating that 'A. Bharati refers in a number of places in his writings to the process of "re-enculturation"' and quoting him on the 'pizza effect', adds

> A somewhat similar kind of process took place in the eighteenth and the nineteenth centuries with respect to the Bhagavad-gītā. When the British first came to power in India in the eighteenth century, Sanskrit texts like the Gītā were not in much use except in some devotional circles and among the traditional pandits.
> ("The *Bhagavad-gītā* as Cross-Cultural Process: Toward an Analysisof the Social Locutions of a Religious Text," *Journal of the American Academy of Religion*, Vol. XLIII, No. 4, December 1965, p. 664)

22 A.L. Basham. 1956. *The Wonder That Was India*, p. 342. London: Sidgwick & Jackson; But also see A.L. Basham, ed. 1975. *A Cultural History of India*, p. 3. Oxford: Clarendon Press.

23 W. Hill. P. Douglas. 1928. *The Bhagavadgīta*, p. 274. London: Oxford University Press.

24 Ibid. The work itself, however, was completed in the year 1290 'according to an entry at the end of the last chapter of the verse' (H.M. Lambert, ed. 1967. *Jnaneshvari*, p. 9. London: George Allen and Unwin). This tradition of Marathi commentaries on the *Gitā* was maintained by Vāman Pandit, who lived in the 17th century, made an 'extended exposition' of the *Bhagavad-gītā*, and 'called it the Yathartha Dipika (true commentary), as opposed to the Bhavartha Dipika (suggestive commentary), which was the alternative title of the Dnyanesvari' (Govind Chimnaji Bhate. 1939. *History of Modern Marathi Literature*, p. 40. Poona: Mahad & A.V. Patwardhan). He also made a literal translation of the Gītā into Marathi called the *Sama-Śloka-Gītā* (see Suniti Kumar Chatterji. 1963. *Languages and Literatures of Modern India*, p. 223. Calcutta: Bengal Publishers Private Ltd). In the same century, Dāsopant wrote the *Gītārṇava*, which 'is said to be in 150 thousand verses' (ibid., 220). I am indebted to Dr Alaka Hejib for these references, who also pointed out that Balarām Dās (c. 1500) composed an Oriya version of the *Bhagavad-gītā* (ibid., 205–6).w

25 Surendrarnath Dasgupta. 1932. *A History of Indian Philosophy*, Vol. III, pp. 119, 120. Cambridge: Cambridge University Press.

26 R.C. Majumdar, ed. 1960. *The Delhi Sultanate*, p. 481. Bombay: Bharatiya Vidya Bhavan.

27 Douglas P. Hill. *op. cit.*, p. 274.

28 Arthur A. Macdonell. 1968. *A History of Sanskrit Literature*, p. 290. New York: Haskell House Publishers, Ltd.

29 Eliot Deutsch and J.A.B. Van Buitenen. 1971. *A Source Book of Advaita Vedānta*, p. 288. Honolulu: University of Hawaii Press.

30 Wasudev Laxman Shastri Pansikar, ed. *op. cit. Passim*.

31 S. Radhakrishnan. 1960. *The Brhama Sutra*, p. 94. London: George Allen and Unwin.

32 Surendranath Dasgupta. *op. cit.*, Vol. III, p. 482.

33 S. Radhakrishnan. *op. cit.*, p. 97.

34 Ibid.

35 R.C. Majumder, et al. 1948. *An Advanced History of India*, p. 1016. London: Macmillan and Co.

36 A.L. Basham, ed. *op. cit.*, p. 291.

37 Ibid.

38 Kalika-Ranjan Qanungo. 1952. *Dara Shukoh*. Vol. 1, p. 102. Calcutta: S.C. Sarkar and Sons.

39 George Hendrik. 1959.*The Bhagavat-Geeta (1785) Translated, with Notes, by Charles Wilkins*, p. A2. Cainsville: Scholar's Facsimiles and Reprints. This was not so much a commercial advertisement as a literary one, and even after it had been discounted for

journalistic hyperbole, the statement remained significant, as attested by the veneration in which the *Gītā* was held.

40 Ibid., p. 23.

41 Ibid., p. 13.

42 Agehananda Bharati's comment in this context is worth noting: 'Another scarcely known fact, but one that must have been grist to Tilak's polemical mills: no less a person than Warren Hastings had written a preface to Wilkins's first English translation, in which he said that the *Gītā* would last when the British Dominion in India shall long have ceased to exist and when the sources which it once yielded to wealth and power are lost to remembrance' (*op. cit.*, p. 275). The relevant question to ask would be, would Warren Hastings contemplate with equanimity the prospect of a work 'scarcely known outside the learned circle of the Pandits' (as the *Gitā* was according to L.S.S. O'Malley [*op. cit.*, p. 230] and presumably Agehananda Bharati outliving the British Empire)?

43 Agehananda Bharati. *op. cit.*, p. 274.

44 See R.C. Majumdar, ed. 1965. *British Paramountey and Indian Renaissance*. Vol. II, Chapter IV. Bombay: Bharatiya Vidya Bhavan.

45 D. Mackenzie Brown. 1958. "The Philosophy of Bal Gangadhar Tilak," *The Journal of Asian Studies*, Vol. XVII, No. 2, February, p. 202. His biographer perhaps tries to gloss over this fact by stating that 'As Sri Krishna, in the Bhagwad Gītā, calls on Arjuna to fight and destroy evil, so does Dayananda call on all to resist evil' (Har Bilas Sarada. 1946. *Life of Dayananda Saraswati*, p. cxxii. Ajmer: Vedic Yant).

46 D. Mackenzie Brown. *op. cit.*, p. 202.

47 Agehananda Bharati. *op. cit.*, p. 275.

48 M.K. Gandhi. 1950. *Hindu Dhamra*, p. 151. Ahmedabad: Navajivan Press.

49 Agehananda Bharati's treatment contains two other 'frivolous blunders'. First, he states that Mohandas Gandhi read Annie Besant's translation of the *Gītā*. Annie Besant's translation wasn't published until 1895 (see W. Hill P. Douglas. *op. cit.*, p. 277). In 1889, Mohandas Gandhi read Edwin Arnold's translation, not Annie Besant's (see M.K. Gandhi. 1993. *An Autobiography*, pp. 67–8 Boston: Beacon Press). Second, he states that by the time Mohandas Gandhi read Annie Besant's impressionistic translation, 'B.G. Tilak (1856–1920) had published his *Gītārahasya* [*sic*] in Marathi' (*op. cit.* p. 275). The Gītārahasya was published in 1911 (see Douglas P. Hill. *op. cit.*, p. 278), and Mohandas Gandhi read the *Gītā* in translation in 1889. Hence, the statement seems to be incorrect.

50 See K.M. Panikkar. 1963. *The Foundation of New India*, pp. 36–43. London: George Allen and Unwin.

51 Madeleine Biardeau. 1985. *Hinduism: The Anthropology of a Civilization*, p. 165. Delhi: Oxford University Press.

52 Swami Vidyananda Saraswati. 1985. *The Brahmasūtra*, p. 17. Bombay: Deva Vedic Prakasana; S. Radhakrishnan. *op. cit.*, p. 22.

53 Edwin Gerow. 1987. "Bādarāyaṇa," in Mircea Eliade, Editor in Chief, *The Encyclopedia of Religion*. Vol. 11, p. 38. New York: Macmillan Publishing Company; but see G.V. Tagare. 1988. *Vayu Purāṇa*, Part II, p. 901, note 2. Delhi: Motilal Banarsidass.

54 Swami Vidyananda Saraswati. *op. cit.*, p. 16; S. Radhakrishnan. *op. cit.*, p. 297, 528, etc.

55 Eliot Deutsch and J.A.B. Van Buitenen. *op. cit.*, p. 34. See Brahmasūtra 1.2.6.

56 Alladi Mahadeva Sastri, ed. *op. cit.*, p. 236.

57 R.C. Zaehner. 1969. *The Bhagavad-Gītā*, p. 335. Oxford: Clarendon Press.

58 Ainslie T. Embree (ed.). 1972. *The Hindu Tradition*, pp. 310–11. New York: Random House. Emphasis added.

59 Robert N. Minor. 1986. *Modern Indian Interpreters of the Bhagavad-gītā*, pp. 223–4. Albany, NY: SUNY Press. The text has been abbreviated.

60 Radhakrishnan. 1929. *Indian Philosophy*, p. 530. London: George Allen & Unwin.

61 As cited in Klaus K. Klostermaier. 1989. *A Survey of Hinduism*, p. 4. Albany, NY: State University of New York Press.
62 R.D. Karmarkar (ed.). 1956. *Arjunopākhyāna*, p. VIII. Poona: Bhandarkar Oriental Research Institute.
63 Ibid.
64 K.T. Telang. 1965. *The Bhagavad-gītā with the Sanatsujātīya and the Anugītā*, p. 198. Delhi: Motilal Banarsidass, first published 1882.
65 S.V. Oka. 1957. *Uttaragītā*, p. XI. Poona: Bhandarkar Oriental Research Institute.
66 Ibid., p. I.
67 R.D. Karmarkar. *op. cit.*, p. i.
68 Ibid., p. IX.
69 I. Theodor. 2016, p. 141.
70 Arvind Sharma. *The Hindu Gītā*, p. 5.
71 S.V. Oka. *op. cit.*, p. XI.
72 But see R.D. Karmarkar. *op. cit.*, p. 28.
73 S.V. Oka. *op. cit.*, p. XI.
74 R.D. Karmarkar. *op. cit.*, p. xii:

> According to the '*Kalpanāvāda*' the creation of the souls and the world is a simple affair. The souls are the fancy of the Highest, and each soul in his own way creates or fancies his world, this again, in its turn can have another world fancied within it and this process can go on endlessly. The result is that there are billions of worlds falsely fancied. This need not frighten the seeker after salvation or the state of a Living-liberated (*Jīvanmukta*). For the whole of this paraphernalia which is merely '*cittadṛṣya*' due to the '*Vāsanā*,' is dissolved when there is '*vāsanākṣaya*' and so the efforts of the '*Mumukṣu*' have to be directed towards the achievement of this end.

75 Ibid.
76 Swami Swarupananda. 1967. *Śrīmad-Bhagvad-Gītā*, p. 406. Calcutta: Advaita Ashrama. Also see N. Gangadharan. 1987. *The Agni Purāṇa*, Part 4, pp. 1068–73. Delhi: Motilal Banarsidass; N.A. Deshpande. 1991. *The Padma-Purāṇa*, Parts 8–9, pp. 2906–70. Delhi: Motilal Banarsidass.
77 A.L. Basham. 1989. *The Origins and Development of Classical Hinduism*, ed. Kenneth Zysk, p. 97. Boston: Beacon Press.
78 W.J. Johnston. *op. cit.*, p. i.
79 A.L. Basham, *The Origins and Development of Classical Hinduism*, p. 79.
80 Ibid., p. 101.
81 I. Theodor. 2016, p. 52.
82 G. Buhler, ed. 1967. *The Laws of Manu*, p. 132. Delhi: Motilal Banarsidass, first published 1886.
83 K. Satchidananda Murty. 1993. *Vedic Hermeneutics*, p. 85. Delhi: Motilal Banarsidass.
84 A.L. Basham. *The Origins and development of Classical Hinduism*, p. 94.
85 See *Manusmṛti*, XII, pp. 88–93.
86 K. Satchidananada Murty. *op. cit.*, p. 40.
87 G. Buhler. *op. cit.*, pp. 512–13.
88 T.M.P. Mamahadevan. *op. cit.*, p. 17.
89 I. Theodor. 2016, p. 72.
90 Ibid., p. 83.
91 Ibid., p. 100.
92 Ibid., 2016, pp. 108–9.
93 R.C. Zaehner. *op. cit.*, Introduction.
94 Robert N. Minor. July 1980. "The Gītā's Way as the Only Way," *Philosophy East & West*, Vol. XXX, No. 3, pp. 339–54.

95 S. Radhakrishnan. 1974.*The Bhagavad-gītā*, p. 20. New Delhi: Blackie & Sons, first published 1946.

96 M. Hiriyanna. 1949. *The Essential of Indian Philosophy*, p. 53. London: George Allen & Unwin. Emphasis added.

97 See Georg Feuerstein. 1974. *Introduction to the Gītā*. London: Rider & Company; W. Hill, P. Douglas. *op. cit*., pp. 188–9; Edgerton Franklin. 1974. *The Bhagavad-gītā*. Cambridge, MA: Harvard University Press Second Part etc. 'Maharshi Mahesh Yogi, the founder of transcendental meditation . . . has even tried to demonstrate how the second verse of the first chapter of the *Gītā* can be interpreted in the light of *all the six orthodox systems* of Hindu thought. He makes this claim about all the verses of the *Gītā*' (Arvind Sharma. Spring 1995. "The Bhagavad-gītā: Its Western and Indian interpretations," *Journal of Vaiṣnava Studies*, Vol. III, No. 2. p. 112.). Could the enterprise be extended to include the non-orthodox systems as well?

Bibliography

Basham, A.L. 1956. *The Wonder That Was India*. London: Sidgwick & Jackson.

Basham, A.L. (ed.). 1975. *A Cultural History of India*. Oxford: Clarendon Press.

Basham, A.L. 1989. *The Origins and Development of Classical Hinduism*. Boston: Beacon Press.

Bharati, Agehananda. February 1970. "The Hindu Renaissance and Its Apologetic Patterns." *The Joumal of Asian Studies*, XXIX(2).

Bhate, Govind Chimnaji. 1939. *History of Modern Marathi Literature*. Poona: Mahad & A.V. Patwardhan.

Biardeau, Madeleine. 1985. *Hinduism: The Anthropology of a Civilization*. Delhi: Oxford University Press.

Bolle, Kees W. 1979. *The Bhagavad-gītā: A New Translation*. Berkeley: University of California Press.

Bouquet, A.C. 1948. *Hinduism*. New York: Hutchinsons University Library.

Buhler, G. (ed.). 1967. *The Laws of Manu*. Delhi: Motilal Banarsidass. First published 1886.

Callewaert, W.M. and S. Hemrai. 1983. *Bhagavadgītānuvāda*: *A Study in Transcultural Translation*. Ranchi: Sathya Bharati Publication.

Chatterji, Suniti Kumar. 1963. *Languages and Literatures of Modern India*. Calcutta: Bengal Publishers Private Ltd.

Dasgupta, Surendrarnath. 1932. *A History of Indian Philosophy*. Cambridge: Cambridge University Press.

Deshpande, N.A. 1991. *The Padma-Purāṇa*, Parts 8–9, pp. 2906–2970. Delhi: Motilal Banarsidass.

Deutsch, Eliot and J.A.B. Van Buitenen. 1971. *A Source Book of Advaita Vedānta*. Honolulu: University of Hawaii Press.

Douglas, W. Hill P. 1928. *The Bhagavadgīta*. London: Oxford University Press.

Edgerton, Franklin. 1974. *The Bhagavad-gītā*. Cambridge, MA: Harvard University Press.

Embree, Ainslie T. (ed.). 1972. *The Hindu Tradition*. New York: Random House.

Feuerstein, Georg. 1974. *Introduction to the Gītā*. London: Rider & Company.

Gandhi, Mohandas Karamchand. 1950. *Hindu Dhamra*. Ahmedabad: Navajivan Press.

Gandhi, Mohandas Karamchand. 1993. *An Autobiography*. Boston: Beacon Press.

Gangadharan, N. 1987. *The Agni Purāṇa*. Delhi: Motilal Banarsidass.

Gerow, Edwin. 1987. "Bādarāyaṇa." In Mircea Eliade (Editor in Chief), *The Encyclopedia of Religion*. New York: Macmillan Publishing Company.
Har Bilas Sarada. 1946. *Life of Dayananda Saraswati*. Ajmer: Vedic Yant.
Hendrik, George. 1959. *The Bhagavat-Geeta (1785) Translated, with Notes, by Charles Wilkins*. Cainsville: Scholar's Facsimiles and Reprints.
Hiriyanna, M. 1949. *The Essential of Indian Philosophy*, p. 53. London: George Allen & Unwin.
Jaini, P.S. 1979. *The Jaina Path of Purification*. Berkeley: University of California Press.
Johnson, W.J. 1994. *The Bhagavad Gītā*. New York: Oxford University Press.
Kapoor, Jagdish Chander. 1983. *Bhagavad-gītā: An international Bibliography from 1785–1979 Imprints*. New York: Garland Publishers.
Karmarkar, R.D. (ed.). 1956. *Arjunopākhyāna*. Poona: Bhandarkar Oriental Research Institute.
Klostermaier, Klaus K. 1989. *A Survey of Hinduism*. Albany, NY: State University of New York Press.
Larson, Gerald James. December 1965. "The *Bhagavad-gītā* as Cross-Cultural Process: Toward an Analysis of the Social Locutions of a Religious Text." *Journal of the American Academy of Religion*, XLIII(4).
Lopez, D. (ed.). 1995. *Buddhism in Practice*. Princeton: Princeton University Press.
Macdonell, Arthur A. 1968. *A History of Sanskrit Literature*. New York: Haskell House Publishers, Ltd.
Mackenzie, Brown D. February 1958. "The Philosophy of Bal Gangadhar Tilak." *The Journal of Asian Studies*, XVII(2).
Mahadevan, T.M.P. 1971. *Outlines of Hinduism*. Bombay: Chetana Ltd.
Majumdar, R.C., et al. 1948. *An Advanced History of India*, p. 1016. London: Macmillan and Co.
Majumdar, R.C., et al. (eds.). 1960. *The Delhi Sultanate*. Bombay: Bharatiya Vidya Bhavan.
Majumdar, R.C., et al. (eds.). 1965. *British Paramountey and Indian Renaissance*. Bombay: Bharatiya Vidya Bhavan. Vol. II, Chapter IV.
Minor, Robert N. July 1980. "The Gītā's Way as the Only Way." *Philosophy East & West*, XXX(3).
Minor, Robert N. 1986. *Modern Indian Interpreters of the Bhagavad-gītā*, pp. 223–224. Albany, NY: SUNY Press.
Murty, K. Satchidananda.1993. *Vedic Hermeneutics*. Delhi: Motilal Banarsidass.
Navaranga, Svāmi Sri Mukundadāsa. 1983. *Gītā Rahasya*. Delhi: Sri Prananatha Mission.
O'Connell, Joseph T. 1995–1996. "Karma in the *Bhagavad-gītā*: Caitanya Vaiṣṇava Views." *Journal of Studies in the Bhagavad-gītā*.
Oka, S.V. 1957. *Uttaragītā*, p. XI. Poona: Bhandarkar Oriental Research Institute.
O'Malley, L.S.S. (ed.). 1968. *Modern India and the West*. Oxford: Oxford University Press.
Pande, Govind Chandra. 1944. *Life and Thought of Śaṅkarācārya*. Delhi: Motilal Banarsidass.
Panikkar, K.M. 1963. *The Foundation of New India*. London: George Allen and Unwin.
Pansikar, W.L.S. (ed.). 1967. *Śrīmadbhagavadgītā*. Bombay: Nimayasagara Press.
Qanungo, Kalika-Ranjan. 1952. *Dara Shukoh*. Calcutta: S.C. Sarkar and Sons.
Radhakrishnan, S. 1929. *Indian Philosophy*. London: George Allen & Unwin.
Radhakrishnan, S. 1960. *The Brhama Sutra*, p. 94. London: George Allen and Unwin.

Radhakrishnan, S. 1974. *The Bhagavad-gītā*. New Delhi: Blackie & Sons. First published 1946.

Sadhale, G.S. (ed.). 1935. *The Bhagavad-gītā with Eleven Commentaries*. Bombay: The "Gujarati" Printing Press

Sastri, A. Mahadeva. 1979. *The Bhagavad-gītā with the Commentar of Śri Śaṅkarācārya*. Madras: Smata Books.

Sharma, Arvind. 1983. *Abhinavagupta Gītārthasaṅgraha*. Leiden: E.J. Brill.

Sharma, Arvind. 1986. *The Hindu Gītā*. London: Duckworth.

Swami, Kripananda. 1989. *Jñāneśvarī*. Albany, NY: State University of New York Press.

Swami, Swarupananda. 1967. *Śrīmad-Bhagvad-Gītā*. Calcutta: Advaita Ashrama.

Swami, Vidyananda Saraswati.1985. *The Brahmasūtra*. Bombay: Deva Vedic Prakasana.

Tagare, G.V. 1988. *Vayu Purāṇa*. Delhi: Motilal Banarsidass.

Telang, K.T. 1965. *The Bhagavad-gītā with the Sanatsujātīya and the Anugītā*. Delhi: Motilal Banarsidass. First published 1882.

Theodor, I. 2016. *Exploring the Bhagavad Gītā; Philosophy, Structure and Meaning*. London: Routledge.

Zaehner, R.C. 1969. *The Bhagavad-Gītā*. Oxford: Clarendon Press.

4

ŚAṄKARA'S DECONSTRUCTION OF THE *BHAGAVAD-GĪTĀ* GROUNDED IN HIS PREUNDERSTANDING

Carl Olson

Over the centuries, the *Bhagavad-gītā* has been interpreted in many ways. This chapter examines the interpretation of the text from the perspective of Śaṅkara and his *Advaita Vedānta* philosophical perspective that he brings with him to his examination of the text. Because of the profoundly theistic nature of the *Gītā*, Śaṅkara's hermeneutical convictions and metaphysical certainties motivated him to deconstruct the theistic features of the *Gītā* by adhering to his beliefs about the role of revelation, his method of sublation, and his philosophical preunderstanding. By using these instruments to deconstruct the text, Śaṅkara also reconstructed the *Gītā* into a document that more accurately reflects his philosophy. This process will be demonstrated through his metaphysics, epistemology, and proposed path to liberation.

There are some scholars of Śaṅkara's philosophical corpus who have questioned the authenticity of his commentary of the *Bhagavad-gītā* because of alleged discrepancies between this commentary and that on the *Vedānta Sūtras*, about God's role and the notion of ignorance (*avidyā*) in the two texts (Hacker 1951). Other Indologists have arrived at the contrary conclusion – that is, Śaṅkara's *Gītā* commentary is authentic (Ingalls 1952, 7–8; Raghavan 1968–9, 283–4; Mayeda 1965) – by comparing his *Gītā* commentary to his authentic works or by using Hacker's criteria against him. Whether or not Śaṅkara wrote a commentary on the text, the commentary that we do have was at least a product of his school of philosophy, a radical non-dualism.

Śaṅkara likely composed commentaries of some *Upaniṣad* texts and the *Vedanta Sūtras* of Bādarāyaṇa, and there are independent works attributed to him such as the *Upadeśasāhasrī*, *Ātmabodha*, *Vivekacūdāmaṇi*, and others. Numerous scholars characterize the *Bhagavad-gītā* as a theistic text (Theodor 2010, 4). Since Śaṅkara represents a philosophical position that is not congruent with theism despite the odd reference to his philosophy as a monotheism (Sinha 1987, 93), it seems reasonable to ask why he would think it necessary to take a primarily theistic text and give it a non-dualist interpretation. On the one hand, like an interpreter, Śaṅkara approaches the text with his own set of presuppositions based on his philosophical convictions that influence any attempt to interpret the text. On the other hand, the *Bhagavad-gītā* achieved the status of an iconic text, giving it an exalted status despite its not being a revealed work, as is true of the *Vedic* literature (Van Buitenen 1981, 7), which for Śaṅkara usually means the *Upaniṣads*. Both of these points need further investigation.

Similar to the Hebrew Bible, the New Testament, Sikh scriptures, and the Quran, the *Bhagavad-gītā* is considered an iconic text by many readers. The iconic nature of the *Gītā* is a status earned over time that implies that it is special, sacred, or different from mundane books. An excellent example of its iconic status is the annual celebration of the *Gītā Jayantī*, the birthday of the text that is observed during the eleventh day of the lunar month of Margashirsha, falling during December and January. Many people celebrating this event believe that the *Gītā* represents the fifth and superior *Veda* because previous *Veda*s were created out of the air, whereas the *Gītā* owes its origin to the mouth of Kṛṣṇa (Waghorne 2013, 193–4). The iconic text is believed by its adherents to give access to a transcendent realm and the truth that it represents. The material nature of the iconic text reveals the normally invisible divine realm to human perception that is not ordinarily capable of such a feat (Parmenter 2013a, 64–5). The iconic text weaves together the visual and the material and enables the creation of social cohesion (Parmenter 2013b, 226). The iconic text can also have political implications when kings, politicians, and priests use it to support their privileged status or to convince ordinary citizens that leaders are on their side. Besides providing leaders with legitimacy, an iconic text gives leaders knowledge that is equated with wealth and power (Watts 2013, 407–9). Moreover, an iconic text is often associated with wisdom, a gift that sets leaders apart from ordinary citizens.

Concerning Śaṅkara's work as an interpreter of the *Gītā*, he is similar to any other interpreter of text in the sense that he brings with him a set of presuppositions that shape his perspective and support his position before he even begins to interpret the text. Without claiming to be exhaustive, there are some obvious presuppositions that Śaṅkara brings with him as he begins to encounter the text. These presuppositions are derived from his study of Bādarāyaṅa's *Vedānta Sūtras* and the *Upaniṣads* and from exposure to his cultural milieu and its intellectual heritage. A fundamental presupposition is his preunderstanding of bondage that is caused by ignorance; the operation of the cycle of causation and how this causes rebirth; the non-dual identity of *Brahman*, ultimate reality; the *Ātman*, the universal self, and freedom as the ultimate value. By accepting freedom as the ultimate value instead of morality, Śaṅkara conceives of freedom as including a person's control of one's environment, others, oneself, and the physical sources of power in the universe (Potter 1972, 3). Śaṅkara accepts the act of renunciation as a means to extricate oneself from a condition of bondage. He also accepts that the *Veda*s, with an emphasis on the *Upaniṣads* as the embodiment of the true message of these texts, represent a sacred revelation (*śruti*) of the truth from divine beings to inspired poets, which gives Śaṅkara's thought a firm foundation in transcendent truth. It is possible to include the illusory (*māyā*) nature of the world and ordinary existence as essential elements of his preunderstanding. These various elements are some of the presuppositions that Śaṅkara brings with him to his interpretation of the *Gītā*. This observation is not intended to be a criticism of Śaṅkara but is instead meant to affirm that there is not only any philosophy devoid of presuppositions, just as there is no interpretation without previously accepted presuppositions that shape an interpreter's reading of any text. In order words, an interpreter's intellectual baggage, worldview, and previous experiences constitute an interpreter's viewpoint before that person begins to make sense of a text.

This observation does not mean that that text gets distorted necessarily by an interpreter when the text is read. There are two levels of reading a text: the plain sense of the text and the second level of a text that represents the pragmatic reading. In the first instance, the plain sense of the text represents the rhetorical context of a text, whereas the second level of reading reveals the otherwise-hidden meaning located in the plain sense (Ochs 1998, 6). If an interpreter is a bit more suspicious, they might recognize that the text is incomplete because it presents an unintended incomplete worldview (Ricoeur 1984, 3: 169). This situation calls for a focus on the reader's response to the text that enables them to react to the stratagems of an author and to find its structure as it is revealed in the text (Ricoeur 1984, 3: 166–7). The structure of the text is grasped through the art of interpretation. It will become evident that Śaṅkara's interpretive commentary of the *Gītā* is not concerned with determining authorship of the text or its sociohistorical context, because he is more concerned with religio-philosophical truth. For Śaṅkara, the *Gītā* represents the essence of the meaning of the *Veda*s. Since the term *Vedānta* means the end of the *Veda*s in the sense of their completion as embodied by the *Upaniṣads*, it appears reasonable also to conclude that the *Bhagavad-gītā* is included in the literature that represents the completion of the *Veda*s.

The assertion that Śaṅkara deconstructs the *Bhagavad-gītā* does not mean that he is following a method of interpretation similar to that of Jacques Derrida, the postmodernist originator of deconstruction. The technique of deconstruction attempts to expose the limitations and illogic of a text by exposing its cracks, traces, limitations, and margins. Derrida denies that deconstruction is a method of interpretation, although it does enable a practitioner to expose the differences in the text and the risky nature of writing. The act of writing is a violent exercise because language is more primary than writing. This claim exposes language as something in which we already exist and exposes that we cannot get outside of language to examine its origin (Derrida 1976, 37). If we assume the role of an interpreter, we discover that writing is characterized by death: "Writing is not an independent order of signification; it is weakened speech, something no completely dead: a living-dead, a reprieved corpse, a deferred life, a semblance of breath" (Derrida 1976, 71). This description of writing and text suggests that it is difficult to interpret a text to discover its truth. At best, the interpreter finds a cluster of truths, but not an absolute truth. The multiple nature of truth is associated with Derrida's philosophical war against what he calls logocentrism, which is identified with metaphysics.

Like Derrida, Śaṅkara is also suspicious of language and texts, although texts can embody the ultimate truth (Olson 2002, 2011). From Śaṅkara's perspective, the fundamental problem with language is that it is a product of ignorance (*avidyā*) that results in erroneous mental constructions that tend to distort reality, even though the great sayings or sentences (*mahāvākya*) of the *Upaniṣads* have the ability to liberate a person regardless of one's ability to understand what they mean (*ŚB*, 1965, 4.3.9). Besides their liberating potential, words are meaningful, although words and texts are inferior in status to the reality of *Brahman*.

Nonetheless, it is possible to refer to Śaṅkara's art of interpretation as a different kind of deconstruction of a text in the sense that he dismantles a work to make it fit into or correspond to his preconceptions before interpreting a text. An excellent example of Śaṅkara's interpreting a part of the *Gītā* is evident at the beginning of chapter 15 and its reference to the upside-down *aśvattha* tree described with its roots extending toward the sky, which is the direction of the abode of the gods. Śaṅkara calls it the tree of *saṃsāra* (rebirth), which he describes as eternal because it rests on a continuous series of births and is continually destroyed every moment. This tree springs from the Unmanifest, its trunk is *buddhi* (intellect), its boughs are sense objects, its leaves and branches represent *dharma* (order) and *adharma* (disorder), its blossoms are pleasure and pain, its fruits give livelihood to all creatures, the tree's roots represent sense impressions that lead to attachment, it functions as the resort of *Brahman*, and it stands for the self that is the essence of *Brahman* (*BhgC* 398). With the example of this inverted tree, it is possible to witness Śaṅkara deconstruct a metaphor for rebirth and identify the meaning of the various parts. The inverted tree is also evident earlier in Indian history, in the *Ṛg Veda* (1.24.7) and the *Kaṭha Upaniṣad* (6.1), but in his commentary, Śaṅkara does not refer to these earlier uses of the image. The inverted tree suggests the difficulty of grasping *saṃsāra* and the origin of evil (Minor 1982, 419).

Since the revealed nature of the *Upaniṣads* embodies the absolute truth, according to Śaṅkara, the correct interpretation of a text, such as the *Bhagavad-gītā*, must be made to reflect the revealed and preordained truth in the *Upaniṣads*, which is more accurately Śaṅkara's conception of these texts, suggested by his philosophical preunderstanding – *Advaita Vedānta*. A reader of Śaṅkara's commentary on the *Bhagavad-gītā* will notice that he not only brings his non-dual philosophy with him to his task but also often cites texts from the *Upaniṣads* and *dharma* literature, such as the *Manusmṛti* to support his interpretation of a passage. With his overall approach in mind, it is possible to grasp how Śaṅkara interprets the *Gītā* by examining his metaphysical stance, aspects of his epistemology, and his understanding of the proper path to liberation.

Metaphysics

Inspired by his reading of the *Upaniṣads*, Śaṅkara affirms that *Brahman* is the highest reality, and this reality is identical to the eternal self (*Ātman*). He defines this ultimate reality from both a positive and negative perspective. From the latter perspective, *Brahman* is *neti neti* (not this, not that). This definition suggests that *Brahman* is not any particular thing in this world that one can indicate with certainty and identify as the ultimate, although being implies that *Brahman* is alone the one real existing being without an origin based on something else, a status that sharply differentiates it from the world, a realm of mere appearances, and it is thus much less real (Śaṅkara 1965–66, 2.2.1).

Śaṅkara's metaphysical reality, or *Brahman*, represents a monism that is difficult to reconcile with the *Gītā*'s monotheistic dualism between matter (*prakṛti*) and self (*puruṣa*). This dualism is reflected through human existence, as is evident, for example, in the opposition between action and inaction, change and changelessness, unitary and multiple forms, sameness and differentiated, and having qualities and not having qualities – which is explained in part by the operation of the three *guṇas* (threads, strands) associated with *prakṛti*. This dualistic metaphysics is complicated further by the role of a theistic deity represented by Kṛṣṇa, who is at the beginning of his commentary on the *Gītā* equated by Śaṇkara as an incarnation of Viṣṇu's wanting to maintain order in the universe (*BhgC* 3). Śaṅkara embraces the text's equation of Kṛṣṇa with *Brahman* (*Bhg* 7.7), whom he defines as having no genus, inexpressible in language, being without qualities and attributes, being without a second, non-objective, unrelated to anything else, and finally *Īśvara* (*BhgC* 347–8). The unity of Kṛṣṇa and *Brahman* in the *Gītā* represents an aspect in the text that coincides with Śaṅkara's metaphysical monism that a reader would expect him to embrace. If Kṛṣṇa is identified with *Brahman*, a reader might wonder, however, why the ultimate reality does not assume the attributes of the monotheistic deity. The answer is connected to Śaṅkara's distinction between the *Saguṇa* and *Nirguṇa* aspects of *Brahman*.

Having defined *Brahman* in both a positive and a negative manner, Śaṅkara draws a twofold distinction between *Saguṇa* and *Nirguṇa*. The former refers to *Brahman* with qualities and attributes such as bodily form, rationality, personality, and ability to communicate in a personal way. Throughout much of the *Gītā*, Kṛṣṇa is depicted in a *Saguṇa* form. The definition of *Brahman* as *Nirguṇa* means that it is without qualities, attributes, or any limiting adjuncts. The *Nirguṇa* aspect is the highest form of *Brahman*. When combined especially with the *neti neti* definition, they together mean that *Brahman* is indefinable, indescribable, lacking qualities, non-relational, and impersonal, which are attributes that apply to the portrait of Kṛṣṇa in the *Gītā*. Śaṅkara is presented with a problem related to making sense of a deity in the text that possesses attributes, is incarnated in a human body, is personal, and enters into relationships with human beings. Moreover, the *Saguṇa* aspect of *Brahman* is equated with ignorance (*avidyā*), whereas the *Nirguṇa* feature is an object of knowledge (*vidyā*), even though this distinction reflects two aspects of the same absolute and not two separate entities. Śaṅkara brings these philosophical convictions about ultimate reality with him to his commentary on the *Bhagavad-gītā*, and they present a challenge to him when he attempts to interpret the *Saguṇa* aspects of Kṛṣṇa depicted in the text.

Kṛṣṇa is depicted in the *Gītā* as a caring, dialogical, intimate, relational, and loving deity who incarnates himself when the socio-cosmic *dharma* (law, order) is threatened or declines. In short, he incarnates himself to restore righteousness and protect the good (*Bhg* 4.7–8). As chapter 11 of the *Gītā* makes lucid with its grand theophany, Kṛṣṇa is indubitably the absolute reality because he is the origin of everything. After asking for a vision of Kṛṣṇa's eternal self, Arjuna is given a celestial eye with which to see the god's transfiguration. During this splendid divine vision, Arjuna sees Kṛṣṇa's body merging into one. For Arjuna and the reader, unity and multiplicity are affirmed (*Bhg* 11.9–13). As he is emotionally filled with wonder, amazement, fear, and terror by his vision, Arjuna sees all the gods in Kṛṣṇa's body (*Bhg* 11.15). And he later witnesses the entire world rushing headlong into Kṛṣṇa's mouth (*Bhg* 11.26–9). Arjuna becomes aware that Kṛṣṇa is the god of gods and not merely an impersonal principle behind the personal gods.

Arjuna also becomes aware that Kṛṣṇa is time, which suggests that the god destroys all things (*Bhg* 11.32). The author of the text connects time with the lower (*prakṛtic*) aspect of Kṛṣṇa's nature that does not pertain to his transcendent nature. This connection of *prakṛti* as God's lower nature suggests that God is dualistic in the *Gītā*, meaning that God has a lower material nature and a higher spiritual nature (*Bhg* 7.5). This predominant dualistic nature of God stands in sharp contrast to the interpretation of God as non-dual, as provided by Śaṅkara in his commentary. Concerning God as time, the *Gītā* teaches that what is about to happen concerning the family war has already occurred. In other words, the destiny of the warriors has already been determined by Kṛṣṇa as time. Since Arjuna cannot alter time, he should fight and be assured of victory. Since Kṛṣṇa is time and has decided the outcome of the war, this aspect of the text suggests that a divine determinism is being promoted.

Śaṅkara's reaction to this depiction of Kṛṣṇa as a personal, all-powerful deity in this part of the *Bhagavad-gītā* is filtered through his conceptualization of *Brahman* in its *Saguṇa* aspect. Although this is an inferior aspect of *Brahman* compared to its *Nirguṇa* aspect and regardless of its ultimate identity with the *Saguṇa* aspect, Śaṅkara refers to this lower aspect of *Brahman* as *Īśvara*, who is viewed as the creator and governor of the universe. Operating as a mediator between *Brahman* and the world, *Īśvara* serves as an object of devotion. However, to refer to *Brahman* as a creator is only true from the standpoint of lower knowledge and ignorance (*avidyā*). Thus, Śaṅkara is forced to admit that Kṛṣṇa is an inferior form of the divine based on what he has stated in his commentary on the *Vedānta Sūtras*.

Kṛṣṇa's subservience to *Brahman* is challenged in the *Bhagavad-gītā* (14.27) when the deity utters the following passage: "For I am the foundation of *Brahman*/ The immortal and imperishable/And of the eternal right/And of absolute bliss." Śaṅkara responds to this passage by arguing that it demonstrates the conditioned nature of *Brahman* when the ultimate reality appears as *Īśvara* in order to bestow his grace to his devotees. Śaṅkara performs a deft interpretive maneuver with his quotation, one that does not cohere with his hermeneutical agenda and the superior status of *Brahman* over a deity.

A different metaphysical problem confronts Śaṅkara in the second chapter of the *Gītā* with the discussion of *jñāna-yoga*, or path of knowledge, which is also called *Sāṅkhya,* and should not be confused with the ancient Indian philosophy that historically had a wide influence in various types of literature until around the 7th century. This path of knowledge is a dualism between *Puruṣa* (self, spirit) and *Prakṛti* (matter, nature) that stresses an absolute separation between them. *Prakṛti* is defined as unconscious and functions as the principles of becoming and differentiation, whereas the *Puruṣa* has neither attributes nor relations, is merely a witness, is pure consciousness, and is discriminating and subjective. The major characteristic of *Prakṛti* that is lacking with the *Puruṣa,* however, is the three *guṇas* (strands, threads): *sattva* (pure, perfect), *rajas* (element of energy and passion), and *tamas* (principle of darkness and inertness). These three *guṇas* exist simultaneously in every physical, biological, or psychomental phenomenon, though in unequal proportion. Although they are separated from each other, when they become located in proximity to each other, this close relationship stimulates an interplay between them that causes the primordial form of *Prakṛti* to transform itself into the world while the *Puruṣa* directly witnesses the transformation. During the phase of transformation, the dual principles assume the characteristics of the other. In short, they become what they are not, forming a metaphysical mistake. Moreover, the purpose of the interaction of the dual principles is to bring about the ultimate release of the *Puruṣa.*

This second chapter of the *Bhagavad-gītā* suggests that the prevailing metaphysical stance of the text is dualistic, whereas Śaṅkara's philosophical position is non-dual (*advaita*). However, it is possible to find passages in the text that are monistic, which is likely indicative of a text that underwent a series of redactions by different authors.

Epistemology

In Śaṅkara's philosophical system, metaphysics meets epistemology in the concept of *māyā* (illusion, unreal): a creative power by which the world comes into being. This metaphysical power lasts for a human until they realize the sole reality of *Brahman.* From an epistemological viewpoint, *māyā* deludes a person into accepting the empirical world as reality, which suggests that *māyā* is epistemologically equated with ignorance (*avidyā*). Why is this the case for Śaṅkara? The reason is related to the power of *māyā* to both conceal reality and distort reality. In summary, the phenomenal world is *māyā* (unreal), and its power produces it. *Māyā* is a power that is used interchangeably with *avidyā* (ignorance) by Śaṅkara, although he gives precedence to *avidyā* over *māyā* when he is explaining bondage and freedom.

In his epistemology, Śaṅkara makes a distinction between two types of knowledge: *paravidyā* and *aparavidyā.* The former represents knowledge of ultimate reality, while the latter is related to knowledge of the phenomenal world. Śaṅkara defines *paravidyā* as sui generis, reached all at once, immediately, and intuitively. Moreover, it is self-validating, implying that another form of knowledge (e.g., inference or perception) cannot refute it. With the achievement of this higher form of knowledge, a person can witness that all other forms of knowledge are tainted by ignorance. In contrast to this intuitive type of knowledge, the lower form of knowledge (*aparavidyā*) is valid just as long as the intuitive vision of *Brahman* is not reached. Although it is considered a lower form of knowledge, it has value as a practical means of knowledge. From a practical perspective, it is useful to know, for example, that a match will burn one's fingers once it has been lit.

Śaṅkara consigns the traditional means of valid knowledge to *aparavidyā* (lower knowledge). Śaṅkara acknowledges six *pramānas* (instruments of knowledge): perception (*pratyakṣa*), comparison (*upamāna*), non-cognition (*anupalabdhi*), inference (*anumāna*), postulation (*arthāpatti*), and testimony (*śabda*). Perception operates by yielding knowledge about the qualities of an object, such as color, size, and texture. It can also provide knowledge about relations that constitute an object, such as the universal nature of a table, and can give knowledge of relations between objects that resemble physical laws. Comparison gives one knowledge derived from judgments of similarity, whereas non-cognition refers to judgments based on the perceived absence of an object at a specific time and place. Inference involves a relation between what is inferred and reason on the basis from which an inference is made. Because it is based on an apprehension of universal agreement between two things, it is a mediated form of knowledge. Postulation is the assuming of some fact in order to make another fact intelligible. If a person gains weight while fasting during the day, one can postulate that the person in question eats at night. Finally, testimony means accepting as true information that one receives from a reliable person (*ŚB* 1.2.21). These six valid means of knowledge presuppose a distinction between knower and what is known. Thus, they are all dualistic types of knowledge and therefore lower than *paravidyā*.

In Śaṅkara's theory of epistemology, he finds a place to discuss the relationship between reason (*yukti*, *tarka*) and revelation (*śruti*). According to Śaṅkara, reason can produce authoritative demonstrations of what is true, as can the revelatory *Upaniṣads*. Halbfass clarifies the role of reason in Śaṅkara's philosophy: "It has its legitimate role under the guidance of and in cooperation with *śruti*" (Halbfass 1991, 154). This observation means that revelation is superior to reason. Moreover, rational arguments indicate that something is possible, but not that it is certain (Murty 1959, 142). It is not possible, for example, to prove that *Brahman* is the Real by rational inference. Because another such argument can refute a rational argument, it is evident that reason deals with probability and not a certainty.

Besides these lower and higher types of knowledge, Śaṅkara includes two additional features of his epistemology: superimposition (*adhyāsa*) and sublation (*bādha*). These procedures are important because they affect his hermeneutics. The practice of superimposition occurs when a person imposes features onto or ascribes features to something such as the self (*Ātman*) that do not inherently belong to it. Therefore, superimposition involves borrowing qualities not immediately present to one's consciousness that properly belong to one thing, using one's memory of previous experiences, and projecting those previous experiences and their qualities and attributing them to something new (*ŚB* 3. 3. 9). Thus, superimposition involves a reference to an erroneous attribution of qualities or memory traces recalled from previous experiences. This process of attribution is akin to a projection of realities onto the world or to the self that is erroneous (Malkovsky 2000, 76). These products of memory are manifested as appearances for Śaṅkara and account in part for incorrect interpretation, an outcome that is also true of sublation.

The procedure of sublation (*bādha*) presupposes that what is real is permanent. It is also assumed that what is real is also eternal and infinite, which can only be the focus of higher knowledge, an immediate intuitive insight. The philosophical guideline is that it is impossible to sublate the real. With a basis in these presuppositions, sublation is more specifically a mental process by which an object or content of consciousness is canceled because a new, more correct experience contradicts it. For instance, imagine walking on a path at twilight and seeing something lying on the path in front of you. This sudden perception causes you to recoil because you think that the object in your path is a snake. When the assumed snake-like object does not move, your curiosity motivates you to examine the object more closely, and you then discover that it is, in fact, a piece of rope and not a snake after all. What has just transpired? An act of sublation has occurred because you changed your judgment after a new experience rectified your previous, erroneous belief (*ŚB* 3.2.21).

In summary, sublation exhibits a three-step process. There is an initial judgment about an object or content of consciousness. There is also a second judgment that radically conflicts with the earlier judgment, rendering it false. Finally, one accepts the new judgment as valid. Thus, to sublate something means that it has a lower degree of reality. Moreover, theoretically, the only thing that cannot be sublated is *Brahman*, a non-dual state of being that cannot be contradicted by any other experience, whereas the realm of appearance can be sublated by other experience. Concerning the spirit of the *Bhagavad-gītā*, a devotee's love of God is a relationship – for example, based on a distinction between the self and the non-self (other). An experience of reality can sublate this experience of the love of a deity because the truly real transcends any distinction based on a relationship.

By the implications associated with the procedures of superimposition and especially sublation, these features of Śaṅkara's epistemology set him on a collision course with a central tenet of the *Bhagavad-gītā*: a devotee's relation to and love of God (6.46–7; 9.31; 18.56). Since this relationship and love represent a lower reality and level of knowledge, it is inferior to the path of knowledge (*jñāna-yoga*), a way that Śaṅkara is convinced represents the higher path to liberation, in contrast to the inferior path of *bhakti* (devotion). Śaṅkara's certainty about the value of each of the three paths espoused in the *Gītā* represents a direct contradiction of the author(s) of the text and a rejection of the conclusion of the text, even though the path of knowledge has a role to play in its theism.

Paths to liberation

Based on his reading of the *Upaniṣads* and the *Vedānta Sūtras*, Śaṅkara is convinced that liberation (*mokṣa*) is attained by practicing a path of *jñāna-yoga* (knowledge). This arduous path requires preparation by an aspirant of specific qualifications. Before entering the quest for liberation, one must develop the ability to discriminate between the real and the unreal, one must renounce any desire to enjoy the results of one's actions, one must desire freedom and wisdom more than anything else, and one must cultivate the mental abilities of tranquility, self-control, dispassion, endurance, intentness of mind, and faith.

Having mastered the required qualifications for entrance into the path, an aspirant must practice three actions: hearing, reflection, and meditation. Hearing refers to receiving instructions from one's teacher about the revealed scriptures and especially the *Upaniṣads* that are the genuine source of *Brahman* intuition. Reflection means to think about the philosophical principles associated with the teachings of *Advaita Vedānta* through reasoning. Finally, meditation calls for intense concentration – for instance, on the truth of *tat tvaṃ asi*, a great saying (*mahāvakya*) that means "that you are." This meditative concentration results in one's becoming completely detached from the phenomenal world and egoism. When a meditator knows oneself to be the one true reality, then notions based on distinctions disappear with this realization. This experience means that one has become the all or the one without a second. Once this intuitive insight dawns and one is enlightened, one is no longer subject to the cycle of causation (*karma*) and rebirth (*saṃsāra*), because one transcends time and causation. This insight suggests that enlightenment does not introduce new things into existence; it does, however, dispel ignorance that enables one to see reality. Thus, it can be affirmed that knowledge that enlightens is a sublating knowledge (Lipner 2000, 68).

There are no degrees associated with the state of liberation. It is merely being, knowing, and experiencing one's true self that is identical to *Brahman*. What the knowing involves in this experience is not an act and thus does not cause further *karmic* residues. What happens in liberation (*mokṣa*) is that the knowledge achieved by the aspirant destroys ignorance (*avidyā*) and terminates all desire, which means that tendencies (*vāsanās*) cannot be carried through to action, and without functioning tendencies, karmic residues cannot determine birth (*ŚB* 1.1.4).

In retrospect, Śaṅkara is convinced that one can achieve certainty through the knowledge that is possible only for a conscious being. This conviction suggests that there is a unity of being and knowing for Śaṅkara that is provided by the revelatory nature of *Vedic* literature and its message about the nature of reality (*ŚB* 2. 1.11). This mode of thinking involves the conviction that the aspirant who gains the intuitive knowledge necessary for liberation has no doubts about whether he has it (Murty 1959, 13). By implication of this certainty, it is possible to recognize two valid sources of knowledge of oneself as *Brahman*: revealed scripture of the *Veda*s and the *anubhava* integral experience (ŚB 4.1.2).

Although Śaṅkara's philosophy advocates persuasively for a path of knowledge as the sole means of attaining liberation (*mokṣa*) from the cycle of causation and rebirth (*saṃsāra*), the *Bhagavad-gītā* offers three paths (*mārgas*) to liberation: *jñāna* (knowledge), *karma* (action, work), and *bhakti* (devotion). As a result of offering these three paths, the text stands conflicted with itself, leading to internal contradictions that challenge the perspective of an interpreter. By offering three valid paths of liberation, the *Gītā* gives the initial impression of being catholic, but such a thought is misleading. Why is a reader given such a misimpression? This situation is due to the author(s) of the text attempts to make a grand synthesis of paths currently being practiced by aspirants at the historical period of the composition of the text. This apparent attempt at a synthesis does not succeed, because the author(s) of the *Gītā* manifests a prejudice for the path of *bhakti* (devotion toward God) as the actual means to liberation and path to attaining one's goal. The path of *karma* supports *bhakti*, while the path of knowledge is ranked third in importance and also supports *bhakti*. In two passages in the text (18.55, 11.54), for example, there is evidence of the author's attempting to reconcile the paths of knowledge and devotion.

The three paths are introduced early in the text in a sequence beginning with the path of knowledge and culminating in *bhakti*. After giving the warrior Arjuna four reasons why he must do his duty and fight in the forthcoming battle, Kṛṣṇa, functioning as the charioteer of the warrior and as his teacher in the narrative, presents to the reluctant and despondent warrior the philosophy of *Sāṅkhya* (*Bhg* 2.39–53). This way is described as a concentrated mental attitude. Thus, the path to salvation is characterized by knowledge, an intuitive realization about the distinction between the self (*puruṣa*) and matter (*prakṛti*). This knowledge is necessary because the cause of bondage is ignorance (*avidyā*) that is more specifically identified as the self's thinking that it is an active actor (*Bhg* 5.16). By being called established wisdom (*Bhg* 2.54), knowledge is described as the abandonment of all desires and being content in the true self (*Bhg* 2.55–7) and realizing the distinction between the true self (*puruṣa*) and the non-self (*prakṛti*).

The discussion of the path of knowledge in the second chapter of the *Gītā* leads seamlessly to a discussion of abandoning attachment to the results of one's actions. What is called *buddhi-yoga* is superior to action because it is a practice that is exemplified by non-attachment to the doing of action and the fruits of action. Although it is impossible not to perform actions by virtue of being a human being, to be unattached to actions and their results means that one is free from rebirth (*Bhg* 2.51). An aspirant can practice non-attached action by using meditation that involves directing the *buddhi* (intellect) inward toward the self (*Bhg* 2. 55). The usually outwardly directed mind finds it necessary to eliminate desires associated with sense attachment by restraining all senses and meditating on Kṛṣṇa (*Bhg* 2.62).

In Śaṅkara's commentary on the *Bhagavad-gītā*, he embraces what the text asserts at this point, by stating that absolute freedom is attained by knowledge alone and not by knowledge conjoined with works (*BhgC* 28). This interpretation of the text by the *Vedāntist* alters the text to a degree, although it does not reach the level of distortion. Śaṅkara has some interesting things to say about the importance of action.

Concerning his commentary on 2.47 of the *Gītā*, Śaṅkara says that it is important for a seeker of knowledge not to allow the anticipated fruits of one's action to become one's primary motive. This cautionary warning is related to his conviction that any thirst for the fruits of actions results in rebirth. However, this viewpoint does not mean that an aspirant should be attached to inaction (*BhgC* 63). By casting off attachment for the fruits of one's actions, a seeker gains purity (*sattva*) of mind, a tranquil mind, and knowledge and rids themselves of both merit and evil (*BhgC* 64, 66). From another perspective, Śaṅkara elaborates on 2.69 of the text by stressing that ignorance is pervasive and authoritative and taints all actions. This intimate relationship of action with ignorance makes it impossible for Śaṅkara to embrace *karma-yoga* as an authentic method for attaining freedom.

Nonetheless, one engages in action in a detached way and regards it as one's duty that has been enjoined by the *Veda*s. The result for the aspirant is that their duty consists of the renunciation of all action and not its performance (*BhgC* 78). An aspect of the *karma-yoga* path that Śaṅkara does not elucidate is Kṛṣṇa's teaching that doing one's duty originates in one's inherent nature (Hiltebeitel 2011, 540). What might be the reason for this oversight by Śaṅkara? It can be something as simple as higher knowledge sublating an inferior kind of knowledge related to action and duty that is tainted by ignorance and transience and has no chance of leading one to freedom. Moreover, based on his philosophical presuppositions, *jñāna-yoga* is superior to *karma-yoga* because intuitive knowledge trumps ordinary modes of knowing and doing deeds, whose fruits a person tends to become attached to, leading one to a destiny of rebirth.

Chapter seven of the *Bhagavad-gītā* marks a change in the text in that it begins to discuss the identity of Kṛṣṇa and the nature of the path of *bhakti* (devotion). In a sense, it is the beginning of a revelation by a deity that reaches its epitome in chapter 11 with the grand theophany of Kṛṣṇa to Arjuna. It also includes instruction in the path of devotion, a more universal and superior path according to the perspective of the author (s) of the text in contrast to the ways of knowledge and action.

Before chapter seven and its teaching about the path of devotion and after discussing the difficulty of controlling one's mind (*Bhg* 6.33–5), this final part of the sixth chapter marks a transition to the next chapter on *bhakti*. It is at this transitional point that Kṛṣṇa teaches Arjuna that the warrior should become fixated on Kṛṣṇa (*Bhg* 6.47). Total fixation on Kṛṣṇa means devotion to him accomplished by faith (*śraddhā*). This instruction implies that the path of devotion is Kṛṣṇa-centric. This Kṛṣṇa-centric point is further enhanced by the injunction that opens chapter seven: one should act by relying on Kṛṣṇa. This act means that reliance is an additional element of faith (*śraddhā*) that implies that Kṛṣṇa will enable one to attain the highest perfection. In this chapter, Kṛṣṇa is the source of the world and its highest reality (*Bhg* 7.6–7). Also, Kṛṣṇa is the source of good and evil (*Bhg* 7.13), and *māyā* (illusion) is his mysterious power (*Bhg* 7.14), which can be penetrated only by humans who are resorting to Kṛṣṇa. In comparison to knowledge (*jñāna*) and deeds (*karma*), the path of *bhakti* is one in which one subordinates oneself to a higher power. This feature of the devotional path is illustrated dramatically when a dying person is instructed to meditate on Kṛṣṇa as that person is about to expire. By having Kṛṣṇa on one's mind as one breathes one's last, this procedure means that one's mind is Kṛṣṇa-centric, a condition that guarantees liberation from the binding forces of the world. Instead of being reborn, a Kṛṣṇa-centered mind enables a dying person to attain Kṛṣṇa's state of being (*Bhg* 8.5). In summary, the path of *bhakti* includes elements of knowledge and works. The element of knowledge involves such practices as concentrating on Kṛṣṇa at the moment of death and having one's mind fixed on God. By contrast, the *karmic* element involves an act of faith, a self-forgetting love, surrender to God, attachment to God, and fulfilling the commands of God.

If a devotee must perform actions because it is impossible not to act by being a human being, the role of action in their life becomes problematic because actions determine the nature of their future rebirth status. To escape the consequences of *karma*, it behooves one to perform one's acts as a gift to God. By resigning all the fruits of one's actions to God, the automatic functioning law of *karma* has no binding effect on a devotee. However, in the final analysis, a devotee is saved through the grace (*prasāda*) of a personal God. Kṛṣṇa is quoted in the text as saying that no devotee of his is ever lost (*Bhg* 9.31). Through his grace, God not only saves his devotees but also reveals himself to them (*Bhg* 11.47). The grace of God also means the granting of supreme peace and salvation (*Bhg* 18.6, 62). In his commentary, Śaṅkara unfortunately says little that is informative about Kṛṣṇa's grace, a situation that appears to be due to his cursory treatment of the path of devotion compared to his treatment of the way of knowledge.

By previously calling attention to fixing one's mind on God at the time of death, the state of one's mind at the moment of death is acknowledged as influential in determining one's state after death. This condition after death raises the issue of the nature of *mokṣa* (liberation). After death, the *Bhagavad-gītā* makes it clear that it does not conceptualize *mokṣa* as a state of oneness or identity with Kṛṣṇa, in sharp contrast to comments by Śaṅkara. The vision of most of the text means that *bhakti* leads not to absorption in Kṛṣṇa but rather to a personal association of the devotee with God. The *Gītā* is vague, however, according to some passages that appear to contract each other. For example, the text includes references to such phrases as "My devotee comes to me" (*Bhg* 7.23), "He goes to the supreme divine spirit" (*Bhg* 8.10), "taking refuge in me" (*Bhg* 4. 10), "dwelling in Kṛṣṇa" (*Bhg* 12.8), and "rests in me" (*Bhg* 6.15). These types of expressions of liberation are relational and unitary, which means that any of these types of explanation risk confusing a reader. If one compares these kinds of statements with a passage from the *Muṇḍaka Upaniṣad* (3.2.9), there is a total absence of ambiguity with the following assertion: "He who knows *Brahman* becomes *Brahman*." In part, these conflicting statements expose the competition between monism and monotheism in the *Gītā*, a competitive situation that presents a challenge for an interpreter.

In Śaṅkara's commentary on the *Bhagavad-gītā*, he demonstrates a penchant for the path of knowledge (*jñāna-yoga*) over the path of devotion (*bhakti*), to the extent of superimposing features of the path of knowledge onto the way of devotion. When he discusses the relationship between knowledge and action and their implication for liberation (*mokṣa*), for instance, Śaṅkara makes it indubitably clear where he stands, by affirming that knowledge is superior to action: "Wherefore the conclusion of the *Gītā* and all the *Upaniṣads* is this, that moksha can be obtained by knowledge alone, unaided (by action)" (*BhgC* 89). Is this what the *Bhagavad-gītā* intends to assert? Although it has already been demonstrated that the *Gītā* is more ambiguous, this point does not stop the intrepid *Vedāntist* from imposing order on the text by superimposing his preunderstanding on it. Śaṅkara performs something similar when he discusses the paths of knowledge and action. He equates the human experience of action and its agent with a being in a state of ignorance, which is defined as those who have not realized the Real (*BhgC* 129). Since action can only be falsely attributed to the self, Śaṅkara equates the action of a sage with inaction in that the sage's actions are consumed in the fire of knowledge (*BhgC* 135).

Śaṅkara's commentary continues its redefinition of *bhakti* by turning it into devotion to knowledge later in the text. This redefinition of devotion into knowledge enables the aspirant to know God as divine and to enter into God (*BhgC* 492). It is implied that the devotee loses their identity in this unitive experience. Again, Śaṅkara comments that the final cessation of rebirth (*saṃsāra*) is attained through devotion to knowledge (*BhgC* 511). What happened to being devoted to God? According to the latter parts of his commentary on the *Bhagavad-gītā* with his emphasis on devotion to knowledge, God has been both eclipsed and replaced by knowledge. From a broader perspective, Śaṅkara has applied superimposition (*adhyāsa*) and sublation (*bādha*) to the *Gītā* by uncompromisingly superimposing his non-dualist philosophy on the text and sublating the path of *karma* and *bhakti* with *jñāna* (knowledge). This development is ironic because in his commentary on the *Vedānta Sūtras*, Śaṅkara associates superimposition and sublation with a realm of appearance, ignorance, misapplication, and incorrect interpretation.

Does this mean that Śaṅkara is distorting or treating the text violently? In both cases, not really. Of course, Śaṅkara brings his preunderstandings and philosophical prejudices with him when he begins to write his interpretive commentary on the *Gītā*. Thereby, he gives the text a non-dualist perspective that is distinct from its predominate dualism between matter and self. Moreover, the paths of action and devotion are eclipsed by a path of non-dual knowledge. The ambiguities and conflicting parts of the original *Gītā* are transformed into a more systematic and coherent message by Śaṅkara, although this result is accomplished at the expense of the original intent of the author(s) of the text and at the neglect of its original context.

Concluding comments

Śaṅkara's concern with metaphysical and epistemological issues in his commentary of the *Gītā* presents an opportunity to reflect further on these matters. The discussion about metaphysics in his commentary on the text should be understood in the context of his previous criticism of the dualistic system of *Sāṅkhya* philosophy. Because the *Bhagavad-gītā* manifests the strong influence of *Sāṅkhya* dualism, Śaṅkara sees it as a threat to a proper understanding of the text, and he views this dualism as an inferior philosophical perspective. Śaṅkara's criticism is also associated with the epistemological problem concerning the relationship between revelation (*śruti*) and reason (*tarka*), which in turn is connected to the relationship between *śruti* and *smrti* (memory). For Śaṅkara, *śruti* has a more authoritative position in its relation to *smṛti*, which is subordinate to revelation. Consequently, since the *Bhagavad-gītā* is a *smṛti* text with a dualistic metaphysical stance, it is inferior to the revelatory *Upaniṣads* that Śaṅkara uses as his philosophical foundation. Since the *Gītā* is dualistic and subordinate epistemologically by definition to the revered *Upaniṣads*, it is implied that the text needs to be saved from itself through a correct interpretation. From Śaṅkara's perspective, the *Bhagavad-gītā* needs to be saved from its internal contradictions and proven to be a more genuinely non-dual text. Thus, Śaṅkara's commentary on the *Gītā* can be understood as an attempt to save the text from itself. In other words, this suggests that Śaṅkara is impelled to deconstruct the text before reconstructing it into a truthful non-dual work.

Śaṅkara's interpretation of the *Bhagavad-gītā* also gives readers an insight into the philosophical mind of a creative thinker with a singular focus expressed as a radical non-dualism. At the same time, this chapter suggests a philosopher falling into errors that he has previously exposed as examples of flawed thinking, as is evident in his notions of superimposition and sublation. It is ironic to find a philosopher of Śaṅkara's exalted status using these epistemological mistakes made by others that he exposed himself.

This result reflects in part Śaṅkara's application of his preunderstanding formed by his adherence to the *Advaita Vedānta* philosophical position. His preunderstanding, accumulated life experiences, and knowledge constitute his contextualized background of further understanding. The dynamic nature of preunderstanding sometimes demonstrates that knowledge and experience are forgotten, although the possibility of being retrieved is always present. Śaṅkara's preunderstanding guides and shapes his commentary on the *Gītā*, even though it may change the meaning intended by the original author(s).

Śaṅkara's commentary on the *Gītā* suggests a text that is in flux. In other words, he helps a reader to witness a text without a fixed meaning. It is also a text that is internally conflicted and at odds with itself, as is evident in its failure to synthesize the three paths to liberation. The text begs someone to unite it. The unification of the text is arguably what Śaṅkara provides. However, he accomplishes this unity at the price of misapplying the tools of a sound hermeneutic and distorting the text by denigrating the path of devotion in favor of the path of knowledge that he presupposes is superior to the other two paths advocated in the text. The intellectual baggage that Śaṅkara brings with him to his hermeneutical task is too heavy a load for the text to carry. Śaṅkara's failure to render full justice to the text and its original author(s) comes with historical and hermeneutical implications in that it opens up the text and invites other interpretations by such figures as Rāmānuja, Madhva, Vivekananda, Gandhi, and others.

Bibliography

Davis, Richard H. 2015. *The Bhagavad-gītā: A Biography.* Princeton: Princeton University Press.

Derrida, Jacques. 1976. *Of Grammatology.* Trans. Gayatri Chakravorty Spivak. Baltimore and London: Johns Hopkins University Press.

Deutsch, Eliot. 1968. *The Bhagavad-gītā: Translated with Introduction and Critical Essays.* New York: Holt, Rinehardt, and Winston.

Edgerton, Franklin. 1972. *The Bhagavad-gītā.* Cambridge, MA: Harvard University Press. Cited as *Bhg* in the chapter.

Hacker, Paul. 1951. "Eigentümlichkeiten der Lehre und Terminologie Śaṅkara: *avidyā, nāmarūpa, māyā, īśvara.*" *Zeitschrift der Deutschen Morgenlandischen Gesellschaft*, 100: 246–86.

Halbfass, Wilhelm. 1988. *Indian and Europe: An Essay in Understanding.* Albany, NY: State University of New York Press.

Halbfass, Wilhelm. 1991. *Tradition and Reflection: Explorations in Indian Thought.* Albany, NY: State University of New York Press.

Hiltebeitel, Alf. 2011. *Dharma: Its Early History in Law, Religion, and Narrative.* New York: Oxford University Press.

Ingalls, Daniel H.H. 1952. "Study of Śaṅkarācārya." *Annals of the Bhandarkar Oriental Research Institute*, 33: 1–14.

Lipner, Julius J. 2000. "The Self of Being and the Being of Self: Śaṅkara on 'That You Are' (*tat tvam asi*)." In *New Perspectives on Advaita Vedānta: Essays in Commemoration of Professor Richard De Smet, S.J.* Edited by Bradley Malkovsky, pp. 51–69. Leiden: Brill.

Malkovsky, Bradley J. 2000. "Śaṃkara on Divine Grace." In *New Perspectives on Advaita Vedānta: Essays in Commemoration of Professor Richard De Smet, S. J.* Edited by Bradley J. Malkovsky, pp. 70–83. Leiden: Brill.

Mayeda, Sengaku. 1965. "The Authenticity of the Bhagavadgītābhāsya Ascribed to Śaṅkara." *Wiener Zeitschrift für des Kunde Sus-und Ostasien*, 9: 155–97.

Minor, Robert N. 1982. *Bhagavad-gītā: An Exegetical Commentary.* Columbia, MO: South Asia Books.

Murty, K. Satchidananda. 1959. *Revelation and Reason in Advaita Vedānta.* New York: Columbia University Press.

Ochs, Peter. 1998. *Peirce, Pragmatism, and the Logic of Scripture.* Cambridge: Cambridge University Press.

Olson, Carl. 2002. *Indian Philosophers and Postmodern Thinkers: Dialogues on the Margins of Culture.* New Delhi: Oxford University Press.

Olson, Carl. 2011. "The Différance that Makes All the Difference: A Comparison of Derrida and Śaṅkara." *Philosophy East and West*, 61(2): 247–59.

Parmenter, Dorina Miller. 2013a. "The Iconic Book: The Image of the Bible in Early Christian Rituals." In *Iconic Books and Texts.* Edited by James W. Watts, pp. 63–92. Sheffield: Equinox Publishing, Ltd.

Parmenter, Dorina Miller. 2013b. "Iconic Books from Below: The Christian Bible and the Discourse of Duct Tape." In *Iconic Books and Texts.* Edited by James W. Watts, pp. 225–38. Sheffield, UK: Equinox Publishing, Ltd.

Potter, Karl H. 1972. *Presuppositions of India's Philosophies.* Westport, CT: Greenwood Press Publishing.

Potter, Karl H. 1981. *Encyclopedia of Indian Philosophies: Advaita Vedānta up to Śaṅkara and His Pupils.* Princeton: Princeton University Press.

Raghavan, V. 1968–69. "Bhāskara's Gītābhāṣya." *Wiener Zeitschrift für des Kunde Süd- und Ostasien*, 12–13: 125–39.
Ricoeur, Paul. 1984. *Time and Narrative*. 3 vol. Trans. Kathleen McLaughlin and David Pellauer. Chicago: University of Chicago Press.
Robinson, Catherine A. 2006. *Interpretation of the Bhagavad-gītā and Images of the Hindu Tradition: The Song of the Lord*. London: Routledge.
Śaṅkara. 1965a. *Commentary on Bṛhadāraṇyaka Upaniṣad*. Trans. Swami Mādhavānanda. Calcutta: Advaita Ashrama.
Śaṅkara. 1965b. *The Vedānta-sūtras with the Commentary of Saṅkarācārya*. Trans. George Thibaut. Delhi: Motilal Banarsidass. Cited as *ŚB* in the chapter.
Śaṅkara. 1965–66. *Commentary on Muṇḍaka Upaniṣad*. In *Eight Upaniṣads*. 2 vols. Trans. Swami Gambhiranda. Calcutta: Advaita Ashrama.
Śaṅkara. 1972. *The Bhagavad-gītā with the Commentary of Śrī Śaṅkarchāryā*. 6th ed. Trans. A. Mahādeva Śāstri. Madras: V Ramaswamy Sastrulu & Sons. Cited as *BhgC*.
Sharma, Arvind. 1986. *The Hindu Gītā: Ancient and Classical Interpretations of the Bhagavad-gītā*. LaSalle: Open Court.
Sharpe, Eric J. 1985. *The Universal Gītā: Western Images of the Bhagavad-gītā*. London: Duckworth.
Sinha, Phulgenda. 1987. *The Gītā as It Was: Rediscovering the Original Bhagavad-gītā*. LaSalle, IL: Open Court.
Theodor, Ithamar. 2010. *Exploring the Bhagavad-gītā: Philosophy, Structure and Meaning*. Surrey: Ashgate Publishing Limited.
Van Buitenen, J.A.B. (trans.). 1981. *The Bhagavad-gītā in the Mahābhārata: A Bilingual Edition*. Chicago: University of Chicago Press.
Waghorne, Joanne Punzo. 2013. "A Birthday Party for a Sacred Text: The *Gītā* Jayanti and the Embodiment of God as the Book and the Book as God." In *Iconic Books and Texts*. Edited by James W. Watts, pp. 283–98. Sheffield, UK: Equinox Publishing, Ltd.
Watts, James W. 2013. "Ancient Iconic Texts and Scholarly Expertise." In *Iconic Books and Texts*. Edited by James W. Watts, pp. 407–18. Sheffield, UK: Equinox Publishing, Lt.
Zaehner, R.C. 1973. *The Bhagavad-gītā with a Commentary Based on the Original Sources*. Oxford: Oxford University Press.

5

THE SOTERIOLOGY OF DEVOTION, DIVINE GRACE, AND TEACHING

Bhagavad-gītā and the *Śrīvaiṣṇavas*

Aleksandar Uskokov

The tradition of *Śrīvaiṣṇavism* is sometimes called *ubhaya-vedānta*, a doctrine based equally on the Sanskrit *Upaniṣad*s and the Tamil hymns of the *Āḻvār*s ('the immersed ones'), collectively known as *Divya-prabandham* (DP). It is a tradition stemming from fine *Vedāntic* philosophy *and* passionate devotion to a personal divinity, Nārāyaṇa. Scholars have long wondered how the two fit together, particularly concerning the tradition's premier representative, Rāmānuja (traditional dates 1017–1037 CE). Arguments have been made that Rāmānuja, who never explicitly quotes the *Āḻvār*s, was a philosopher later co-opted by *Śrīvaiṣṇavism* (Lester 1966, 281–2; Carman 1974, 230–1) and that, conversely, it was he and his fellow *Vedāntin*s who co-opted Tamil spirituality and stripped it of its emotionalism (Hardy 1983, 46).

In an important paper, however, Nancy Ann Nayar (1994) had demonstrated that Rāmānuja made a real synthesis of the two streams, and he did so in his commentary on the *Bhagavad-gītā* (*Bhg*). She showed, specifically, that Rāmānuja's idiosyncratic language in describing God's characteristic of purity (*amalatvam*) and the devotee's inability to find sustenance for the soul in separation from God were reflections of *Āḻvār* spirituality and were modelled on the vocabulary of the DP. Rāmānuja, like his predecessor Yāmuna (ca. 917–1037 CE), had a dual agenda: establishing the respectability of *Śrīvaiṣṇava* doctrine in the wider Brahmanical world and incorporating major *Āḻvār* themes in normative *Vedāntic* discourse. While his *Vedāntic* works were more about the first task, he accomplished the second in the *Bhg* commentary. To use a hackneyed phrase, then, one cannot emphasize enough how important a scripture the *Bhg* is for the *Śrīvaiṣṇava*s. In a sense, it is the linchpin that keeps *Upaniṣadic* philosophy and Tamil religious devotionalism together.

The corpus of writings on the *Bhg* in *Śrīvaiṣṇavism* is varied but can be grouped under three general headings. There is, first, Yāmuna's *Gītārtha-saṅgraha*, 'Summary of the *Bhagavad-gītā*' (*GAS*), a 32-verse hermeneutic frame that has shaped *Śrīvaiṣṇava* readings of Kṛṣṇa's song. There is, second, Rāmānuja's much more famous *Bhagavad-gītā-bhāṣya* (*BhgBh*). Both were interpreted by Vedāntadeśika (1269–1370 CE), in the *Gītārtha-saṅgraha-rakṣā* (*GASR*) and the *Tātparya-candrikā* (*TC*). The first is particularly useful for appreciating the significance of Yāmuna's work, as its major part consists of stitching together all the sections of the *BhgBh* where Rāmānuja paraphrases or quotes the *GAS* in important transitional points, such as chapter conclusions and introductions (van Buitenen 1968, 9–12).[1]

Finally, there are numerous interpretations of what became the *carama-śloka* of the *Bhg*, verse 18.66, its most important teaching. These concern the *Śrīvaiṣṇava* doctrines of surrender to the Lord (*prapatti*) and his divine grace (*prasāda*) as the ultimate means of liberation. *Bhg* 18.66 was discussed primarily in the *rahasya* genre of writings in Sanskritized Tamil (Maṇipravāḷa), the most relevant of which are the *Mumukṣuppaṭi* by Piḷḷai Lokācārya (1205–1311 CE) and Vedāntadeśika's *Rahasya-traya-sāra* (*RTS*), although Deśika also wrote a Sanskrit essay on the topic, titled *Nikṣepa-rakṣā*, and a long comment on the verse itself in the *TC*.

In this brief overview of the *Bhg*'s role in *Śrīvaiṣṇava* theology and philosophy, I will focus on its soteriological significance across the three main headings in which it was interpreted. In the first part, I will follow the *GAS* and the *GASR*, paying attention to the quotations from the *BhgBh*, to reconstruct what may be described as the textual and soteriological structure of the *Bhg* in *Śrīvaiṣṇava* reception history and arguably Yāmuna's most important contribution to the wider readings of the *Gītā*, namely its division in three hexads of six chapters. Next, I will move to the *carama-śloka* and the doctrines of surrender. Coming back to the *BhgBh*, I will finish the chapter with a brief account of Rāmānuja's arguments against *Advaita Vedānta* under 2.12, geared as they were towards showing that the *Bhg*'s soteriological significance would be impossible under *Advaita* ontological presuppositions.

The textual and soteriological structure of the *Bhagavad-gītā*

It is well known that the *Bhg* is sometimes divided into three groups of six chapters each. Several classical commentaries mention such a division. For instance, the 16th-century *Advaitin* Madhusūdana Sarasvatī (2000) in his *Gūḍhārtha-dīpikā* (*GAD*) presents a scheme in which the whole *Bhg* is an exposition of the paradigmatic identity statement 'That You Are', *tat tvam asi*, of the sixth chapter of the *Chāndogya Upaniṣad*. The first six chapters are about ascertaining the meaning of 'You', to refer to an aspirant after liberation who must perform *karma-yoga* first and then renounce all action. The second hexad or group of six chapters is about the category of 'That', understood as steadfast devotion to the Lord, accompanied by the deliberation on the *Upaniṣadic* statements. The final six chapters are about knowing the identity of 'You' and 'That'. This division, in fact, mirrors the common division of the *Veda*s, in three parts:

> It is the highest and complete state of Viṣṇu which is Being, consciousness and bliss in nature for the attaining of which the *Veda*s consist of three

> sections. These are, in order, action, meditation, and knowledge. In conformity with them, the *Gītā* of eighteen chapters has three sections.
>
> *(Sarasvatī 2000, Introduction, verse 3–4)*

The *Dvaita Vedāntin* Rāghavendra Tīrtha likewise says that the first hexad of the *Bhg* is about the means of acquiring knowledge, the second set is about practice, and the third is an elaboration of what had already been discussed. The *Gauḍīyas* Viśvanātha Cakravartin and Baladeva Vidyabhūṣaṇa present a similar scheme. According to the first, to illustrate, the respective groups are primarily about *karma*, *bhakti*, and *jñāna*. Such an arrangement is a reflection of *bhakti*'s being the most esoteric – shielded on both sides – and of its being the support without which the other two, unmixed with it, would not be efficacious (Burton 2011, 217).

This classification, however, is absent from the oldest commentaries on the *Bhg*, those of Śaṅkara, Bhāskara, Abhinavagupta, and Rājānaka Rāmakaṇṭha. Other than *Śrīvaiṣṇava* theology, in fact, the three-hexad division does not appear in *Bhg* commentaries well until early modernity, and for all we know, it appears for the first time at the beginning of the *GAS*. This three-hexad approach to the *Bhg*, then, is Yāmuna's major innovation that had influenced, through the *BhgBh*, the reception history of Kṛṣṇa's song, not only in classical Sanskrit writing but in Indological scholarship as well.

In what follows, I will briefly show that this approach to the *Bhg* was a device through which Yāmuna wanted to accomplish two things: present *bhakti* or devotional meditation on Nārāyaṇa as the sole means of attaining liberation, the highest good, and work out an interpretation frame in which the other *yoga*s of the *Gītā* would be soteriologically relevant by participating in a model of liberation based on mediate soteriological causality.

Yāmuna's thesis in the *GAS* stated in verse 1 is that the *Bhg* is all about Nārāyaṇa, the supreme *Brahman* who can be attained solely by devotion, *bhakti*, which devotion on its part must be brought about by the performance of one's duties, knowledge, and dispassion. There is, then, a central position accorded to *bhakti* in the text, which is bidirectional: as the means of attaining Nārāyaṇa, it looks ahead towards him; insofar as it is not the starting point of one's soteriological aspirations, however, and must first be brought about, it looks back towards three things as its conditions. In verses 2 and 3, this bidirectionality of *bhakti* is presented in more detail with reference to the first two hexads of the *Bhg*:

> In the first six chapters, two practices are enjoined, consisting of action and knowledge respectively, terminating in *yoga*, adorned, with the aim of achieving success in the direct experience of the Self. The middle six chapters discuss the *yoga* of devotion, which can be brought about by knowledge and action, and whose purpose is attaining correct understanding of the truth of the Blessed Lord.
>
> (GAS *2–3)*

For Yāmuna's commentators, this bidirectionality of *bhakti* organizes the three *yoga*s of the *Bhg* in a developmental sequence towards the supreme Lord in which *bhakti* is the sole direct means, but the other two obtain mediate soteriological efficacy as well. Deśika says this explicitly in *TC* in 18.66: the three *yoga*s are called *dharma* because they are the means to the highest good, and they are so either mediately, *paramparayā*, or directly, *sākṣāt*. He repeats the same under verses 2 and 3 of the *GAS*: the first hexad presents the means that are remote, whereas the second presents the means that are proximate to the supreme.

This, then, presents the three *yoga*s as three legs on the journey towards the highest good: everything that is discussed in chapters one through six is meant to prepare one for the practice of *bhakti*. In Rāmānuja's and Deśika's readings, more specifically, chapters two through five should bring one to the level of knowing oneself as *Brahman*, or rather the knowing of the self as identical with *Brahman in kind* and the corresponding vision of sameness, after which a meditation on the self that is described in chapter six can begin. They can do that either in sequence, such that the practice of *karma*, where one ascribes agency to prime matter (*prakṛti*) or to the Lord transforms into *jñāna*, or through the practice of *karma* alone, one which contains knowledge within itself (*GASR* 1–2, 7). The practice of meditation on oneself as *Brahman* in kind, on the other hand, brings one to the direct experience of the nature of the self, perfect *jñāna*, and only then is one ready to engage in *bhakti*, meditation on the Lord. The first six chapters, then, delineate the mediate means of liberation: they are about the preconditions of *bhakti*. Naturally, the next six chapters are about *bhakti*, the direct means and the true nature of the Lord, who is the object of attainment.[2]

We will not go into the details of hexads two and three. Yāmuna describes the last as a supplement of the first two, meant to clarify their topics but not to introduce anything new. It is crucial to appreciate, however, that Yāmuna developed this frame of reading the *Bhg* in terms of mediate and immediate soteriological causality on the basis of verses 54 and 55 of chapter 18.[3] This is clear from *GAS* 26:

> When one had seen oneself as a follower of the Supreme, all ignorance has been destroyed, and one had obtained the higher devotion, by means of that devotion alone one attains his abode.

Vedāntadeśika rightly recognizes 18.54–5 as the background of Yāmuna's statement. In these two verses, Kṛṣṇa says that only when one has become *Brahman* and has attained the vision of equality does one attain supreme devotion, by means of which one truly understands him and enters into him. Becoming *Brahman* is a goal on the road to liberation, but only as a juncture point: it terminates in supreme devotion, which in its turn leads one to Kṛṣṇa.

This reading of the text in groups of chapters that are concerned directly and indirectly with liberation obviously negotiates between working out a soteriological system out of the *Bhg* and devising a frame in which it can be read as a coherent text: it is both normative and interpretative. To conclude briefly, then, in the early *Śrīvaiṣṇava* reading of the *Bhg*, the conclusion of the text was 18.65–66, where *bhakti* is presented as the ultimate means of liberation. *Bhakti*, however, was not only a means: it was also the goal of the other *Bhg yoga*s, and this was predicated on *Bhg* 18.54–5.[4] We are justified, I believe, in taking 18.54–5 as the hermeneutic key through which the *Bhg* obtains textual cohesion as a book on liberation.

The ultimate verse (*carama-śloka*)

We saw in the previous section that for early *Śrīvaiṣṇava*s, *bhakti-yoga* was the conclusion of the *Bhg*. We need to appreciate, however, that *bhakti-yoga* in this conceptual universe stood for *meditation* on Nārāyaṇa, its most common synonyms being *dhyāna* and *upāsana* and its theology being informed by the *Brahma-sūtra*. In Deśika's definition, *bhakti-yoga* was uninterrupted mentation – like the flowing of oil – that has the clarity of perceptual awareness (*GASR* 1). It was supposed to be practised until death, and it came with the typical caste and gender restrictions that govern ritual: it was not available to *śūdra*s, women, and outcastes. It was *bhakti* because of the elements of affection for and dedication to the Lord (*GAS* 24), but they were overlaid on a *Vedic* substratum. No wonder that post-Rāmānuja theology moved towards rejecting such association with Vedism, and a crucial role in this was played by one *Bhg* verse. It was 18.66, where Kṛṣṇa says to Arjuna, 'Giving up all *dharma*s, come to me alone for refuge. I will protect you from all faults, grieve not!'

The verse, bearing the epithet of the *carama-śloka* or the 'ultimate verse', became one of the three most important *mantra*s in *Śrīvaiṣṇavism*, along with the so-called *tiru-mantra* and the *dvayam*. The three, labelled *rahasya*s or 'secrets', became the principal topic of the so-called *rahasya* genre and 'the main vehicle for explicating *Śrīvaiṣṇava* soteriology' (Mumme 1992, 73).

The first known use of the term *carama* with respect to *Bhg* 18.66 comes from the final verse of the *Aṣṭa-ślokī* of Parāśara Bhaṭṭar, the son of Rāmānuja's most intimate student, Kureśa:

> Certain in my eternal dependence on you, Hari, I sink, filled with sorrow, not competent to perform the means such as *karma-yoga*, or to give them up, or even to surrender to you. Nevertheless, remembering the final sentence of the charioteer, I am firmly convinced that you will destroy all my transgressions, as I have gotten this knowledge.

To the *Śrīvaiṣṇava*s, the 'final sentence' expressed in the 'final verse' was final because it introduced the 'final means' to liberation, the Lord himself, through the act of full surrender to him, *prapatti*.

In the *BhgBh* on 18.66, Rāmānuja offered two alternative interpretations of the verse. In the first, the respective *dharma*s that Kṛṣṇa wanted Arjuna to give up were the three *yoga*s that we saw in the previous section, including *bhakti*.[5] To be precise, Kṛṣṇa wanted Arjuna not to stop performing them but rather to renounce the sense of personal agency and to consider the Lord as the agent, the object of worship, the goal, and the means, all at once. In the second interpretation, Kṛṣṇa, realizing Arjuna's despair born of the sense of his being embodied and having but limited time yet endless accumulated faults, told his friend to forget about it all and give up all *dharmas*. These *dharmas* were now expiation rites required for the purification of faults, the freedom from which is the prerequisite for the engagement in *bhakti-yoga*. Kṛṣṇa as the ocean of parental affection would personally remove such faults and thus facilitate Arjuna's taking up of *bhakti-yoga*.

In post-Rāmānuja doctrine, the two interpretations have essentially merged into one, giving rise to the idea of *prapatti* as an independent soteriological practice, in which the act of surrender precisely *is* considering the Lord to be agent, the object of worship, the goal, and the means, but in the spirit of personal desperation out of a sense of incompetence, an act which is not for the sake of preparation for *bhakti-yoga*. There developed, however, major disagreements over *prapatti* and the continual value of *bhakti-yoga*, which have split the *Śrīvaiṣṇava* tradition into the two familiar brands: *Tĕṉkalai* (southern) and *Vaṭakalai* (northern) (Mumme 1988).

In the fifth chapter of *Mumukṣuppaṭi*, the *Tĕṉkalai* theologian Piḷḷai Lokācārya and his commentator Maṇavāḷamāmuni (1370–1443 CE) claimed that *bhakti-yoga* and its auxiliaries were for those who did not fully understand the soul's utter dependence on the Lord and were under the illusion of having something positive to do for the attainment of liberation, depending partly on their own agency.[6] The process of *prapatti*, on the other hand, was for those who understand that their soul is utterly dependent on the Lord and meant for his enjoyment. Both processes were merely a pretext for the Lord to grant his divine grace, which is the sole means of liberation, yet the second was incomparably easier than the first and was not contingent on gender or caste differences. In a reversal of *BhgBh* 18.66, the three *yogas* in any case had to transition into *prapatti* before the Lord would grant his grace. Piḷḷai Lokācārya compares their function to that of a log which people fasten on a cow's neck to keep her from wandering astray. Their performance keeps the practitioners self-controlled yet simultaneously exhausts them so much that they finally give it all up and gladly accept the Lord as the sole means.

What is *prapatti*? It is simply understanding – a mental phenomenon, never a physical or a verbal act – of one's essential dependence on the Lord. More specifically, it is an understanding that neither the effort towards nor the benefit of liberation are one's own but rather of the Lord, who takes upon himself the responsibility of rescuing one from faults, *pāpa*, which is now not the bad *karma* that prevents one from taking up *bhakti-yoga*, as in *BhgBh* 18.66, but is equivalent to *saṁsāra*, or the life of transmigration. In this, one's agency does not extend even to the acceptance of the means: even that happens on the Lord's initiative, through the fact of his soteriological exploits in various *avatāras*. All that one is expected to do is *stop being averse* to accepting God's saving grace. Liberation, thus, is not a consequence of doing anything but simply of understanding one's true nature as utterly dependent on the Lord. Such understanding, however, and the acceptance of God as one's saviour, must be preceded by the giving up of all other means which presuppose even the slightest trace of personal agency, including *bhakti-yoga*.

Vedāntadeśika as a *Vaṭakalai* theologian was much closer to Rāmānuja's *BhgBh*, but he introduced a third reading of 18.66, one in which *prapatti* is not only an auxiliary to *bhakti-yoga* but an independent alternative as well.[7] There could be several reasons why one may prefer the second over the first, but the most important are as follows: first, being ineligible for *bhakti-yoga* on the account of social considerations – *prapatti* unlike *bhakti-yoga* is open for everyone – and, second, the desire to attain liberation immediately. The second is peculiarly interesting, since *prapatti* is a real alternative to *bhakti-yoga* only when one has the competence for both. In such a case, *prapatti* may be appealing because it is easy to perform and brings the desired result immediately.

To elaborate, *bhakti-yoga* brings liberation only after the *karma* which had started bearing fruit (*prārabdha*) has been exhausted. This may take many lives: the characteristic *bhakti-yogī* for our *Śrīvaiṣṇava*s is the *jñānī* of the *Bhg* 7.16–19, one who attains Kṛṣṇa 'at the end of many lives'. *Prapatti*, on the other hand, brings liberation immediately upon performance, and one remains embodied solely through the desire to serve the Lord in the temple or similar considerations.

How precisely are *bhakti-yoga* and *prapatti* alternatives? Here we get a glimpse into further developments of the doctrine of *bhakti*. *Prapatti* is an alternative to the *parā bhakti* from *Bhg* 18.54–5, the one which was supposed to be brought about by *karma* and *jñāna*, and it is an alternative insofar as it does not require the prior two *yoga*s. Both are, however, just *means*, *sādhana* or *upāya*, and are equally followed by direct perceptual experience of the Lord, which Deśika calls *para-jñāna* or highest knowledge, which further culminates in a state called *parama-bhakti*, supreme devotion: 'an excessive and unsurpassed love for the Lord similar to that felt by a man suffering from great thirst at the sight of a tank' (*RTS* pp. 108–9). This is a reabsorption of *prapatti* in the doctrine of *bhakti*, but it is also a conceptual clarification of *bhakti* as the means in one sense and the goal in another.[8]

Deśika also did not quite like the *Tĕṉkalai* doctrine that *prapatti* was only an understanding, a mental act. While such understanding was certainly a precondition, it was supposed to be followed by the verbal act of affirmation of one's surrender and the bodily act of prostration. Mental *prapatti* was self-sufficient, yet the other two were its natural overflow (*RTS*, p. 109).

The difference between the two interpretations becomes most obvious when we compare their reading of the sequence from *parityajya* to *śaraṇaṁ vraja* in 18.66. For Piḷḷai Lokācārya, 'having given up', *parityajya*, was an injunction (*vidhi*) of renunciation as a prerequisite for *prapatti*, making *prapatti* an exclusive process such that the final meaning of the verse is as follows: 'you have to give up the three other *yoga*s and then surrender to me'. For Deśika, *parityajya* was what *Mīmāṁsaka*s call *anuvāda*, a statement of a prior condition obtaining – one is eligible for and interested in *prapatti* – making the whole injunction conditional: 'Given that *prapatti* is for you but might not be for someone else, and you prefer it, come to me for refuge'. In terms of actual practice, however, these distinctions do not seem to be particularly significant, since neither camp considered the renunciation of other means to be factually required and laboured hard to show that the other *yoga*s would be in any case included in what a *Vaiṣṇava* does or is, only in different spirit.

The critique of monism

Unlike his other two major works, the *Śrī-bhāṣya* and the *Vedārtha-saṅgraha*, Rāmānuja's *BhgBh* is non-polemical (Van Buitenen 1968, 18, 28). There are just two verses under which Rāmānuja engages in a prolonged disputation, 2.12 and 13.2, and it is clear from both that he was not interested in sustained critique: 'enough of these incorrect doctrines' and 'enough of this prolixity'. To the extent that he does argue with others, however, his critique can be characterized as emphasizing a single point: the context of the *Bhg* does not make much sense on the ontological presuppositions of the two prior major commentators: Śaṅkara and Bhāskara. This is so because the *Bhg* involves teaching, an action that cannot take place without presupposing ontological diversity.

We will focus on 2.12, where the critique is more developed. This is the verse where Kṛṣṇa says to Arjuna that the two of them and the other kings on the battlefield have always existed and will never cease to exist. Kṛṣṇa specifically uses the plural number of the personal pronoun 'we', *vayam*. Śaṅkara (2012) was alarmed by this use of 'we' because, at face value at least, it implies ontological pluralism. He claimed, therefore, that the plural was in the sense of different bodies, not different selves, implying, perhaps, that the difference was stated from the standpoint of conventional truth (*vyāvahārika-satya*), but not absolute truth (*pāramārthika-satya*). This is how, in any case, Rāmānuja (2009) read Śaṅkara's comment, and his initial argument is one of simple exegesis: the occasion was not one of conventional reality, as in our daily life, where we use pronouns to refer to embodied beings.[9] It was, rather, that of 'absolute eternity', because Kṛṣṇa's statement concerns Arjuna's confusion that needs to be removed. If Kṛṣṇa were using the pronoun intending bodily difference, he would be simultaneously removing and reinforcing Arjuna's confusion.

The simple exegetical argument, however, quickly turns into the critique that we introduced earlier: the impossibility of teaching on the ground of non-dualist ontology. The critique concerns particularly *Advaita Vedānta*, because it was there that instruction became the process of liberation *par excellence*. In Śaṅkara's system, liberation was the result of the removal of ignorance by means of inquiry into *Brahman* through the three processes of theological and philosophical reasoning with a teacher (*śravaṇa* and *manana*) and personal reflection (*nididhyāsana*). This obviously posed the problem of justifying the teacher/student distinction on which instruction was predicated, under the assumption that the teacher is a liberated knower of *Brahman* yet in some way continues seeing duality. Liberation is the result of a direct experience of the self, which is featureless, permanently unchanging consciousness, a vision which occasions a cognitive defeat of the vision of duality. How is teaching, the crucial *Advaita* soteriological practice, possible, when the teacher should not be aware of themselves and the student as being distinct? Advaitins seem to want to have it both ways: a teacher who should not see duality under the requirements of liberation yet cannot but see duality under the requirements of teaching, the process of liberation.

This is variation of the familiar problem of *jīvan-mukti*, liberation while living, and Advaitins have grappled with it in various ways. Generally, its defence depended on positing some karmic inertia that perpetuates the cognition of duality, like in the classical *Sāṅkhya-kārikā* instance of the potter's wheel that keeps rolling because of the final impulse yet will inevitably stop in the near future. Another favourite example, one which Rāmānuja puts in his opponent's mouth, is that of a burnt piece of cloth that keeps its shape but has ceased being cloth as a substance. Rāmānuja, however, accentuates the incoherence of the idea in the context of teaching, by insisting on its functional and factual impossibility.

If such cognition of duality is possible, it would have to be purely formal, not functional. *Advaitin*s illustrate the continuation of the vision of duality upon full knowledge with instances of cognitive faults where the subject knows that the object that he sees is false yet continues seeing it because the cause persists. A mirage is caused by a refraction of light, and a double moon is caused by astigmatism. Their cognition persists, but its veracity has been defeated by testimony: one may keep seeing the mirage but wouldn't want to drink from it. Precisely such is *not* the case with teaching, however, where the enlightened teacher goes on instructing what could only be 'his own reflection seen in jewels, knives, mirrors and such, knowing them to be non-different from oneself'. Saying that a burnt cloth may keep its form is one thing, but making a jacket out of it another. And that is what *Advaitin*s precisely need: an ignorance that remains functional and superimposes yet again the agent/patient/action distinction.

But Rāmānuja does not make even that concession. The persistence of mirage and the double moon is due to the persistence of the cause: the refraction of light or astigmatism. Their cognitive defeat concerns their veracity, such that they are no longer veridical cognitions, but they do persist as awareness episodes. The vision of duality, on the other hand, has ignorance *as its cause*. As an awareness episode, the vision of the student is caused by ignorance, and the removal of such ignorance should not only defeat its veracity but also remove it as an awareness episode, just as the removal of astigmatism should remove the vision of the double moon.

By the time of Rāmānuja, *Advaitin*s have started justifying ignorance in the student–teacher relationship by talking about 'imagination', generally on the part of the student. We may illustrate this with a piece from Sarvajñātman's (10th century) *Pañca-prakriyā*, where our *Advaitin* says that the student who is about to undergo an instruction in the *Upaniṣadic* identity statements approaches a teacher for the sake of clarifying their meaning. The characteristics of this teacher are, obviously, important: he has personally realized *Brahman*, is liberated while living, has been purified of all faults by the knowledge of *Brahman*, and yet is 'just imagined to be a teacher by the student's own ignorance, as a teacher that one might see in a dream', surrounded by equally imagined thousands of students. The teacher is liberated, but the student imagines his presence just as one might in a dream: there is no teacher to begin with (Kocmarek 1985, 52).

Rāmānuja picks up this 'dreamlike imagination' possibility at the end of *BhgBh* 2.12; his comment is terse, so I will focus on Vedāntadeśika's elaboration. Imagine that the student imagines the teacher and the teacher's knowledge. There are several problems with it; the teacher might figure out that he is imagined by the student and choose not to liberate the student, since such liberation would necessarily be the teacher's own end. In other words, the teacher would decline to show the means of liberation to the student, the cause of the teacher's own destruction. The student would also likely figure out that the teacher is a dreamlike illusion, in which case the student would not hear from the teacher: if the student realizes that the teacher and his knowledge are the student's own imagination and that he himself is the object of their imagination, constituted as a student in an act of double imagination, why would the student listen to the teacher? Wouldn't the student already know what the teacher might tell him, as it is his own mind that projects the teacher? The teacher's knowledge is the student's own knowledge, so what use of imagining a teacher? And knowing this, wouldn't the student simply wait to wake up on his own?

Deśika imagines other possibilities of imagination, for instance that both the teacher and the student are imagined by someone else or that the student is self-awakened, both of which go a long way in showing not only that teaching's instrumentality in liberation would be impossible on *Advaita* ontological presuppositions but that it would be useless as well.

Conclusion

I have focused this overview of *Śrīvaiṣṇava* readings of the *Bhg* on the soteriological value of Kṛṣṇa's song for the *Śrīvaiṣṇava* tradition, guided somewhat by the agenda set already by Yāmuna:

> Enjoying solely in exclusive and absolute servitude, he attains the Lord's abode. This scripture is primarily about that: thus, the summary of the Gītā. (GAS *32)*

We saw how the early tradition promoted *bhakti-yoga* as the essence of the *Bhg* – through the scheme of three groups of six chapters that proved a lasting innovation – and how soon the doctrine of *prapatti* took over and eventually split *Śrīvaiṣṇavism* into two doctrinal communities. While *Śrīvaiṣṇava*s unanimously held 18.66 as the most important verse of the *Bhg*, and of scripture in general, we saw that for textual cohesion, equally important were 18.54–5; in fact, 18.66 proved to be more of a wedge than a linchpin. I hope, finally, that I have managed to illustrate the richness of *Bhg*'s reception history in *Śrīvaiṣṇavism*, by my supplementing the general account of soteriology with the specific critique of *Advaita Vedānta*.

Curiously, in doing so, we traversed *backwards* the full extent of Kṛṣṇa's song:

> Kṛṣṇa spoke this speech, *beginning* in 'There never was a time' (2.12) and *ending* in 'I will protect you from all faults, grieve not!' (18.66) concerning the real nature of the individual and the Supreme Self, and the *yogas* of *karma*, *jñāna* and *bhakti*, which are the means of attaining the Supreme.
>
> (BhgBh *2.10)*

Notes

1 All quotes from *Bhg* and *GAS* are given according to verse number; *GASR*, *BhgBh*, and *TC* are quoted based on the verse number they are commenting on. *RTS* is quoted by page number of the English translation; *GAD* is quoted by verse number of the introduction (see References). All translations from Sanskrit are mine, and those from Maṇipravāḷa are from the English translations, in References.

2 We should mention that *bhakti* for the *Śrīvaiṣṇavas* is the means not only to liberation but to prosperity and isolation as well, modelled on *Bhg* 7.16.

3 The verses run as follows:

> He who has become *Brahman* is always content and does not grieve or desire. Equal to all beings, he attains the highest devotion to me. One understands me truly, as I am, by devotion. Once one had known me in truth, he then enters into me.

4 *Bhg* 18.65–6:

> Absorb your mind in me and become my devotee. Worship me and pay homage to me. To me you shall come, I promise you truly, because you are dear to me. Giving up all *dharmas*, come to me alone for refuge. I will protect you from all faults, grieve not!

5 Remember the definition of *dharma:* a means, *sādhana*, to something desirable.

6 Piḷḷai Lokācārya (1987, 150–207).

7 The following section is based on RTS, chapters eight to 13 and 29 (Vedāntadeśika 1946, 94–140; 465–565).

8 The sequence of *para-bhakti* to *para-jñāna* and to *parama-bhakti* comes, in fact, from Rāmānuja's *Śaraṇāgati-gadya* (Lester 1966, 271–2).

9 Deśika explicitly names Śaṅkara as representing the *prima facie* view.

References

Primary literature

Bhagavad-gītā with *Gītārtha-saṅgraha* of Yāmuna; *Gītārtha-saṅgraha-rakṣā* of Vedāntadeśika; *Gītā-bhāṣya* of Rāmānuja; and *Tātparya-candrikā* of Vedāntadeśika, edited by Sri Kanchi. P.B. Annangaracharyar. Kanchipuram 1941: Srimath Vedantadesika Granthamala.

Gūḍhārtha-dīpikā of Madhusūdana Sarasvati, edited by K.S. Āgaśe. Ānandāśrama Sanskrit Series 45. Poona 1901: Ānandāśrama.

Parāśara, Bhaṭṭar. 1969. *Aṣṭa-ślokī*, in *Stotramālā*. Ed. P.B. Annangaracharyar. Kanchipuram: Grantamala Office.

Secondary literature and translations

van Buitenen, J.A.B. 1968. *Rāmānuja on the Bhagavad-gītā*. Delhi: Motilal Banarsidass.

Burton, Adrian P. 2011. *Temples, Texts, and Taxes: The Bhagavad-gītā and the Politico-Religious Identity of the Caitanya Sect*. PhD Dissertation, Australian National University.

Carman, John Braisted. 1974. *The Theology of Rāmānuja: An Essay in Interreligious Understanding*. New Haven: Yale University Press.

Hardy, Friedhelm. 1983. *Viraha Bhakti: The Early History of Kṛṣṇa Devotion in South India*. Delhi: Oxford University Press.

Kocmarek, Ivan. 1985. *Language and Release: Sarvajñātman's Pañcaprakriyā*. Delhi: Motilal Banarsidass.

Lester, Robert. Winter 1966. "Rāmānuja and Śrī-Vaiṣṇavism: The Concept of Prapatti or Śaraṇāgati." *History of Religions*, 5(2): 266–82.

Mumme, Patricia V. 1988. *The Śrīvaiṣṇava Theological Dispute: Maṇavāḷamāmuni and Vedānta Deśika*. Madras: New Era Publications.

Mumme, Patricia V. 1992. "Haunted by Śaṅkara's Ghost: The *Śrīvaiṣṇava* Interpretation of *Bhagavad-gītā* 18:66." In *Texts in Context: Traditional Hermeneutics in South Asia*. Edited by Jeffrey R. Timm, pp. 69–84. Albany: State University of New York Press.

Nayar, Nancy Ann. 1994. "The Tamilizing of a Sacred Sanskrit Text: The Devotional Mood of Rāmānuja's BhagavadgītāBhāṣya and Āḻvār Spirituality." In *Hermeneutical Paths to the Sacred Worlds of India: Essays in Honour of Robert W. Stevenson*. Edited by Katherine K. Young, pp. 186–221. Atlanta: Scholars Press.

Piḷḷai, Lokācārya. 1987. *The Mumukṣuppaṭi. With Maṇavālamāmuni's Commentary*. Trans. Patricia V. Mumme. Bombay: Ananthacharya Indological Research Institute.

Rāmānuja. 2009. *Gītā Bhāṣya*. Trans. Ādidevānanda Svāmī. Chennai: Sri RamaKṛṣṇa Math.

Śaṅkara. 2012. *Bhagavad-gītā With the Commentary of Śaṅkarācārya*. Trans. Gambhirananda Swami. Kolkata: *Advaita* Ashrama.

Sarasvatī, Madhusūdana. 2000. *Bhagavad-gītā. With the Annotation Gūḍhārtha-Dīpikā*. Trans. Gambhirananda Swami. Calcutta: Advaita Ashrama.

Vedāntadeśika. 1946. *Śrīmad Rahasyatrayasāra*. Trans. M.R Rajagopala Ayyangar. Kumbakonam: Agnihotram Ramanuja Thathachariar.

6

KARMA IN THE *BHAGAVAD-GĪTĀ*

Caitanya Vaiṣṇava views[1]

Joseph T. O'Connell

The *Bhagavad-gītā*, which may be considered a *Vaiṣṇava* text, has enjoyed wide currency in India for two millennia or so.[2] It is thus reasonable to ask how the *Caitanya Vaiṣṇava*s – i.e., those devotees of Kṛṣṇa revering Śri Caitanya Mahāprabhu (1486–1533) as the divine paradigm of loving devotion, *prema-bhakti* – have understood the *Bhagavad-gītā*. It is a bit surprising to find that not until the end of the 17th century, more than a century and a half after the passing away of Caitanya, did any *Caitanya Vaiṣṇava* produce a commentary on the *Gītā* that is extant today. This chapter does not attempt to survey more-recent *Caitanya Vaiṣṇavas*' commentaries on and translations of the *Gītā*. Rather, it confines its attention to two relatively early but influential theologians who may be presumed to represent mainline *Caitanya Vaiṣṇava* views: Kṛṣṇadāsa Kavirāja and Viśvanātha Cakravartin. Even here it is not their overall interpretations of the *Bhagavad-gītā* that are examined but rather their treatment of *karma*, work or action understood as a religious category. This particular focus reflects my concern to understand how Caitanya *Vaiṣṇavas*, especially in the formative period of their movement, have understood the relationship between religious faith – in their case, devotion to Kṛṣṇa – and mundane sociopolitical life.[3]

In the 16th century, presumably, there would have been available to Caitanya and his *Vaiṣṇava* associates the commentary on the *Gītā* by Śrīdhara Svāmin (circa 1400), whose commentary on the *Bhāgavata Purāṇa* they so much admired. Although Śrīdhara's *Bhāgavata* commentary received much praise and citation by Caitanyaites, his *Gītā* commentary seems to have gone largely unmentioned. Nor did the existence of Śrīdhara's respected commentary on the *Bhāgavata* dissuade prominent associates of Caitanya (e.g. Sanātana and Jīva) from trying their hands at *Bhāgavata* commentaries of their own; yet they refrained from doing so for the *Gītā*.

Advaita Ācārya, a senior contemporary and highly regarded associate of Caitanya, is reported to have taught on the *Gītā*, and the *Advaita-prakāśa* claims that he wrote a commentary on it. But had he produced a formal written commentary, it is surprising that his descendants and spiritual successors, otherwise jealous of their heritage from *Advaita*, would have let it slip into oblivion.[4] *Advaita* had learned the devotional interpretation of the *Bhagavad-gītā*, it is reported, from his preceptor, Mādhavendra Puri (the *guru*'s *guru* of Caitanya). Apart from the small circle of Mādhavendra's disciples, however, there were few scholars of Sanskrit texts at Navadvīpa, the town in Bengal where Caitanya was born, who did not subordinate the teachings on devotion (*bhakti*) to the teachings on knowledge (of a gnostic and impersonal sort, *jñāna*) or on work (in the sense of traditionally ascribed ritual and social actions, *karma*), or so one of the best of Caitanya's biographers, Vṛndāvanadāsa, laments.[5] The lament of the biographer points directly at the problem which the *Gītā* posed for the *Caitanya-Vaiṣṇavas*: it can be argued that it does not give unambiguous enough pre-eminence to devotion over the other spiritual disciplines of knowledge and work. In particular, the *Gītā* is silent on the winsome sports of Kṛṣṇa as a child and on his amorous sports (*Līlās*) as an adolescent boy, sports which the *Caitanya-Vaiṣṇavas* confidently believe to reveal the essence of divine life and the perfection of human religious life, loving devotion (*prema-bhakti*).[6] Advaita Ācārya himself is reported to have for a time slipped into a more *jñāna*-oriented mode of teaching, from which Caitanya is reported to have restored him to proper emphasis on *bhakti*. It is not out of the question that the allegedly lost commentary on the *Bhagavad-gītā* by *Advaita*, if there was one, might have reflected more influence of *jñāna* than was considered acceptable in mainline *Caitanya Vaiṣṇava* circles.

Evidently, several of the biographers of Caitanya were well versed in the *Gītā*, since they quote it with some frequency. The famous six *Gosvāmins* of *Vṛndāvana*, most of whom made substantial contributions to the Sanskrit literature of the *Caitanya Vaiṣṇava* movement, were aware of the *Bhagavad-gītā* but generally were sparing in their citation of it, according to the tables prepared by S.K. De. Only the second generation, Jīva Gosvāmin, quotes the *Gītā* with any profusion. None of the six is known to have authored a commentary on the famous text. Of much more importance to them, as to the *Caitanya Vaiṣṇava*s generally, were the *Bhāgavata Purāṇa* and other *Vaiṣṇava* texts telling of the amorous pastimes of Kṛṣṇa.[7] The first extant *Caitanya Vaiṣṇava* commentary on the *Bhagavad-gītā* is the *Sārārtha-varṣiṇī* (also mentioned as *Sārārtha-darśinī*) of Viśvanātha Cakravartin, a *brāhmaṇa* born in northern Bengal in the second half of the 17th century. Most of his copious writing in Sanskrit was done as a recluse at or near Vṛndāvana. He was steeped in the distinctive *Caitanya Vaiṣṇava* literature, especially that of Rūpa Gosvāmin that dealt with the mood of loving devotion (*prema-bhakti-rasa*).[8]

There is another commentary on the *Gītā*, by a *Vaiṣṇava* from Orissa, said to have been a disciple of Viśvanātha, namely Baladeva Vidyābhūṣaṇa. I have not considered this 18th-century document in this chapter, because the philosophical theology of Baladeva is thought to reflect aspects of Madhva's thought, with which he was also acquainted. His work is certainly significant and deserving of more scholarly attention than it has received, though it may be something of a hybridization of Caitanya and Madhva elements.[9] Likewise, I have not considered the ideas of the *Gauḍīya Maṭh* and several related revival movements in the past century or the views of Swami A.C. Bhaktivedanta and the International Society for Kṛṣṇa Consciousness. It is *Caitanya Vaiṣṇavas'* exegetical use of the *Bhagavad-gītā* – and in particular their view of "work" (*karma*) – in their formative period with which this chapter is concerned, not with subsequent developments, interesting as these may be.

The one document after the *Bhāgavata Purāṇa* that is the most influential among the *Caitanya Vaiṣṇavas* is the *Caitanya-Caritāmṛta*, a Bengali biography and theological compendium completed probably in 1612 by Kṛṣṇadāsa Kavirāja, heir to the intellectual and spiritual legacy of the *Gosvāmins* of Vṛndāvana. What I propose to do in this chapter is examine the ways Kṛṣṇadāsa and Viśvanātha respectively exegete passages from the *Bhagavad-gītā* in the historical context in which the *Caitanya Vaiṣṇava* movement emerged and matured, namely Bengal and Vṛndāvana ruled by independent Muslim sultans or by imperial Mughal officers. In the examination of Kṛṣṇadāsa's and Viśvanātha's interpretations of the *Gītā*, I focus on their treatment of *karma*, traditional socio-ritual work. This is because it is in work (*karma*) that sacredness and particular forms of mundane social (and even political, if one considers *rāja-dharma*) organization may become fused. In the epic context which the *Bhagavad-gītā* portrays the sacred normative order (*dharma*) is that characterized by the Brahmanical system of castes (*varṇa*) and states in life (*āśrama*). A good king is one who enforces *varṇāśrama-dharma*, a good warrior one who risks his life in defence of it. The *Bhagavad-gītā* explicitly affirms and legitimates on sacred grounds the system of *varṇāṣrama-dharma*, even though it has much else to say about the religious life. The *Caitanya Vaiṣṇavas*, on the contrary, tend to withdraw both legitimation and censure from the social and political spheres by confining the area of genuinely sacred activity to the interior devotional life of the individual and to congregational devotional exercises.[10]

I. Kṛṣṇadāsa's interpretation of the *Gītā*

The chart appended to this article lists those verses of the *Bhagavad-gītā* which Kṛṣṇadāsa quotes in the *Caitanya Caritāmṛta* and indicates where these occur in the editions of the *Caitanya Maṭh* and of *Rādhā Govinda Naṭh*.[11] Since our present concern is the attitude *Vaiṣṇavas'* take on traditional patterns of action which may simultaneously have ritual and social – and even economic, political and military – significances, i.e. their attitude toward performance of work (*karma*), I have simply noted but not elaborated on, the several passages which have little or no relevance to the question of work but which speak to some other theological question. The next group includes passages which appear to be more or less favourable to the performance of work. Kṛṣṇadāsa's exegesis of such passages is quite interesting and, theologically speaking, rather daring. Finally, there are those passages, slightly more numerous, which seem to be unfavourable to the performance of work, passages which Kṛṣṇadāsa, like the *Caitanya Vaiṣṇavas* generally, interprets in a way favourable to devotion, but not favourable to work or knowledge (*jñāna*).

Verses neutral in attitude to *karma*

Passages from the *Bhagavad-gītā* quoted by Kṛṣṇadāsa but having no direct bearing on the issue of *karma* address the following points: God pervades and upholds the universe (*Gītā* 10:41–2); God has a spiritual nature beyond matter (*Gītā* 7:4–5); a display of Kṛṣṇa's majesty (*aiśvarya*) diminishes the spontaneity of love (*Gītā* 11:41–2); fools despise Kṛṣṇa in his human form (*Gītā* 9:11); and those who deny the supremacy of Kṛṣṇa go to perdition (*Gītā* 16:19).

Verses favourable to performance of *karma*

Kṛṣṇadāsa (1962) quotes four verses from the *Gītā* early in the first book of the *Caitanya Caritāmṛta* to support one basic point: 'If (the Lord) Himself does not perform it, *dharma*, normative order, fails to be propagated' (*CC* 1:3.2.1). The verses appealed to are *Gītā* 4:7–8, which state that whenever *dharma* is in decline and its opposite in the ascendancy, the Lord himself takes birth age after age for the rescue of the good, the destruction of the wicked and the establishment of *dharma*; *Gītā* 3:24, which states that, if he did not perform his work, these worlds would perish, he would be the agent of mixing (of castes) and he would thus destroy these creatures; and *Gītā* 3:21, which states that whatever the best do, lesser men imitate and whatever standard such a one sets, the world follows. Kṛṣṇadāsa goes on to say that while a mere portion of the deity, a partial *avatāra*, is capable of establishing the normative order appropriate for any particular age (*yuga-dharma*), only the Lord in person is able to distribute the love appropriate to Kṛṣṇa's pastoral village (*vraja-prema*) (*CC* 1:3.26). Caitanya is Kṛṣṇa in person descended for two purposes: the propagation of the *dharma* of *kali* age, i.e. propagation of the divine name (*namer pracāra*) (*CC* 1:3:40), and the more transcending work of loving devotion (*prema-bhakti*). Kṛṣṇadāsa thus, like other *Caitanya Vaiṣṇavas*, maintains the traditional idea of a divine descent to propagate a system of normative order (*dharma*) but by having recourse to the notion of several ages (*yuga*) radically alters the kind of *dharma* now valid. In place of the 'just war' to maintain the *brāhmaṇical* system of socially and ritually exclusive castes, the work now required to support *dharma* is a combination of singing the names of God and fostering amorous devotion to Kṛṣṇa and his beloved Rādhā. Kṛṣṇadāsa, interestingly enough, says nothing at all about the word *saṅkarasya*, 'of mixing' (castes), a problem that looms large in Kṛṣṇa's charge to Arjuna in the *Bhagavad-gītā*.

One of the verses just mentioned, *Gītā* 3:21, stating that lesser men follow the example of the best, appears again in the *Caitanya Caritāimṛta* (2:17.178), not as a sanction for rigor in upholding the order of castes and states in life, as the context in the *Gītā* seems to require, but as justification for laxity. Kṛṣṇadāsa appeals to this verse to explain why Caitanya, contrary to the usual practice of a *brāhmaṇa* ascetic (*saṁnyāsin*), took food at the house of a *brāhmaṇa* of questionable ritual purity. The explanation is that Caitanya simply followed the precedent of that excellent person, Mādhavendra Purī, the *guru* of Caitanya's own *guru*, who had eaten at the same house years before.

Another passage in the *Bhagavad-gītā* (4:11) enunciates the principle that the Lord favours his devotees in ways proportionate to how they worship him; after all, people tread the way to him in all sorts of paths. This principle can be construed broadly enough to include the performance of social and ritual duties, as the *Gītā* does. However, as Kṛṣṇadāsa applies the verse the first time, it seems restricted to the interpersonal, devotional relationships of child to father, friend to friend and lover to beloved. The second citing of the verse is in a special context bearing on dramatic symbolism of amorous devotion. Kṛṣṇadāsa explains that the promise of Kṛṣṇa (in *Gītā* 4:11) to respond to his devotee in proportionate or reciprocal fashion appears to be violated in the incident in the *Bhāgavata Purāṇa* where young married women longing to meet Kṛṣṇa are kept locked in their houses. In this case, as Kṛṣṇadāsa explains, Kṛṣṇa indeed allows them to meet him, but in their meditation. Neither of these applications of *Gītā* 4:11 explicitly rules out the performance of social and ritual duties as worthwhile expressions of devotion, but neither do they give any endorsement to such an interpretation.

A related idea appears in *Gītā* 7:16, where Kṛṣṇa states that four types of well-behaved people worship him: the suffering, those desiring knowledge, those seeking rewards and those possessing knowledge. 'Well behaved' (*sukṛtino*) may, as Caitanyaite editors and commentators take it, refer to fidelity to the *dharma* of castes and states in life. Hence, the mere citation of the verse constitutes a mild endorsement of the performance of *karma* in line with *Varṇāśarma-dharma*. Kṛṣṇadāsa even says that the four types of well-behaved people are most fortunate (*mahābhāgyavān*) (*CC* 2:14.91) but quickly adds that they should abandon the corporal and spiritual desires which motivate them and become exclusively motivated by devotion (*śuddha-bhaktimān*). He has nothing more to say in this section about being well behaved: neither precisely what it involves nor whether it is a sine qua non of further development or a coincidental, but not essential, circumstance.

One of the foremost principles in the *Bhagavad-gītā*, especially in the early chapters in which the issue of righteous warfare in behalf of *dharma*, including *varṇāśrarma-dharma*, is that it brings rewards and repercussions in this life and beyond; however, all such rewards and repercussion should be dedicated to Kṛṣṇa. On this principle, public and domestic activities can be of major religious importance. This pivotal idea is almost entirely ignored in the more than 10,000 couplets of the *Caitanya Caritāmṛta*. The idea is suggested, however, in *Gītā* 9:27, which is cited once (*CC* 2:860); an intimate associate of Caitanya, Rāmānanda Rāya, is presented as reciting to Caitanya a series of scriptural statements on the goal of religious discipline. The first suggestion is that devotion comes from the exercise of the *dharma* proper to oneself (*svadharma*). Caitanya says that this is superficial (*bāhya*) and asks for something more. Then Rāmānanda says, 'Dedication of one's works to Kṛṣṇa, this is the essence of all piety' and recites *Gītā*

9:27 in support. Again, Caitanya puts this suggestion aside as superficial, and the two move on towards ever-more-intimate modalities of loving devotion.

There is explicit mention of work in *Gītā* 6:3 (*karma*) and *Gītā* 6:4 (*karmasu*), both of which are cited by Kṛṣṇadāsa (*CC* 2:24.153–4). The first states that for one desirous of attaining *yoga*, the instrumental cause is *karma*; the second says that when a person is no longer attached to sense objects or to works (*karmasu*) and has abandoned all schemes, they are said to have reached *yoga*. The context in the *Caitanya Caritāmṛta* is a laborious exposition of the 64 ways Caitanya was able to construe a verse from the *Bhāgavata Purāṇa*) (1:7.10; i.e., *ātmārāmāśca*) to show that various types of holy men authentically worship Kṛṣṇa, not because of the varieties of knowledge (*jñāna*) or release (*mokṣa*) to which they are aspiring or which they have attained but because they have grown attracted to Kṛṣṇa by his grace, directly or by associating with his devotees (*CC* 2:24:155). There is no discussion of the significance of *karma* in this case; it is referred to only as part of the scriptural passage cited to fill out the 64-fold interpretation.

Moderation in spiritual discipline is the theme of *Gītā* 6:16–17, moderation in eating, sleeping, rest and works. Kṛṣṇadāsa relays these verses as part of an advice by an older ascetic, Rāmacandra Puri, to Caitanya, who had grown thin from excessive fasting. There is no consideration of moderation in domestic or public affairs on the part of householders (*CC* 3:8.61–7).

Thus we see that the 11 verses from the *Bhagavad-gītā* cited in the *Caitanya Caritāmṛta* which more or less explicitly seem to endorse the performance of *karma*, traditional social and ritual work do not receive any comment or application by Kṛṣṇadāsa such as would constitute endorsement of efforts to maintain or re-establish *varṇāśrama-dharma*, despite the didactic character of the book. At most, it is admitted that exercise of one's proper dharma and dedication of one's work to Kṛṣṇa are valid but superficial types of devotion. Coincidental mention of *karma* or *dharma* in a few verses cited as scriptural may suggest that some value attaches work that is supportive of maintaining social order. But whether *varṇāśrama-dharma* in its *Brahmanical* form is intended as the exclusive norm or is merely cited as one concrete but historically contingent example of responsible social order is not specified. Indeed, it is not specified whether the *varṇāśrama-dharma* referred to in the *Gītā* as valid in Kṛṣṇa's time (in the *Dvāpara* age) remains authoritative (and, if so, to what extent) in the current *kali* age. In any event, no effort is made to inspire the reader to work for the fulfilment of *varṇāśrama-dharma* in the present context.

Rather, the overwhelming concern of Kṛṣṇadāsa is to expound devotion to Kṛṣṇa as revealed through Caitanya. Other matters are ignored or subordinated to this one. The *dharma* appropriate to the present age is said to be recitation of the names of Kṛṣṇa. The ultimate *dharma*, surpassing all others, is *prema-bhakti*, loving devotion, to Kṛṣṇa as epitomized in his beloved Rādhā. To establish firmly both these *dharmas* is the purpose of Kṛṣṇa's descent as Caitanya. To save the world from the mixing of castes is the least of Caitanya's objectives, or so it would seem from a reading of the *Caitanya Caritāmṛta* of Kṛṣṇadāsa.

Verses not favourable to *karma*

Several verses from the *Bhagavad-gītā* which state, or might be construed to imply, that the performance of work is unnecessary or baneful in the quest for devotion find their way into the *Caitanya Caritāmṛta.* A few of these are cited three times, presumably reflecting the author's high regard for them as scriptural proof texts. One such text is the *Gītā* 10:10, which states that the Lord gives to those who constantly and attentively worship him with love a mental control (*buddhi-yogam*) by which they may reach him. This is offered as proof of a statement (*CC* 1:1.47) that Kṛṣṇa, by guiding the soul from within, i.e. as *antaryāmī*, reveals himself as a teacher. It appears again (*CC* 2:24.167) in that 64-fold interpretation of how saints are saved, to support the contention that devotion does not grow into love without a person's being attentive or disciplined. Later in the same exegesis (*CC* 2:24.186), the verse reappears after a paraphrase of it in the Bengali text. There is no extended discussion of the *Gītā* verse in any of the contexts in which it is cited. While there is here no overt disparagement of work in the service of *dharma* – and, indeed, *karma* is not even mentioned – there seems to be more than a hint that it is by the more direct intervention of Kṛṣṇa himself, rather than by work, that devotion, at least the higher loving devotion, develops in a person. *Gītā* 10:8, cited as *CC* 2:24.183, has similar import.

Another of the verses from the *Gītā* that Kṛṣṇadāsa cites three times is *Gītā* 7:14, which states that by resort to Kṛṣṇa one passes beyond the snares of material illusion (*māyā*), which is also an aspect of Kṛṣṇa. Kṛṣṇadāsa uses this text to support these assertions: by the mercy of Kṛṣṇa extended through holy men and scriptures, souls long caught in *māyā* pass beyond it (*CC* 2:20:121); release comes not from knowledge which is without devotion but from devotion to Kṛṣṇa (*CC* 2:22.23); and release from *māyā* depends on that release which is focused on Kṛṣṇa (*CC* 2:24.131). Like the previous example, this contains no explicit denigration of the performance of *karma* but simply ignores it. It directs human attention towards an awareness of Kṛṣṇa as the effective element in the process of salvation. The only extended passage from the *Gītā*, i.e. 12:13–20, carried into the *Caitanya Caritāmṛta* (2:23.100–7) has much of the same force. The virtues of the person who is dear to Kṛṣṇa are listed at length. They emphasize tranquillity, indifference to changes in the external environment and trusting devotion to Kṛṣṇa but do not recommend *karma.*

The next example is much the same, although the verse in the *Gītā* (18:54), stating that the soul which is at peace and has realized *Brahman* attains to the highest devotion to the Lord, seems to attribute slightly less instrumental significance to devotion than do the assertions it is called up to support. *CC* 2:8:65 illustrates yet another of the relatively superficial types of piety – i.e. knowledge mixed with devotion (*Jñāna-miśra bhakti*) – that is set aside by Caitanya in favour of unadulterated devotion. *CC* 2:24.127 supports the principle that one whose release is through devotion worships Kṛṣṇa, while one whose (alleged) release is through dry knowledge (*śuṣka-jñāne*) falls into sin (*aparādhe*). It appears a third time (*CC* 2:25.148) to prove that one should continuously sing the praises of Kṛṣṇa's name to receive liberation through love. In these passages, there is evidence of a consistent *Caitanya Vaiṣṇava* polemic against the claim of knowledge (*Jñāna*) as a means of genuine release. The parallel polemic against work (*karma*) would depict a discipline of pure work as folly and work mixed with devotion as effective, but not optimally so, with pure devotion as the active ingredient in the mix. This polemic against work does appear in *Caitanya Vaiṣṇava* literature, but not with the frequency and urgency of the polemic against knowledge, which presumably was a greater challenge at the time.

A forceful statement of the polemic against work is *CC* 2:9.263: 'All scriptures advise disparagement of work (*karma-nindā*) and the abandonment of work (*karma-tyāga*). Loving devotion for Kṛṣṇa never comes from work'. In support of this, Kṛṣṇadāsa appeals to *Gītā* 18:66, wherein Kṛṣṇa recommends that one forsake all *dharmas* and promises that he will save from all sins. The context of this is a discussion in which Caitanya is presented as criticizing the view of one *Raghuvarya Tirtha* that the best religious practice is dedicating to Kṛṣṇa one's *dharma* of caste and state in life and that the best religious attainment is enjoyment of five-fold release. *Gītā* 18:66 reappears (*CC* 2:22.91) to substantiate the statement: 'Forsaking all the foregoing and also the *dharma* of caste and state in life becoming humble, one attains the sole refuge of Kṛṣṇa' (*CC* 2:22.90). The third occurrence of *Gītā* 18:66 is in *CC* 2:8.63, where it supports the Rāmānanda Rāya's advocacy of abandoning one's proper *dharma* as the essence of beatitude, one of the views that Caitanya sets aside as superficial.

Gītā 18:64–6 has Kṛṣṇa reveal the highest secret to Arjuna, i.e. he is going to save Arjuna, if Arjuna remains devoted to him, because Arjuna is dear to him. Kṛṣṇadāsa writes that Kṛṣṇa gave this message through Arjuna to the whole world. Kṛṣṇadāsa goes on to declare that 'The former directives – for *Vedic dharma*, work, *yoga*, knowledge – all are terminated and the final directive is in force. If there is trust (*śraddhā*) in this directive, then one abandons all work and worships Kṛṣṇa' (*CC* 2:22.60). The crucial point then becomes trust in Kṛṣṇa. So long as this is wanting, there is some scope for other religious practices; when it is effectively present, only devotion to Kṛṣṇa is appropriate.

Kṛṣṇadāsa draws on two verses (*CC* 3:4.177–8) from the *Gītā* to explain Caitanya's willingness to embrace two allegedly defiling people, Haridāsa, the *Vaiṣṇava* saint of Muslim background and Sanātana, the Brahman *Vaiṣṇava* who was disgraced in some circles for close association with Muslims and who was at the time diseased. *Gītā* 6:8 says that a *yogī* sees no difference between a clod of earth and a piece of gold; *Gītā* 5:18 says that the wise look upon cow and dog and upon *Brahman* and eater of dogs as equivalent. Caitanya's behaviour does not seem to have been part of an effort to do away with caste and ritual pollution altogether, as some modern interpreters have contended, but it was sufficiently liberal in these regards to gain for him a contemporary reputation for universal love of people whom others would dare not touch.

The basic policy of Kṛṣṇadāsa in appealing to passages from the *Bhagavad-gītā* which do not favour the performance of traditional social and ritual work is to argue from them to the fundamental superiority and uniqueness of devotion. Since devotion is the active ingredient in the mixtures of devotion, work and knowledge and since Kṛṣṇa by his grace bestows devotion on whom he will, there is no basic need for work or knowledge in the ultimate religious quest.

II. Viśvanātha Cakravartin's commentary on the *Bhagavad-gītā*

Viśvanātha Cakravrtin composed the *Sārārtha-varṣiṇī*, a commentary on the *Bhagavad-gītā*, towards the end of the 17th century. His views are close to those of Kṛṣṇadāsa in most respects. Viśvanātha says that the first six chapters of the *Gītā* deal with the discipline of work free of desire (*niṣkāma-karma-yoga*), the middle six deal with devotion (*bhakti-yoga*), and the final six deal with knowledge (*jñāna-yoga*). Like Kṛṣṇadāsa, Viśvanātha considers work and knowledge to be effective only when mixed with some devotion. Devotion receives the central position in the *Gītā*, he says, because it is the most secret, the most respected (since it gives vitality to the other two disciplines) and the most rare.[12] If we take the rareness (difficulty of attainment, *durlabhatvāt*) in a quantitative sense, there would be a difference of mood from Kṛṣṇadāsa's enthusiasm over the current ease of access to devotion, but the word may simply indicate excellence. There is a major difference between the two *Vaiṣṇavas* in their treatment of Caitanya and a wide divergence in concern for contemporary history. While the biographer subordinates the *Gītā* to the demands of explaining Caitanya's life and teachings in concrete historical scenes, the commentator salutes Caitanya in couplet at the outset and thereafter ignores him and anything having to do with contemporary history.

There are a great many passages in the *Sārārtha-varṣiṇī* wherein Viśvanātha shows how one can subordinate work, and knowledge, to devotion. I focus attention, however, on those relatively few passages in which his comments on work (*karma*) give some inkling of his view of the significance (or lack of it) of domestic and public affairs to a committed *Vaiṣṇava*. The examples selected are from Viśvanātha's comments on the first six chapters of the *Gītā*, that portion of the basic text which he says is dedicated to works without desire for results (*niṣkāma-karma*).

Two extended passages in the *Gītā* explicitly refer to the social implications of action: a warrior's fighting in war (1:26–46) and a leader's duty to lead (3:21–5). Viśvanātha says next to nothing about these verses apart from grammatical or lexical notes, a fact in itself suggestive of his priorities. It is interior religious discipline and not social ethics with which he is concerned. He does mention, in commenting on *Gītā* 3:16–17, that a person who is incapable of working without desire should continue the traditional *Vedic* practices which nourish the gods, the ancestors and the living in what might be called the great cycle of sacred ecology. He also devotes seven lines of explanation to *Gītā* 3:35, which states that one should perform one's proper *dharma*, even if badly, in preference executing another's *dharma* well. Viśvanātha restates Arjuna's appeal that he would rather do something less violent than the *dharma* of a warrior and then paraphrases the requirement stated by Kṛṣṇa. This is an explicit admission that violence in some cases is or at some time has been obligatory, but it is a rather perfunctory one, presumably reflecting the general *Caitanya Vaiṣṇava* preference for a nonviolent way of life (and possibly reflecting the paucity of *kṣatriyas* among the Hindus of Bengal on whom such an injunction could be binding). Like Kṛṣṇadāsa, Viśvanātha shared the conviction that the higher *dharma* of the current age is devoted singing of the names of God.

Viśvanātha has little else to say explicitly about domestic and public responsibilities, but his brief references to the notion of 'holding the world(s)/people(s) together' or 'the general welfare' (*loka-saṁgraham*) are pertinent. The expression occurs in *Gītā* 3:20, where Viśvanātha briefly glosses it as 'You should do work to uphold teaching, (i.e., good example) in the world' (*loke śikṣā-grahanārtham*). In his one line of comment on *Gītā* 3:25, where the expression appears again, he fails to mention it. In another document of his, however, a commentary on the *Bhakti-rasāmṛta-sindhuḥ* of Rūpa, Viśvanātha quotes *Gītā* 3:20 precisely because of the idea of 'holding the world together'. In that context, Rūpa is quoting the *Bhāgavata Purāṇa* 3:33:6 (*yannāmadheya*) to sustain his contention that devotion can efface the effects of sins that have already begun to bear fruit (*prārabdha*), i.e. have caused a person's current birth in a defiled tribe or caste. The verse says that even an eater of dogs, i.e. a *Caṇḍāla*, is fit for the oblations of *Vedic* sacrifice (*savanāya*) if they have taken the name of God. Viśvanātha and the other commentators, Jīva and Mukunda, agree that in practice *Vaiṣṇava Caṇḍālas* do not participate in *Vedic* sacrifices, but they differ in explaining the discrepancy between bold principle and cautious practice.[13]

Visvanātha answers the objector's query – why the *Caṇḍāla* fails to sacrifice if he is qualified – by asserting that since the person is a pure devotee such a person has no trust (*śraddhā*) in work (*karma*, i.e., *Vedic* ritual). Hence, they do not perform it. On the other hand, he points out, it is true that householders of good families (who also are pure *Vaiṣṇavas*) perform such work for the sake of holding the world together, though they too lack trust in it. Here he quotes *Gītā* 3:20. He then adds that the *Caṇḍāla Vaiṣṇava* is further deterred from performing work for which he is qualified by fear of censure from people not acquainted with devotional scriptures. Unfortunately for our purposes, but quite understandable in view of the context into which the proof texts from the *Bhāgavata* and the *Gītā* have been drawn, there is no precise delineation of what Visvanātha means by 'holding the world together' (*loka-saṁgraham*). Could it embrace a sense of public responsibility in a world not governed on the pattern of *varṇāśrma-dharma*? Do actions other than *Vedic* rituals and *varṇāśrma-dharma* contribute to holding the world together? Were there no scoffers to censure them, would *Vaiṣṇava Caṇḍālas* perform and *Vaiṣṇava Brāhmaṇas* discard *Vedic* rites? Does *loka-saṅgraham* suggest merely negative avoidance of discord or a more positive commitment to physical and social well-being? Viśvanātha does not say.

What Viśvanātha does say about work seems to exclude two extreme positions: *varṇāśrma-dharma* is wrong in itself and must be opposed, and *varṇāśrma-dharma* is necessary to the ultimate religious quest, devotion to Kṛṣṇa. Between these extremes, there seems to be an open field for situationally appropriate resolutions of the tension between devotion to Kṛṣṇa and everything else in the world. The crucial factor, according to Viśvanātha, is trust (*śraddhā*). If a person is performing work with their trust anywhere but exclusively in devotion to Kṛṣṇa, then, according to *Gītā* 3:26, they should not create conflict in conscience for themselves, should not try to undermine their confidence in what they are doing (so long as there is a vein of trust in devotion also running through their trust in knowledge, work, etc.). But once they trust devotion alone, it is a different matter:

> Knowledge depends upon purity of the mind and this purity depends upon performing work without desire. Devotion, however, depends upon its own efficacy and is not dependent upon anything, not even upon purity of mind. If one should be able to arouse trust (*śraddhā*), in devotion, then (one should create) conflicts in conscience (*buddhi-bhedam*) on the part of those who perform work, because there is no eligibility for work on the part of those who trust in devotion.
>
> (Comment on *Gītā* 3:26)

Performance of work even without desire may serve some extrinsic purpose, but neither it nor knowledge is intrinsic to the attainment of the fundamental religious goal, devotion to Kṛṣṇa.

Like most Sanskrit texts (other than sacred biographies of Caitanya) composed by *Caitanya Vaiṣṇavas*, the *Sārārtha-varṣinī* almost completely ignores contemporary history and the relationship between devotion and mundane responsibility. It would be unwarranted, however, to assume from this silence a fundamental *Caitanya Vaiṣṇava* denial of value to living in history, although the earlier renunciation of family and world by most of the authors of these Sanskrit texts indicates that those individuals were themselves inclined in such a direction. Viśvanātha's commentary leaves open a wide range of ways of coping with the tensions between the historical and the eternal, the world and Kṛṣṇa. I am inclined to view this reticent stance of Viśvanātha and other *Caitanya Vaiṣṇavas* as indicative of a policy of flexibility and freedom for the individual *Vaiṣṇava* and for local groups of *Vaiṣṇavas* in fostering devotion while participating in domestic and public affairs in ways appropriate to their situations. The *Caitanya Vaiṣṇava* interpretation of the *Bhagavad-gītā*, especially as represented in the most influential Bengali document of the movement, the *Caitanya-caritāmṛta* of Kṛṣṇadāsa, seems to be open to a fairly modern and even secular orientation to conditions of religious plurality and sociocultural historical change. Secular in this context, of course, does not mean anti-religious or anti-spiritual but rather viewing a wide range of mundane activities as religiously neutral, as in principle independent of ascribed ritual and social forms, as fit to be engaged in alongside people of differing religious faith and communal affiliation. Such at any event was the pattern of

APPENDIX: TABLE 6.1 Verses of the *Bhgavad-gītā* cited in the *Caitanya-caritāimṛta*

Gītā	*Gauḍīya Maṭh*	*Nath*	*Gītā*	*Gauḍīya Maṭh*	*Nath*
3:21	1:3.25	4	7:16	2:24.89	29
	2:17.178	10	9:11	2:25.38	7
3:24	1:3.24	3	9:27	2:8.60	5
4:7	1:3:22	–	10:8	2:24.183	68
4:8	1:3.23	2	10:10	1:1.49	20
4:11	1:4.20	2		2:24.167	59
	1:4.178	28		2:24.186	70
5:18	3:4.177	7	10:41–2	2:20.373–4	61–2
6:3–4	2:24.153–4	53–4	11:41	2:19.199	28
6:8	3:4.178	8	11:42	2:19–	29
6:16–17	3:8.65–66	4–5	12:13–20	2:23.100–7	50–7
7:4	2:6.164	–	16:19	2:25.39	8
7:5	1:7.118	6	18:54	2:8.65	8
	2:6.165	12		2:24.127	41
	2:20.116	10		2:25.148	43
7:14	2:20.121	12	18:64–5	2:22.57–8	23–24
	2:22.23	7			
	2:24.133	45	18:66	2:9.265	22
				2:22.91	–
				2:8.63	7

behaviour exemplified by Caitanya and his associates in Husain Shahi Bengal as conveyed by the *Caitanya-caritāmṛta* as a whole (and other sacred biographies of Caitanya as well), but that is another story.

Book, chapter, and verse numbers are given in full for the Gauḍīiya Maṭh edition of the *Caitanya-caritāmṛta.* Radha Govinda Nath numbers Sanskrit verses independently within each chapter; his chapter and book numbering coincides with that of the Gauḍīya Maṭh.

Notes

1 This chapter was originally published as an article in the *Journal of Vaishnava Studies.*

2 To say that the *Bhagavad-gītā* may be considered a *Vaiṣṇava* text does not mean that it cannot be interpreted plausibly from other Hindu viewpoints as well or that it does not have an inclusive structure tending to integrate multiple viewpoints. For an informed historical view of the *Gītā*, including its Vaiṣṇava aspects, see chapter on *Gītā* in A.L. Basham. 1989. *Origins and Development of Classical Hindusim*, ed. Kenneth G. Zysk. Boston: Beacon Press.

3 An earlier *Bhāgavata* version of the substance of this article was published as part of a longer article, in 1976. "Caitanya's Followers and the *Bhagavad-gītā*: A Case Study in Bhakti and the Secular," in Bardwell L. Smith (ed.), *Hinduism: New Studies in the History of Religion*, pp. 33–52. Leiden: E.J. Brill.

4 Krishnadāsa Kavirāja, *Caitanya-caritāmṛta*, ed. Bhakti Vilas Tirtha. 5th ed. Mayapur, West Bengal: Caitanya Math, G.A 470 or A.D. 1956 (hereafter cited as CC),

1:13.64 states that Advaita spoke (*kahe*) on *Gītā* and. For discussion of Advaita and the *Advaita-prakāśa*, see Biman Behari Majumder. 1959. *Caitanya-cariter upādān*, 2nd ed. Calcutta: University of Calcutta, pp. 412–63; and Chakrbarty Ramakanta. 1985. *Vaiṣṇavism in Bengal, 1486–1900*. Calcutta: Sanskrit Pustak Bhandar, pp. 122–32. N.N. Basu, ed. *Viśvakoṣa*, Vol. 22. Calcutta, B.A. 1318 or A.D. 1911. 138 mentions one Suryadāsa Paṇḍita as author of a commentary on the *Gītā* but does not identify him as the person by the same name who was the father-in-law of Caitanya's associate, Nityānanda; I have not noticed mention of such a text in standard reference works on *Caitanya Vaiṣṇava* literature.

5 Vṛndāvanadāsa. 1961. *Caitanya-bhāgavata*, 3rd ed., ed. Bhakti Kevala Audulomi. Calcutta: Gauya Mission, 1:2.72–3.

6 S.K. De. 1961. *Early History of the Vaiṣṇava Faith and Movement in Bengal*. Calcutta: Firma K.L. Mukhopadhyay; Edward C. Dimock Jr. 1966 (reprint 1989). *The Place of the Hidden Moon*. Chicago: University of Chicago Press. Both are valuable accounts of the *Caitanya Vaiṣṇava* movement, though I do not agree with Dimock's contention that certain of Caitanya's early associates were of the sahajiyā type (cf. O'Connell, J.T. Spring 1993. "Rāmānanda Rāya: A Sahajiyā or a Rāgānuga Bhakta?" *Journal of Vaiṣṇava Studies*, Vol. 1, No. 3, 36–58).

7 S.K De. *Early History*. *op. cit*., 201, 220, 253, 414–15.

8 Viśvanātha Cakravartin, *Sārārtha-varṣiṇī, in Bhagavad-gītā*, ed. Adhara Natha Cakravartin. Calcutta: Tara Library, B.A. 1361 or A.D. 1954). Hereafter the *Bhagavad-gītā* will be cited as *Gītā* and the Sārārtha-varṣinī as Comment (on *Gītā*).

9 The two philosophic theologians on whom Surendranath Dasgupta relied most heavily for his treatment of *Caitanya Vaiṣṇava* thought in *History of Indian Philosophy*, Vol. 4, *Indian Pluralism* (Cambridge: Cambridge University Press, 1961) are Jīva Gosvāmin and Baladeva Vidyābhūṣaṇa.

10 For an extended discussion of these issues, see J.T. O'Connell. May 1993. "Religious Movements Is Social Structure: The Case of Caitanya's Vaiṣṇavas in Bengal," in *Socio-Religious Movements and Cultural Networks in Indian Civilization*, Occasional paper 4. Shimla: Indian Institute of Advanced Study.

11 Another good-quality, if not strictly critical, edition of Kṛṣṇadāsa's *Caitanya-caritāmṛta* is that edited by Radha Govinda Nath, 6 vols, 4th ed. Calcutta: Pracyavani Mandir, n.d.

12 Comment on *Gītā* 1;1.

13 Rūpa Gosvāmin, *Bhakti-rasāmṛta-sindhuḥ*, with commentaries by Jīva, Mukundadāsa and Viśvanātha, ed. Haridas Das. Navadvip: Haribol Kuti, G.A 475 or A.D. 1961, 1:1.21–2.

Bibliography

Basham, A.L. 1989. *Origins and Development of Classical Hinduism*. Ed. Kenneth G. Zysk. Boston: Beacon Press.

Basu, N.N. (ed.). 1911. *Viśvakoṣa*. Vol. 22. Calcutta, B.A. 1318 or A.D 1911. 138 mentions one Suryadāsa Paṇḍita as author of a commentary on the *Gītā*.

Caitanya, Vaiṣṇava thought in *History of Indian Philosophy, Vol. 4, Indian Pluralism* (Cambridge: Cambridge University Press, 1961). See: Jīva Gosvāmin and Baladeva Vidyābhūṣaṇa.

Chakrbarty, Ramakanta. 1985. *Vaiṣṇavism in Bengal, 1486–1900*, pp. 122–32. Calcutta: Sanskrit Pustak Bhandar.

De, S.K. 1961. *Early History of the Vaiṣṇava Faith and Movement in Bengal*. Calcutta: Firma K.L. Mukhopadhyay;

Edward, C. Dimock Jr. 1966 (reprint 1989). *The Place of the Hidden Moon*. Chicago: University of Chicago Press.

Kṛṣṇadāsa, Kavirāja, 1956. *Caitanya-caritāmṛta.* Ed. Bhakti Vilas Tirtha. 5th ed. Mayapur, West Bengal: Caitanya Math, G.A 470 or A.D. [hereafter cited as CC], 1:13:64

Kṛṣṇadāsa, Kavirāja, 1962. *Caitanya-Caritāmṛta*, Ed. Radha Govinda Nath. 6 vols. 4th ed. Calcutta: Pracyavani Mandir.

Majumder, Biman Behari. 1959. *Caitanya-cariter upādān*, 2nd ed., pp. 412–63. Calcutta: University of Calcutta.

O'Connell, Joseph T. 1976. "Caitanya's Followers and the *Bhagavad-gītā*: A Case Study in *Bhakti* and the Secular." In *Hinduism: New Studies in the History of Religion.* Edited by Bardwell L. Smith, pp. 33–52. Leiden: E.J. Brill.

O'Connell, Joseph T. 1993. "Religious Movements Is Social Structure: The Case of Caitanya's Vaiṣṇavas in Bengal." In *Socio-Religious Movements and Cultural Networks in Indian Civilization, Occasional paper 4.* Shimla: Indian Institute of Advanced Study.

O'Connell, Joseph T. Spring 1993. "Rāmānanda Rāya: A Sahajiyā or a Rāgānuga Bhakta?" *Journal of Vaiṣṇava Studies*, 1(3), 36–58.

Rūpa, Gosvāmin. 1961. *Bhakti-rasāmṛta-sindhuḥ, with Commentaries by Jīva, Mukundadāsa and Viśvanātha.* Ed. Haridas Das. Navadvip: Haribol Kuti.

Viśvanātha, Cakravartin. 1954. "Sārārtha-varṣiṇī." In *Bhagavad-gītā.* Edited by Adhara Natha Cakravartin. Calcutta: Tara Library, B.A 1361 or A.D. 1954).

Vṛndāvanadāsa. *Caitanya-bhāgavata.* Ed. Bhakti Kevala Audulomi. 3rd ed. Calcutta: Gauḍīya Mission, 1961, 1:2:72–3.

7

THE GREATNESS OF THE *GĪTĀ*, AS ICON AND MANTRA

Richard H. Davis

In general, the *māhātmya* is a common genre of medieval literature concerned with the exaltation of the greatness of a particular place, ritual or implement charged with religious power. Most often the *māhātmya* centers on a *tīrtha* or holy pilgrimage place, but in some special cases, a verbal text can also be the subject of a *māhātmya*. The best known of the *māhātmyas* focused on texts, evidently, was the *Bhāgavata-māhātmya*, exalting the greatness of the *Bhāgavata Purāṇa*. So too with the *Gītā-māhātmyas*, which are texts glorifying and exalting the *Bhagavad-gītā*. These are often considered to have been spoken by gods or seers or may even be an integral part of the *Gītā* itself.

> Assistance comes quickly when one undertakes the *Bhagavad-gītā*. Wherever the *Gītā* is discussed, recited, read, or heard, there I most certainly always dwell. I reside in the *Gītā* as my *āśrama*. The *Gītā* is my highest home.

This is what the god Viṣṇu tells the goddess Earth in the "Greatness of the *Gītā*" (*Gītā-māhātmya*) chapter of the *Varāha Purāṇa*.[1]

In the *Bhagavad-gītā*, Kṛṣṇa promises that his teachings will be efficacious for future readers and listeners: "One who promulgates this ultimate secret to my devotees," he says, "shows the highest devotion to me and will undoubtedly come to me" (*Bhg* 18.68). The dissemination of Kṛṣṇa's teachings in the *Gītā* is a form of *bhakti* and a way of reinforcing the mutual relationship between devotee and God: "Among all humanity, no one shows greater love to me than such a person, and no one on earth shall be dearer to me" (*Bhg* 18.69). Benefits are not confined to those who transmit the dialogue, but rather, those who recite it to themselves and those who simply listen to it also share in them:

> I believe that one who recites this righteous dialogue between the two of us offers to me a sacrifice of knowledge. And as for the person who listens

> to it with faith and without rancor, he will also be liberated and reach the pleasant worlds of those who have done good deeds.
>
> (Bhg *18.70–1)*

Kṛṣṇa envisions that this dialogue will enjoy a long life in great time through these human acts of transmission and reception.[2]

But in his statement to Earth, Viṣṇu goes one step further. The recitation of the words of Kṛṣṇa, as recorded in the *Bhagavad-gītā*, actually invokes the presence of the god. The *Gītā* is the abode of Viṣṇu-Kṛṣṇa, so when one mentally or orally constructs that abode, Viṣṇu-Kṛṣṇa comes to reside there, inhabiting his own words. The first person to perceive the conversation of Kṛṣṇa with Arjuna, thanks to his "divine eye," is Sanjaya, who observed to his interlocutor, King Dhṛtarāṣṭra, that these two figures bring about beneficial results wherever they are present:

> Wherever Kṛṣṇa the Lord of Yoga and the archer Arjuna are, there will be good fortune, victory, wealth, and wise conduct. That is my view.
>
> (Bhg *18.78)*

Here in the *Gītā Māhātmya*, Viṣṇu asserts that Kṛṣṇa becomes present when his teachings in the *Bhagavad-gītā* are recited or heard.

This suggests a different conception of listening or reading. Viṣṇu is not suggesting that one must study and grasp the meaning of the words of Kṛṣṇa's teachings in the *Bhagavad-gītā* for the text to be valuable, though that may be a good thing. One does not require the elaborate interpretive efforts of the *Vedānta* commentators in medieval times or the thoughtful applications of the Indian nationalists in the 20th century. Rather, the sheer act of making the words of the *Gītā* manifest, whether through reading or reciting, creates a verbal icon. Reciting its words becomes an invocation, an act of worship that brings one into communion with God. And the presence of God in these words can act with powerful force on the reciter and on those nearby. Within Viṣṇu's statement lies a devotional theory of the oral text.

The *Gītā* as verbal icon

In a classic 1954 work of what came to be called new criticism, W.K. Wimsatt Jr adopts the phrase "verbal icon" to emphasize the objective status of the poem or literary work, as a self-standing unit or repository of meaning. Stressing the iconicity of the work, Wimsatt seeks to direct the act of interpretation away from matters like the author's intention (the intentional fallacy) or the emotional responses evoked in a reader (the affective fallacy) and toward the inherent qualities of the text, the highest abode of literary significance: "The outcome of either Fallacy, the Intentional or the Affective," argues Wimsatt, "is that the poem itself, as an object of specifically critical judgment, tends to disappear" (1954, 21). Rather, the poem or text should be recognized as the true location of meaning and therefore the primary target for literary interpretation.

One can of course approach the *Bhagavad-gītā* in this way. But in the "Greatness of the *Gītā*," Viṣṇu suggests a different way of understanding the *Gītā* as a verbal icon, one much closer to an older sense of the term. Adopted from the Greek *eikōn*, the word "icon" denotes a physical representation or symbolic object that partakes in some way in the sacred reality it represents. As the physical location for the actual presence of a god, it is necessary therefore to treat the enlivened icon with veneration or worship.[3] The recited words of the *Gītā*, Viṣṇu proclaims, can serve as just such a physical icon.

In the *Bhagavad-gītā*, Kṛṣṇa advances a theology of his own recurrent incarnation.

> Even though I am unborn, and even though I am the imperishable Lord of all Beings, I take birth by entering into my own physical form, by my own supernal power. For whenever there is a decline in righteousness (*dharma*) and an increase in unrighteousness, Arjuna, then I emanate myself. For the protection of good people, for the destruction of evil-doers, and for the restoration of righteousness, I take birth in age after age.
>
> (Bhg *4.6–8)*

In early medieval India, followers of Viṣṇu elaborated and greatly expanded this incarnational theology. Kṛṣṇa is taken as one of ten or more living incarnations (*avatāra*) of Viṣṇu. The list also includes supernal animals like the fish, tortoise and boar; half-human figures like the man-lion Narasimha; and human incarnations like Kṛṣṇa and Rāma (the hero of the epic *Rāmāyaṇa*). This is only the start, as far as Vaiṣṇava theologians like Rāmānuja are concerned. Viṣṇu also makes himself present inside the hearts of his devotees. And, most relevant to our case, Viṣṇu graciously enters into a variety of physical forms, such as stone or bronze images fabricated by humans. These objects become supports or "*āśramas*" for the divine presence or "bodies" (*mūrti*) that God can animate. God's entry into and manifestation in the icon transforms it into a living being and makes it suitable for devotional interaction with worshipers. The theologians refer to such icons as *arcāvatāra*, "incarnations for the purpose of worship."[4]

If the supreme Lord can make himself manifest or present in these other physical forms, it is not surprising that the Lord also can be present wherever his words recorded in the *Bhagavad-gītā* are pronounced. Like a physical icon, sound can also be a location for divine presence. As a result, the recitation of the *Gītā* acts with a remarkable autonomous potency. This is the basic argument of the several *Gītā-māhātmyas* (Greatness of the *Gītā*) incorporated in the Purāṇas.

The *māhātmya* is a common genre of medieval literature concerned, writes Greg Bailey (1995, 23), with "the exaltation of the greatness of a particular place, ritual or implement charged with religious power." Most often the *māhātmya* centers on a *tīrtha* (a holy pilgrimage place), but in some special cases, a verbal text can also be the subject of a *māhātmya.* The best known of the *māhātmyas* focused on texts, evidently, was the *Bhāgvata-māhātmya*, exalting the greatness of the *Bhāgavata Purāṇa.*[5] So too with the *Gītā-māhātmyas*: the text serves as the focus of exaltation.[6] Here I will concentrate on the section found in the *Padma Purāṇa*, the lengthiest and most interesting of the Purāṇic *Gītā-māhātmyas*.[7]

At the opening of this *Gītā-māhātmya*, we are told of a conversation between Viṣṇu and Lakṣmī. Viṣṇu is trying to describe to his wife his higher nature, the Absolute. It transcends duality and non-duality, he explains. It is free from both being and nonbeing, devoid of either beginning or end and uniquely beautiful as the highest joy. And, he adds, it is praised in the *Gītā*. Quick to spot a possible contradiction, Lakṣmī immediately challenges him: "If you are the highest joy, beyond the reach of speech and mind, how can the *Gītā* make you known? Please clear up this doubt of mine" (*PP* 175.20). Lakṣmī poses the same paradox that the *Vedānta* commentators have wrestled with. If we accept the absolute qualities of the Highest Person, which place it in a realm beyond our powers of verbal description or mental cognition, how can we gain access to this Supreme? How could the *Bhagavad-gītā*, a composition made up of words, enable us to approach the Absolute?

Viṣṇu answers that his essential being or soul (*ātman*) is firmly established in the *Gītā*. He goes on to explain that each chapter of the work constitutes a part of his body: the first five chapters are his five faces, the next ten make up his ten arms, one is his belly and the final two are his feet. Thus, he summarizes, "the *Gītā* with its eighteen chapters is my body (*mūrti*) made of words" (*PP* 175.28). According to Viṣṇu, the *Bhagavad-gītā* is not just a metaphoric body of discourse. It is a real body of sound, in which his own soul dwells. And because of Viṣṇu's presence, recitation of the *Gītā* can create enormous merit and can counteract even mortal sins. "So a strong-minded person who concentrates on a chapter of the *Gītā*, or half of one, or a single verse, or even half a verse," he concludes, "can be liberated, just as Suśarman was" (*PP* 175.29). Lakṣmī naturally asks him who this Suśarman was.

The *Gītā* as *mantra*

Just as Viṣṇu has asserted that each chapter of the *Bhagavad-gītā* is a portion of his body, now he tells Lakṣmī eighteen stories, each one extolling a particular chapter of the *Gītā*. In these narratives, the powers of the *Gītā* extend not just over humans but over other categories of living beings as well, including gods, animals, trees and ghosts. They often cover long stretches of time, allowing for the death and rebirth of protagonists. Although each story promotes the virtues of a particular chapter, Viṣṇu makes no attempt here to comment on the doctrines or ideas of those chapters. Rather, each demonstrates the great liberating power that simply reciting or even just hearing the chapter has for the characters in the story.

Since Lakṣmī asked about Suśarman, let us take that story as a point of departure. Suśarman is born into a family of *brāhmaṇas* who fail to act as *brāhmaṇas* ought. They do not meditate, recite the *Vedas*, perform sacrifices or honor guests. Growing up in this lax household, Suśarman himself takes to eating meat and drinking liquor, and he becomes addicted to the chewing of betel leaves. Once when he sneaks into a sage's orchard to steal some leaves, a poisonous snake bites him and he dies. As a result of his misdeeds, Suśarman is reborn as a bull. He becomes the property of a disabled man who rides on his back and works him mercilessly until the bull finally collapses. Passersby feel pity for the prostrate animal. A compassionate sex worker, who is unaware of the inner religious merit (*puṇya*) she possesses, inadvertently transfers some of her hidden merit onto the expiring bull. When the bull dies, he is reborn into a family of virtuous *brāhmaṇas*, thanks to the sex worker's transposed virtue. In his new birth, Suśarman is able to remember his past life as a bull, and he decides to seek out the sex worker to thank her and to inquire into how it is that a sex worker, ordinarily considered a most sinful person in the *brāhmaṇic* moral scale, has come to possess such an overabundance of merit.

The sex worker explains that she has a parrot who incessantly recites the first chapter of the *Bhagavad-gītā*. She must have gained merit from her parrot. Suśarman then questions the parrot. Once he was a learned man, the parrot replies, but he became proud of his knowledge and full of disdain for others. This moral failing resulted in a series of painful rebirths, finally leading to birth in a family of parrots. The unfortunate parrot lost its parents at a young age. The orphan bird was captured and caged and ended up in the *āśrama* of some sages. There the sages were teaching the first chapter of the *Gītā* to their young pupils, and the parrot listened in on the constant recitation. Eventually a fowler stole the caged bird from the *āśrama* and sold it to the sex worker. In the sex worker's apartment, the parrot constantly repeated what it learned in the *āśrama*, the first chapter of the *Gītā*.

Viṣṇu concludes this tale by telling his audience that the parrot, through its *Gītā* repetition, removed its past sins, cleansed its soul and gained release from all sorrow. Likewise, he adds, Suśarman and the sex worker also attained liberation. Viṣṇu's first story gives us a clear sense of the expansive potency of the *Bhagavad-gītā*. From the sages' teaching the text to their young students, to the parrot who memorizes and recites it, to the sex worker who hears the parrot's chant and gains inner merit, to the expiring bull who profits from the sex worker's sympathy and returns as a virtuous *brāhmaṇa*, all categories of beings gain spiritual benefits when the words of the *Gītā* are given voice. The sounds of the *Gītā* act as a *mantra*, insofar as their sheer repetition – apart from any understanding of their conventional meaning – has a transformative effect on speakers and listeners.[8] So too can it be effective for others, Viṣṇu tells Lakṣmī: "Therefore, for one who recites the first chapter, or hears it, or remembers it, or practices it, the ocean of existence will not be difficult to cross" (*PP* 175.54).

In the stories that follow, the recitation of different parts of the *Bhagavad-gītā* act in various powerful ways. In some, it creates merit that counteracts past misdeeds, as in the story of Suśarman. The recitation of the *Gītā* can be effective where other forms of virtuous action may fail. As one snake explains to his son, "Going to pilgrimage places, giving gifts, performing austerities, or offering sacrifices cannot free me. Only the seventh chapter of the *Gītā*, made of nectar, can do that" (*PP* 181.26–7). In other cases, the recitation of the *Gītā* can form a protective shield of Viṣṇu's presence against the threat of sin (*PP* 183.49–60).

The potency of *Gītā* recitation does not rely on a speaker's intention. In one story, a pair of ghosts (*preta*), formerly a degenerate *brāhmaṇa* couple, sit down under a palm tree. They are overcome with hunger and thirst, and the ghost husband wonders in despair how they can ever be freed from their troubles if they don't undergo proper spiritual instruction. Perplexed, his ghost wife asks him, "O best of men (*puruṣottama*), what is the *brahman*? What is the inner spirit? What is action?" (*PP* 182.15). She has inadvertently quoted the exact questions that Arjuna asks Kṛṣṇa at the start of chapter eight in the *Gītā*. Miraculously a divine chariot appears and transports the couple up to heaven. The palm tree under which they have been sitting happens to overhear the accidental *Gītā* quotation and has its soul cleansed of past sins. It turns out that the tree had formerly been a *brāhmaṇa* who had engaged in all kinds of evil conduct. Once he drank so much palm wine that he died and was reborn for his misconduct as a palm tree. Now freed of this unhappy incarnation, the former palm tree carefully writes down the half verse he has overheard, goes to Varanasi and devotes himself to the constant recitation of that passage from the *Gītā*. Eventually he receives Viṣṇu's full grace.

The *Gītā* can lead to moral realizations and transformations not only among ghosts and trees but even among the gods. The final story in this *Gītā-māhātmya* tells of Indra, king of the gods, ruling in Amarāvatī on the peak of Mount Meru. Once as he is sitting regally on his throne, enjoying the delightful music of the divine Gāndharvas, another divine-looking figure marches up and quickly overcomes Indra with his fiery brilliance. The denizens of Amarāvatī immediately shift their allegiance and anoint the victor as the new Indra. The fickle Gāndharvas redirect their sweet songs to the new ruler. The old Indra is astonished by this rapid turn of events and goes to find Viṣṇu, asleep on the ocean of milk, to get an explanation for what has just happened. Indra asks,

> Viṣṇu, in the past I performed a hundred sacrifices to please you. Through the merit of that act I gained my position as Indra, king of the gods. But now some new god has become Indra in heaven. He did not carry out any righteous acts, and he did not perform any sacrifices. So how is it that he has seized my heavenly lion-throne, Viṣṇu?
>
> (PP *192.47–9)*

Viṣṇu tells Indra that the new Indra has done something much more pleasing than austerities, gifts or sacrifices: he has recited five verses from the eighteenth chapter of the *Bhagavad-gītā*. With that merit, he has acquired Indra's imperial sovereignty over the gods.

Indra decides to see for himself the power of the *Gītā*, so he assumes the appearance of a *brāhmaṇa*, travels to the holy Godavari River and finds himself a teacher who knows the *Gītā*. Indra learns from him the eighteenth chapter of the *Gītā*, and through the merit resulting from his recitation of this, he attains union (*sāyujya*) with Viṣṇu. He realizes as well that, in comparison with this, his former status as lord over all the gods has been insignificant. So rather than return to Amarāvatī to challenge the new Indra, the old Indra instead goes to Vaikuṇṭha, the city of Viṣṇu, where he enjoys the presence of the Lord.

The *Gītā's* greatness in medieval times

The *Gītā-māhātmyas* contained in the *Varāha Purāṇa* and the *Padma Purāṇa* extol the expansive soteriological power of the *Bhagavad-gītā.* They propose a distinctive understanding of its transformative potential. Since the *Gītā* is an aural icon, Viṣṇu's body filled with his innermost being, the words of the *Gītā* act as *mantra* powers, efficacious sounds that do not require any comprehension of the reciter or listener to exercise their force. As the *Varāha Purāṇa*'s version explains,

> Through repetition of the *Gītā*, one attains the highest form of liberation. A dying person firmly adhering to *Gītā*-recitation will find a good path. Even a great sinner who zealously listens to the *Gītā* will get to Vaikuṇṭha and rejoice together with Viṣṇu.
>
> (GM *17–18)*

The *Gītā-māhātmya* therefore encourages us to take refuge in the *Gītā*, in emulation of exemplary rulers of the past:

> Starting with King Janaka, many kings who have taken recourse to the *Gītā* have been freed of their sins and, celebrated in the world, they have reached the highest state.
>
> (GM *20)*

The work goes on to suggest that it too – the *Gītā Māhātmya* itself – is a necessary ancillary part of this transformative *Gītā* practice:

> For one who reads the *Gītā* but fails to read the *Māhātmya*, that person's reading becomes useless and the effort is for naught. But one who recites the *Gītā* along with this *Māhātmya* will obtain its full fruits, and reach a path otherwise difficult to gain.
>
> (GM *21–2)*

The expansive praise of the greatness of the *Gītā* as icon and *mantra* articulated in the *Gītā-māhātmyas* raises a historical question: how broadly was this vision of *Gītā* power shared in medieval Hindu circles? Scholarship on the history of the *Bhagavad-gītā* during the medieval period has focused almost entirely on the erudite Sanskrit commentaries of *Vedānta* philosophers such as Śaṅkara, Rāmānuja and Madhva and to a lesser extent on other philosophers outside the *Vedānta* field, like Abhinavagupta.[9] The quantity of *Vedānta* commentaries, the erudition of their interpretive disquisitions and the evident influence of the key commentaries on subsequent

Indian philosophy all warrant this attention. But the medieval audience for such commentarial explication would have necessarily been quite restricted, and it is clear that this was not the only circle in which the *Gītā* circulated during this period.

One indication of the greater reach of the *Bhagavad-gītā* in medieval India is the proliferation of other gods' *Gītās*. Kṛṣṇa's teachings in the *Bhagavad-gītā* evidently inspired other competing divinities to imitate the *Gītā* form. This became a popular genre of religious poetry, found most often in the Purāṇas. Gods engage in dialogues with human or divine interlocutors. Often the human approaches the god in a state of despair, much as Arjuna requires Kṛṣṇa's guidance in the *Bhagavad-gītā*. So in the *Kūrma Purāṇa*, the god Śiva delivers the *Īśvara Gītā* to a despondent Rāma, whose wife has been abducted by a demon, and the god Gaṇeśa presents his teachings to a despondent prince Vareṇya in the *Gaṇeśa Gītā*, part of the *Gaṇeśa Purāṇa*.[10] The different gods provide authoritative instruction to their listeners, just as Kṛṣṇa gives to Arjuna, though the gods' teachings reflect the diverse schools of thought of their followers. In the *Īśvara Gītā*, accordingly, Śiva delivers a message that echoes the *yoga*-based Śaiva Pāśupata system of belief and practice.

Although the Sanskrit *Mahābhārata* was retold widely in vernacular languages during medieval times, there are few signs that the *Bhagavad-gītā* was translated into vernacular Indian languages before the 19th century. One often-cited exception is the remarkable Marathi poem *Bhāvārthadīpikā*, more commonly known as the *Jñāneśvarī*, by the poet Jñānadeva.[11] This is not actually a translation, nor is it a commentary exactly, but rather, it is a large new devotional poem in Marathi constructed on top of the Sanskrit *Bhagavad-gītā*. Seven hundred verses in the original *Gītā* generate 9000 Marathi verses in the *Jñāneśvarī*. Jñānadeva explains in his poem that as he has been praising the god, Kṛṣṇa has filled him up with himself. In this state of devotional merging of identity, Jñānadeva becomes a channel for Kṛṣṇa to expand on the teachings that he formerly gave to Arjuna, now updated for medieval Maharashtra and delivered in the Marathi language.

Jñānadeva compares the *Bhagavad-gītā* to the wish-granting gem Cintāmaṇi. Here the devotional approach of the Marathi poet parallels the attitude of the Sanskrit authors of the *Gītā-māhātmyas*. Like the many facets of that remarkable jewel, the words of the *Gītā* also send off beams of sound that achieve tremendous results for those who read, recite or hear those efficacious words. The *Gītā-māhātmyas* reveal an important way that some in medieval India envisioned the potency of this famous religious poem. They proclaim that the highest god, Viṣṇu-Kṛṣṇa, comes to inhabit the words of the *Bhagavad-gītā* whenever those words are spoken or heard, much as God can inhabit a physical icon. And through the divine presence within the sounds of the *Gītā*, its sounds exercise a transformative effect on those who speak or hear it.

Abbreviations

Bhg *Bhagavad-gītā*
GM *Gītā-māhātmya* in the *Varāha Purāṇa*
PP *Padma Purāṇa*

Notes

1 *Gītā-māhātmya* of the *Varāha Purāṇa*, vv. 6–7, in Besant and Das (1973, xlii). This *Gītā-māhātmya* of 23 verses is also found in Sadhale (1985, 23) (originally published in 1935). However, the *Gītā-māhātmya* is not included in the critical edition of the *Varāha Purāṇa*. The editor of the *Varāha*, Anand Swarup Gupta (1981), does mention numerous works attributed to the *Varāha*, including the *Gītā-māhātmya*. Bhandarkar (1884, 54) reports a manuscript version of this text, and Aufrecht lists this in the *Catalogus Catalogorum*.

2 This chapter derives from outtake writings on the *Bhagavad-gītā* that did not fit into my book, *The Bhagavad Gītā: A Biography* (Davis 2015). I thank the National Endowment for the Humanities for support of this work, Bard College for enabling me to pursue it and Fred Appel at the Princeton University Press for first inviting me to contribute to the series Lives of Great Religious Books.

3 See Davis (2005) on the veneration of images.

4 See Narayanan (1985) for a useful summary of the Śrī Vaiṣṇava theology of incarnation. For a general treatment of early medieval Hindu theologies of image worship, see Davis (1997, 15–50).

5 Rocher (1986, 211–12). This work occurs just after the *Gītā-māhātmya* in the Uttarakhaṇḍa of the *Padma Purāṇa* and has circulated in numerous separate publications. See Hawley 2015 for a full discussion of the importance of the *Bhāgavata Māhātmya*.

6 See Bailey (1995, 23–5) for brief treatment of *māhātmya* as a Purāṇic genre. Sharma (1986, 12–15) briefly notices the species of *Gītā-māhātmyas*. See Chatterjee (1967, 81–2) for a list of numerous *Gītā-māhātmya* manuscripts, which indicates that these *māhātmyas* circulated as self-standing texts and are incorporated as part of larger Purāṇas like the *Padma*. The *Bhagavad-gītā* is not the only text that is so exalted. The *Bhāgavata Purāṇa* also merits a *māhātmya* in the *Padma Purāṇa*, which, as Ludo Rocher (1986, 211–12) observes, is much more popular than the *Gītā-māhātmya*, judging from the number of separate manuscripts and publications.

7 The *Padma Purāṇa's* (2007) *Gītā-māhātmya* occupies chapters 175–92 in the Chowkhamba edition. It was also published separately by the Ganapatikrsnaji Press in 1871 (see Rocher 1986, 211). I use the Chowkhamba Sanskrit Series edition, published in Varanasi, 2007. Prabhanjanacharya (1996) retells the stories of this text with commentary.

8 For a brief treatment of *mantra*, see Smith (2005).

9 This section draws on my brief overview of the *Bhagavad-gītā* in medieval India, in Davis (2015, 43–71). On the *Vedānta* philosophical commentaries, a good accessible explication is Sharma (1986). Also see Mainkar (1969).

10 A brief account is in Davis (2015, 51–3). A full treatment may be found in Bhattacharjee (1926). Recent translations include Bailey (1995) of the *Gaṇeśa Gītā* in the *Gaṇeśa Purāṇa*, Brown (1998) of the *Devī Gītā* and Nicholson (2014) of the *Īśvara Gītā*.

11 Davis (2015, 65–71). See Kripananda (1989) for an accessible full translation.

References

Bailey, Greg. 1995. *Gaṇeśapurāṇa. 2 vols. Purāṇa Research Publications, Tubingen.* Wiesbaden: Otto Harrassowitz Verlag.

Besant, Annie and Bhagavan Das. 1973. *The Bhagavad-gītā*. London: Theosophical Publishing Society. First published 1905.

Bhandarkar, R.G. 1884. *Report on the Search for Sanskrit MSS in the Bombay Presidency. Bombay.*

Bhattacharjee, Umesh Chandra. 1926. "The *Gītā* Literature and Its Relation with Brahma-Vidya." *Indian Historical Quarterly*, 2, 537–46, 761–71.
Brown, Mackenzie C. 1998. *The Devī Gītā: The Song of the Goddess*. Albany: SUNY Press.
Chatterjee, Asoke. 1967. *Padma-Purāṇa – A Study, Calcutta Sanskrit College Research Series*. Calcutta: Sanskrit College.
Davis, Richard H. 1997. *Lives of Indian Images*. Princeton: Princeton University Press.
Davis, Richard H. 2005. "Images: Veneration of Images." In *Encyclopedia of Religion*. Edited by Lindsay Jones. Detroit: Thomas Gale.
Davis, Richard H. 2015. *The Bhagavad-gītā: A Biography, Lives of Great Religious Books*. Princeton: Princeton University Press.
Gupta, Anand Swarup. 1981. *The Varāha Purāṇa*. 2 vols. Varanasi: All-India Kashiraj Trust.
Hawley, John Stratton. 2015. *A Storm of Stories: India and the Idea of the Bhakti Movement*. Cambridge, MA: Harvard University Press.
Kripananda, Swami. 1989. *Jnaneshwar's Gītā: A Rendering of the Jnaneshwari*. Albany: State University of New York Press.
Mainkar, T.G. 1969. *A Comparative Study of the Commentaries on the Bhagavad-gītā*. Delhi: Motilal Banasidass.
Narayanan, Vasudha. 1985. "Arcāvatāra: On Earth as He Is in Heaven." In *Gods of Flesh/Gods of Stone: The Embodiment of Divinity in India*. Edited by Joanne Punzo Waghorne and Norman Cutler, pp. 53–66. Chambersburg, PA: Anima Publications.
Nicholson, Andres J. 2014. *Lord Śiva's Song: The Īśvara Gītā*. Albany: State University of New York Press.
Padma-Purāṇam. 2007. 6 vols. Chowkhamba Sanskrit Series. Varanasi: Chowkhamba Sanskrit Series Office.
Prabhanjanacharya, Vyasanakere. 1996. *The Glory of the Bhagavad-gītā (Tales from the Padmapurāṇa), S.M.S.O. Sabha Publication*. Chirtanur, AP: Sriman Madhwasiddhantonnahini Sabha.
Rocher, Ludo. 1986. *The Purāṇas*. Ed. Jan Gonda. Vol. II.3. Wiesbaden: Otto Harrassowitz.
Sadhale, G S. 1935. *The Bhagavad-gītā with Eleven Commentaries*. Bombay: Gujarati Printing Press. Reprint, 1985, in Parimal Sanskrit Series, No. 17.
Sharma, Arvind. 1986. *The Hindu Gītā: Ancient and Classical Interpretations of the Bhagavad-gītā*. LaSalle, IL: Open Court Publishing.
Smith, Frederick M. 2005. "Mantra." In *Encyclopedia of Religion*. Edited by Lindsay Jones. Detroit: Thomas Gale.
Wimsatt, Jr., W.J. 1954. *The Verbal Icon: Studies in the Meaning of Poetry*. Lexington, KY: University of Kentucky Press.

8

THE *BHAGAVAD-GĪTĀ* AND INDIAN NATIONALIST MOVEMENT

Tilak, Gandhi, and Aurobindo

James D. Ryan

The Sanskrit *Mahābhārata*,[1] the world's longest extant epic poem, is part of India's DNA. Nearly every region of India has translated this remarkable story into the regional vernacular. Sometimes these are quite popular adaptations, as in *Telugu*, whereas sometimes they are not as culturally central. In addition to the vernacular literary versions are folk versions in dramas or tales that retell the extraordinary tale in more-accessible terms. In the Tamil folk-drama, the *Terukūttu*, which is a street dance-drama, scenes from the *Mahābhārata* (*MBh*) are central to the repertoire, where the troupes used to give rural performances for the people in long overnight presentations lasting eight hours or longer (Frasca 1990). All over India, the names of Arjuna and Bhīma, the *Pāṇḍava* heroes, are the first names or part of the first names for hundreds of thousands of men. Composed circa 600 BCE–100 CE, the *MBh* was so popular centuries later that the Muslim emperor Akbar[2] commissioned two full translations of the full epic into Persian (Truschke 2012, 239). Dara Shikoh, Akbar's grandson, and numerous others made translations, commentaries, or prose summaries into Persian of the *Bhagavad-gītā*, itself a section of the *MBh*.[3]

So, putting aside its values in terms of philosophy, religion, and theology, the *Bhagavad-gīta* whose action takes place at a crucial juncture of the *MBh* was well-placed to be culturally highlighted from the earliest times. Certainly, at least from the time of Śaṅkarācārya (circa 7th century to 9th century), the *Bhg* was seen as an independent text worthy of erudite commentary by the *Vedāntins*. The commentaries on the *Bhg* in Sanskrit among the major *Vedāntins* continued into the 15th century with a commentary by Vallabha, and lesser *Vedāntins* continued to comment on the *Bhg* in Sanskrit through the 18th century at least. Even the *Śaivite* Abhinavagupta (circa 10th century) wrote a Sanskrit commentary on the *Bhg*, showing that this *Vaiṣṇava* philosophical treatise had begun to cross sectarian lines in its influence long ago. As noted earlier, the *Bhg* was also translated or commented on numerous times in Persian during Muslim times (circa 1200–1800 CE) showing a robust cultural interest in that era even with a Muslim audience.

The *Bhg*'s adaption into Indian vernaculars has not yet seen the scholarly study it deserves. There were most definitely translations and adaptions of it into the vernaculars, as vernacular literature in India most often began with local versions of the epics *Mahābhārata* or the *Rāmāyaṇa* (Pollock 2006, 396). Pampa (10th century) did a loose version of *MBh* in Kannada that is well known, Peruntēvaṉār (9th century) wrote a version of *MBh* in Tamil, Nannaya (11th century) and Tikkana (13th century) did so in Telugu, Harivaravipra (circa 14th century) wrote a version in Assamese and later versions were created by the 15th century in Oriya and Malayalam (Pollock 2006, 396). Clearly, there were vernacular versions of the *Bhg* in these works that have yet to find significant scholarly attention. Well known is the popular and powerful Marathi version of the work by Jñānadeva (13th century), *Jñāneśvarī*. Although many of these local *Bhgs* are not yet subjects of wider study, the presence for at least 1,000 years of sectarian stories, in both Sanskrit and the vernaculars, labeled as *Gītās*, obviously echoing the Sanskrit classic's name, clearly show the *Bhg*'s pervasive cultural impact from the time of its inclusion in the *MBh*.

Nagappa K. Gowda begins his insightful book *The Bhagavad-gītā in the Nationalist Discourse*, by saying with 'No religious text has been as frequently invoked or as passionately deployed by the Indian nationalists as the *Bhagavad-gītā*' (Gowda 2011, 2). In addition to the three nationalist leaders to be discussed in this chapter, many other nationalist leaders or champions of independence for India, like Bankimchandra Chattopadhyay,[4] S. Radhakrishnan, and Vinoba Bhave, engaged deeply with and commented on the *Bhg*. The foreign-born Annie Besant, who headed the Indian National Congress in 1917, wrote a translation of *Bhg*. Even the person who eventually became Pakistan's foremost poet, Muhammed Iqbal, embraced the *Bhg*, declaring that 'in the *Gītā* is contained the *Qur'ān* and in the *Qur'ān* the *Gītā*' (Bilimoria 2016, 1).

The reasons for this modern embrace of the *Gītā* are several. Those who fought for independence from Britain on the Indian side quite often believed that their subjugation under the British (and earlier under the Muslims) was due in part to spiritual impoverishment and the decay of India's spiritual values over time. Many of the reforms of Indian society championed at the time, like the abolition of untouchability, the elimination of child marriage, allowing widows to remarry, and the banning of *satī* were seen as efforts to correct *spiritual* wrongs done in the past. Some saw the Indian body politic weakened by caste divisions and held back by the oppression of women, so these reforms were, early on, brought forth as remedies to strengthen it. In short, the intellectuals who led the nationalist enterprise by and large believed that the spiritual and the political could not be separated in the struggle for independence. In a certain sense, *mokṣa*, the release from the cycle of birth and rebirth, took on a dual meaning, implying that 'release' from the British was as much a spiritual project as it was a political one.

So in the context of a political battle that sought spiritual underpinnings and guidance, the traditional textual resource that sought to bolster it was found readily in the *Bhg*. The *Mahābhārata* had a mixed sectarian profile, containing many references to Śiva, while containing, via the *Bhg*, a strong association with an *avatāra* of *Viṣṇu*, *Kṛṣṇa*.[5] The *Bhg*, a venerable philosophical treatise also treated as an independent text for centuries, clearly had transcended sectarian boundaries, a significant example being Abhinavagupta's commentary. Similarly, the many Persian translations, commentaries, and so on engaging the *Bhg* may be a sign of its having influence among Muslims also in the times of Muslim rule. By the 19th century, certainly, the *Bhg* had clearly become a 'non-sectarian' text and was looked to by most, including some non-Hindus, for inspiration, despite its strong *Vaiṣṇava* framework.

The fact that the story focused on a battlefield certainly suited the political context in late 19th and the first half of the 20th century as the nationalist struggle intensified. Traditional commentators, including all the *Vedāntins* and the tantric Abhinavagupta, looked at the battle before Arjuna as a spiritual battle and did *not* emphasize lessons about war itself that might be interpreted there. This, of course, was despite the fact that this was such a crucial juncture in the story of the *Pāṇḍavas*. There was no 'just war theory' discussed among commentators.

If one looks at the text carefully, one finds that the 'battle' for Arjuna is made into a spiritual battle, as it were, after the second chapter. In *Bhg* II.37, the battle seems concrete: 'arise, son of Kunti, resolved to battle' (*uttiṣṭha kaunteya yuddhāya kṛtaniścayaḥ*). See also II.38: 'ready yourself for battle' (*yuddhāya yujyasva*). But even in chapter II, as Śrī Kṛṣṇa begins to describe *yoga* and *karma yoga*, the exhortation becomes more general, as in II.48: 'Do (your) actions steadfast in *yoga*' (*yogasthaḥ kuru karmāṇi*). In chapter III, as *karma yoga* is more fully developed, Kṛṣṇa says in his exhortation (III.19), 'Without attachment, perform always work that must be done' (*tasmād asaktaḥ satatam kāryaṃ karma samācara*). Clearly, this is a general call, moving beyond the specific context of the battle. After continuing, in this chapter, to speak more about action and the need to act in the world as opposed to renouncing it, to speak about *prakṛti* and the need to control the senses, and about countering desire, Kṛṣṇa applies the battle metaphor to *yoga* against desire (III. 41): 'Therefore, best of the *Bhāratas*, first control your senses, and slay this sinful destroyer of wisdom and discrimination' (*tasmāt tvam indriyāny ādau niyamya bhartarṣabha| pāpmānaṃ prajahi hy enaṃ jñānavijñānanāśanam*). Also, the battle becomes metaphorical in III.43, the last verse of the chapter: 'Thus, knowing that which is beyond the discriminative mind, steadying the self by the self, mighty-armed one, kill the enemy in the form of desire, hard to get at' (*evaṃ buddheḥ paraṃ buddhvā saṃstabhyātmānamātmanā| jahi śatruṃ mahābāho kāmarūpaṃ durāsadam*). Chapter IV, which speaks of devotion to Kṛṣna, *yoga*, wisdom, and action ends metaphorically with battle images (verse 42): 'Therefore, having cut asunder with this sword of wisdom the doubt in your heart that is born of ignorance, resort to *yoga* and stand up'. As Arjuna has asked several questions in uncertainty, I argue that the 'doubt' being spoken of here should not be understood as the same doubt expressed by Arjuna at the end of chapter I and beginning of chapter II, though, in the largest sense, Kṛṣṇa may be answering that doubt too. From this point forward in *Bhg*, Kṛṣṇa expatiates on the three *yogas*: *bhakti*, *jñāna*, and *karma yogas*, not again directly referring to battle, concrete or metaphorical.[6] It is only at the end of the text's last chapter, chapter XVIII, that Kṛṣṇa returns to the theme of battle and advises Arjuna that he will be compelled to fight (verse 59): 'If you take recourse in ego and think, "I will not fight", this resolve is vain. *Prakṛti* will compel you'. Kṛṣṇa implies that because Arjuna is a warrior, if he does not fall into self-centered and self-pitying notions, he will be compelled by his nature to enter the battle before him. Now clearly the epic might not have turned out the way it did if Arjuna had been urged by Kṛṣṇa to *not* step forward. But in a later verse of the same chapter, verse 63, Kṛṣṇa says, 'Thus this wisdom more secret than all secrets has been declared by me to you. Having reflected on it fully, do as you choose'. In other words, God is not commanding Arjuna to act but asking him to judge the truth of what he has said. In the end, verse 73, Arjuna says, 'I will carry out (*kṛ*) your words'. Having referred here to all the passages that speak directly to 'warring' or battling in regard to Arjuna in the *Gītā*, we see how the narrative moves from reference to the concrete battle to a set of more-metaphorical statements about battling against desire and doing *yogic* action – except for Kṛṣṇa's final statement in the last chapter (verse 59), after 14 chapters about *yoga* alone. It is for this reason that no traditional commentator dwells on the '*dharma-yuddha*', 'the religious war' highlighted at times by modern nationalists, looking on the *Gītā* as a guide to life and salvation and not centrally on the question of war.

In summary of this discussion, Arjuna's fight becomes a fight against the pull of the senses and against *karma* itself. At the most, the *Gītā* may enjoin members of the warrior class to do their warring duty, but this is an incidental message in the larger philosophical backdrop. In the nationalist struggle, however, the battlefield context was used by many to, in fact, even justify violence in a political arena. Nationalists as different as Bal Gangadhar Tilak and Aurobindo Ghose believed that using violence in the political realm was justified by the *Gītā*.

But the battle metaphor may have been less important than another core lesson of the *Gītā*, the lesson of *karma yoga*, the *Yoga* of Action. If the nationalists were looking for spiritual guidance in their travails, most of them would not be likely to look to the *Vedas* themselves, which were honored but too distant from the modern to afford practical aid. Nor could the myths of the gods found in the *Purāṇas* be central poles to support the nationalist tent, as these, again, seemed to speak to the past alone for these primarily English-speaking, often-British-educated intellectuals inclined toward a certain 'rationalism'. The *Upaniṣads* were certainly inspiring and drew due attention among this nationalist cohort. But the *Upaniṣads* and the *Vedāntic* tradition associated with them tended to point away from the world. It was in the *Gītā*, then, that the secret to merging political action and spiritual pursuit was found.

The *Gītā* seems to have been aimed at the issue of social participation;[7] one imagines the challenges offered, at the turn of the first millennium CE, to the *brāhmaṇical* systems by the renunciant-led heterodoxies: Buddhism and Jainism. The heterodox challenge to the *Veda*s and *brāhmaṇism* impacted the *brāhmaṇa*-led traditions themselves. The renunciation of the world was soon enshrined in the *Upaniṣads* also, where it was declared in some places that one would be forever bound by *karma* if one remained in the village and could escape the grip of *karma* only by going to the forest to meditate upon *Brahman*. 'Orthodox' ascetics who were aligned with the *Brāhmaṇical* tradition began to appear also in the *MBh* and *Rāmāyaṇa* and in the critiques of the early Buddhists and Jains, orthodox ascetics who practiced *tapas* as bodily mortification.[8] In part, the *Bhg* seems to have the purpose of redirecting these cultural tendencies toward renunciation back toward the world. The *Vedas* (including the *Brāhmaṇa* portions), of course, are life affirming compared to their heterodox opponents and revel in long life, family life, progeny, health, and prosperity. They are profoundly of this world in terms of preserving society as a communal endeavor. The world, according to the early *Vedic* tradition (up to the *Upaniṣads*), is most definitely not the 'sorrow' (*duḥkha)* or the *karmic* 'trap' that the heterodoxies and parts of the *Upaniṣads* themselves understood.

So in the *Gītā* is offered a compromise, as it were, with the cultural embrace of renunciatory ideals. Kṛṣṇa declares clearly that true renunciation (*saṃnyāsa*) has nothing to do with leaving the world.[9] He declares definitely that going away from the world in isolation does not solve the problem of *action* (*karma*). That is a mistaken impression; one must understand, says Kṛṣṇa, that true renunciation is not a movement away from the world but rather renouncing the fruits of one's actions. Though, in traditional fashion, not forbidding endeavors that lead one from the world, Kṛṣṇa's call is to undertake 'action that must be done' (*kāryaṃ karma*) (*Bhg* III.19), however burdensome it might be. The lesson is a difficult one, because it means that one should forge forward in the world to keep it together and going (*lokasaṃgraha*) in any situation. And, of course, declared to Arjuna amid his existential crisis, it is particularly poignant because it means that he cannot escape into renunciation, as he hints at doing (*Bhg* II.5). He must 'arise and fight'. This spiritual call to act and not 'retreat' was certainly a primary reason why the *Bhg* was the Indian nationalists' text of choice.

Aurobindo Ghose (1872–1950) shared for some years, if not a political alliance, an agreement on political ends with his senior in Indian political action, Bal Gangadhar Tilak (1856–1920). Both were members of what was termed the 'extremist faction' that split the Indian National Congress in 1905–8, declaring the goal of complete independence from Britain by any means necessary. Previous Congress Party leadership, from their point of view, was much too timid, fearing to even bring up the notion of absolute independence. Tilak had famously in 1897 invoked the *Gītā* in saying that killing in a just cause (in this case against the British) was justified, if it was not done with an attitude of anger (Chakraborty and Majumdar 2013, 71). Aurobindo in his early direct political actions, after moving to Bengal in 1905, held the same views in seeing India as a fierce 'Mother' resembling Durgā who should militantly oppose the British at every turn. He suggested that even killing in political activity was justified by the *Bhg* (Chakraborty and Majumdar 2013, 73). In the Alipore case of 1909, Aurobindo Ghose was caught up in an assassination plot that his brother Barindra executed, intending to kill a British magistrate with a bomb, but only killing the magistrate's wife and her friend. Aurobindo was eventually freed in 1910, when the chief witness against him (a conspirator turned informer) was shot with a pistol in jail and killed. Soon after, Aurobindo retreated to Pondicherry and slowly ceased direct involvement in politics.

But even in the earliest declaration of militant action, in the pamphlet *Bhavani Mandir* (Temple of the Mother) of 1905, which envisioned India as the divine *Śakti*, or spiritual power, Aurobindo phrased his nationalism in religious terms. For him, then, as later, the political and the religious or spiritual had to be joined for an authentic freedom struggle. Aurobindo believed, like many, that India had become weak and needed to connect with a higher spiritual energy, the divine *Śakti*, to overthrow the British and break its chains. In his first major pamphlet, Aurobindo directly references the three *yogas* of the *Gītā* – *bhakti*, *jñāna*, and *karma yogas* – which he declared should be brought together in the struggle (Aurobindo 2003b, 75). Aurobindo discusses the *Bhg* once again in a longer discussion of the *MBh*, dated between 1893 and 1906 (Aurobindo 2003a, 324–32). There Aurobindo emphasizes that Kṛṣṇa's focus is on action and not 'quiescence' (Aurobindo 2003a, 324). He speaks of Kṛṣṇa's call as a 'gospel of action' (Aurobindo 2003a, 327). But, even here, in contrast to both Tilak and Gandhi later, he says that this action must be action surrendered to God alone, and he makes clear that because it is action for its own sake, as it were, it cannot be aimed only at some worldly end. While certainly personally inspired to act in political terms by *Bhg*, Aurobindo Ghose (later under the name Śrī Aurobindo) saw a fuller, more 'integral' message in the text beyond the simple *karma yoga*. Here he finally rejected Tilak's views and Gandhi's views, which saw the *Bhg*'s call as being world oriented, in the end, and called for social action centrally.

If one reads the many articles of Aurobindo in first *Bande Mataram* (1906–08) and then *Karmayogin* (1909–10),[10] both nationalist journals in English, one only rarely finds a direct reference to the *Bhg*, but its backdrop as a touchstone must be seen as ever-present. In the *Bande Mataram* on 5 April 1907 (Aurobindo 2003b, 237–8), Aurobindo discusses at some length the distinction between the '*pravṛtti marga*' 'path of involvement in the world' and the '*nivṛtti marga*' ('the path of renunciation'), criticizing the later and praising the former in terms of nationalist philosophy. Clearly, the *pravritti marga* is best outlined in the *Bhg*. Here, Aurobindo echoes the sentiments of his elder, Tilak, as Tilak had chosen the *Bhg* as the 'bible' for his militant call for self-rule (*svarāj*) and called on fellow nationalists to avoid the renunciatory notions of *Vedānta* in favor of *karma yoga*.

In jail at Alipore from 1908 to 1909, Aurobindo spent his time immersed in reading the *Bhg*. His devotion to the text was so strong that he experienced a mystical vision, when he was put in the docket, where he saw the docket, the judge, the prosecutor, and his own magistrate as being only Kṛṣṇa himself. Coming out of jail, Aurobindo gave one public speech where he discussed, again, the *Bhg* at length. In a speech in 1909 and recorded by government agents, Aurobindo seems to go out of his way to discuss the *Gītā* in specific but apparently apolitical terms. One suspects here, and in other nationalist contexts, that a discussion of the *Bhg* had become an encoded nationalist signal that one should keep up the struggle. In this long speech, Aurobindo says, 'It is *yoga* that gives utter perfection in action. The man who works for God is not shaken by doubts' (Aurobindo 2003c, 53). This may have been meant to say that if you trust in God and do the 'yoga' of *Bhg* and the struggle, you can be assured of success in liberating India from foreign domination.

Like his senior in the nationalist struggle, Tilak, Aurobindo seems to have reached his truest engagement with the text in jail. But it was Bal Gangadhar Tilak, the prominent Maharashtrian nationalist leader, who composed the first extensive commentarial work on the *Gītā* in English in the Mandalay jail in Burma, 1910–11, where he was jailed in exile for six years (Minor 1986, 44). This was his influential *Gītā Rahasya* (*Esoteric Import of the Gītā*). Aurobindo's extensive commentary on the *Bhg* came years later (1916–20), when he had already focused on spiritual practice in exile, and he would soon bear the title Sri Aurobindo.

We shall first discuss Tilak's work. Tilak in his thoughtful and provocative book *Gītā Rahasya* rejected the previous Sanskrit commentaries on the *Gītā* as limited and tendentious. On one hand was the camp of Śaṅkarācārya that emphasized gnostic knowledge (*jñāna*) as the central and primary goal of *Bhg*. On the other hand were the *Vaiṣṇava* commentators led by Rāmānuja, who insisted that the central goal of the *Gītā* was *bhakti*, or devotion to God. Tilak determined that the essence of the teaching of the *Gītā* was *karma yoga*: *karma yoga* based on devotion founded in knowledge (*jñānamūlaka bhakti-pradhāna karma yoga*) (Thomas 1987, 57). His highlighting of the *yoga* of action (*karma-yoga*) was the first such emphasis in the long history of *Gītā* commentary, but it was crucial to his political agenda. Tilak, then, like M.K. Gandhi after him (but unlike Aurobindo), saw that the be-all and end-all of the *Gītā* was the gospel of *karma yoga*, the *yoga* of action (Thomas 1987, 58). Tilak, in this, does not lose sight of the final goal of liberation of the self, but he believed that the central means was action in the world (Thomas 1987, 60). This somewhat paradoxical view is maintained by the notion that whatever action one is engaged in, it must be carried out without regard for its fruits (*niṣkāma)* (Thomas 1987, 64).

Along with his focus on *karma yoga*, Tilak took up the term *sthitaprajña* (one of steadied wisdom),[11] which he saw designated 'the completely integrated person' (Gowda 2011, 53). This person whose reason was steadied by *karma yoga* combined with *jnāna* and *bhakti*, whose heart throbs with the heart of all humanity, Tilak saw as the sort of ethical exemplar for modern India in the liberation of India from the British (Gowda 2011, 53–4). Gowda argues here that this was Tilak's way of bridging the gap between the elite and the masses by including the devotional call for the independence fighter (Gowda 2011, 54).

Perhaps most influential in the nationalists' reinterpretation of the *Gītā* was the term *lokasaṅgraha* (*Bhg* III.20 and III.25). The term in its original sense probably meant something like 'holding (keeping) the world together'. Its meaning surely was involved in the *Gītā*'s sense of a higher *dharma*. Given that the *Gītā* was arguing against turning one's back on the world and against renouncing the world itself, this term must have been coined to suggest that part of duty (*dharma*) was to hold the world together, i.e. participate in the world and society one was born into (rather than resort to renunciation). Kṛṣṇa goes out of his way in chapter III to urge that one must keep the wheel of the world going (III.16). To make this point, Kṛṣṇa says that even he, God, must act (III.22–24), and therefore Arjuna and others too must act, to keep the world together (III.25).

Tilak gave a deep analysis of the notion of *lokasaṅgraha*:

> The word *loka* in the phrase '*lokasaṅgraha*' has a comprehensive meaning, and includes the putting, not only of mankind, but the entire world, on a proper path, and making a '*saṅgraha*' of it, that is maintaining, feeding, protecting and defending it in a proper way, without allowing it to be destroyed.
>
> *(Tilak 1971, 962)*

Tilak insisted that the 'duty' of maintaining the world was not just for an enlightened elite but rather for all (Thomas 1987, 36). Tilak understood that the term *lokasaṅgaha* went beyond the world (*loka*) of humankind. He read it to include the world of the fathers, the gods, and so on (Thomas 1987, 38). Thus, one's duty (*dharma*) extended beyond even this world. But most important about his analysis was that he believed that the *Gītā* was charting individual, liberatory goals and was guidance toward universal welfare and the public welfare of the country. His considered view most certainly had a strong impact on the nationalists fighting for Indian independence. Other intellectuals like S. Radhakrishnan and activists like M.K. Gandhi had similar views, and the term *lokasaṅgraha* became the hub of the nationalists' melding of the spiritual and the political.[12] However, it must be reiterated that before the 19th century, no commentator on the *Bhg* saw *karma yoga* as the central *yoga* in the *Bhg*.

When Aurobindo Ghose, who was soon to become Sri Aurobindo, wrote his original *Essays on the Gītā*[13] from 1916 to 1920, as installments in the journal *Arya* in Pondicherry, M.K. Gandhi had just returned to India to become involved in the independence struggle. Here Gandhi began his rise to prominence in the nationalist movement of India not long after Aurobindo had all but retired from it. As has been previously stated, Aurobindo disagreed with his fellow nationalist interpreters of the *Gītā* on the meaning of the crucial word *lokasaṅgraha*. Here Aurobindo was adamant that this 'maintaining of the world' is not to be understood in purely 'modern' terms as a call to 'social, humanitarian motives, principals, ideals' (Aurobindo 1996, 31). This did not mean, however, that he looked at the *Bhg* from one of the more ancient viewpoints that did not make *karma yoga* central. Aurobindo, like many of the modern nationalists (particularly Tilak) who went to the *Gītā* for guidance, believed that one should not focus on what the meaning of the *Gītā* might have been in its time, but instead, one should extract the 'living truth it contains' (Sartori 2013, 57). While insisting on a more 'integral' reading of *Bhg*, Aurobindo saw that the text could guide to a 'new age of development' in which humanity would look to its 'perfection and highest spiritual welfare' (Sartori 2013, 57).

Now there may be a change in Aurobindo's attitude toward action in his spiritual retreat in Pondicherry. It is likely that he would have embraced the cause of 'worldly ends' more fully as a political activist (Sartori 2013, 62), but even in his increasing retreat from the nationalist struggle, he could understand that 'duty has its place in worldly affairs, but the divine should not be reduced to a mere social relation; on the contrary the social relation should be raised to the divine' (Sartori 2013, 63). In this way, Aurobindo did not seek to deny the possibilities of *karma yoga* in the world but simply insisted that social action alone was not sufficient. It must be part of a larger spiritual agenda of perfecting being. Essentially, Aurobindo and his spiritual, co-*yogin* Mother never distanced themselves from ideals of social transformation. They would call for human unity and global peace, as part of their spiritual quest. Even the Mother's establishment of the 'utopian city', Auroville, was aimed at these goals. So the view on *karma yoga*, later, simply went beyond the local demands of the Indian nationalist movement to look toward a larger transformation of the whole world, but certainly, it did not mean that Aurobindo had forgotten his nationalist compatriots; consequently, he took great pleasure in the fact that India's independence was declared on his own birthday, 15 August, in 1947. Here, Aurobindo was seeing what he saw as a logical outcome of his occult integral *yoga*, which meant to transform the world, but he certainly had not forgotten the Indian independence struggle.

The *Bhg* is a crucial touchstone for Sri Aurobindo's development of his integral *yoga*, laid out in his book *Synthesis of Yoga*. Where Tilak and Gandhi and many other nationalist leaders emphasized *karma yoga* as the centrally important *yoga* in *Bhg*, using their understanding of it to inspire social and national change, Aurobindo, from the beginning, saw the three *yogas* of the *Gītā* – *jñāna*, *bhakti*, and *karma* – as being a map to the development of 'integral' being. *Jñāna yoga* was to be developed to refine the cognitive aspect of being; *bhakti* was needed to divinize, as it were, the emotional aspect of being; and *karma yoga* was there to develop the more physical aspects of being to, in the end, produce the integral person, who, in their apotheosis, would be fully divine, as laid out in his book *Life Divine*. Where Tilak focuses on the development of the *sthitaprajña* (one of steadied wisdom) as the exemplar for the nationalist struggle, Aurobindo had grander goals than even the liberation of India. The most highly developed person, who had integrally perfected the *yogas* of the *Gītā*, would in essence become divine. Aurobindo aimed not merely at national transformation but at global transformation. Although he rejected the usual nationalist reading of the *yogas* and their understanding of *lokasaṅgraha* in the *Gītā*, he still held that 'spiritual men should dominate the future India and the nationalist regeneration should lie in the establishment of the kingdom of God' (Gowda 2011, 135). While focusing more on spiritual goals, Aurobindo still kept his nationalist flame burning.

Aurobindo spoke of the notion of *avatāra* in the *Gītā* in reliably nationalist terms too. Aurobindo regarded nationalism itself as an *avatāra*, coming from God (Gowda 2011, 140). As Gowda puts it,

> Aurobindo's understanding of nationalism as the *avatāra* is implicit here. The object of the *avatāra* is to stand witness to the truth of the vision, to give humanity a call to prepare itself and help all souls to the spiritual call. The *avatāra* can be interpreted more in the nature of a promise or hope of the future perfection of mankind. It is in this sense that Aurobindo regarded nationalism as an avatāra that had come from God as it promises and affords and opportunity to rouse the spiritual consciousness of the Indians.
>
> *(Gowda 2011, 141)*

Although he, in the end, varied from his fellow nationalists in interpreting the *Gītā*, the differences did not lead him to deny either the efficaciousness of *karma yoga* or the importance of the development of the right people into *sthitaprajñas*, as Tilak projected (Gowda 2011, 141). To Aurobindo, the *sthitaprajña*, one steady in wisdom, could be seen as someone who was perfecting the knowledge aspect of being through *jñāna*. Like his compatriots Tilak and Gandhi, Aurobindo saw a full merging of the nationalist enterprise with spirituality. He, like Tilak before him and Gandhi after him, openly declared that 'Nationalism is not a mere political programme; Nationalism is a religion that has come from God' (Aurobindo 2003b, 818).

Mohandas Karamchand Gandhi (1869–1948) arrived back in India in 1915, after having been educated in England in law and after years of agitation and political organizing in South Africa. By 1921, he had become the leader of the Indian National Congress. By this time, Indian National Congress itself had openly adopted the program of '*svarāj*' (self-rule), which in Tilak's and Aurobindo's early years had been considered an extremist agenda. Also, as a tool in the fight was the call for boycotts of British manufactured goods (*svadeshi*), which was also considered an extremist tactic when it was embraced by Tilak and Aurobindo. Gandhi, who eventually earned the name Mahātmā, Great Soul,[14] like his fellow nationalists, took the *Bhg* as a guidebook for action in the political realm. He, like Tilak and Aurobindo before him, did not approach the *Gītā* dogmatically or reflexively, because he understood that all sacred texts must be read through the lens of reason (Thomas 1987, 84). Although Gandhi famously claimed to have no knowledge of *Bhg* before he encountered Edwin Arnold's English translation in 1889 in England (Gowda 2011, 169), he went on to intimately engage with it and went on to declare of the *Gītā* that 'it is my mother. I lost my earthly mother who gave birth to me long ago, but this Eternal Mother has completely filled her place by my side ever since' (Thomas 1987, 86).

Throughout Gandhi's political career, the *Bhg* was a backdrop, as it was for many others. Gandhi particularly opposed interpretations of the *Gītā*, like those of Tilak and Aurobindo, that sought to justify violence in the name of politics (Gowda 2011, 170). He believed that the spiritual and *yogic* elements of *Gītā* were paramount, and thus, justifying warfare by appeal to the text was a serious misreading: 'In the characteristics of the perfected man of the *Gītā*, I don't see any need to correspond to physical warfare. Its whole design is inconsistent with the rules of conduct governing the relations between warring parties' (Gowda 2011, 175).

Not only did Gandhi believe that the *Bhg* did not, in the end, show the way to political violence, but also Gandhi claims even to have been inspired by the *Gītā* in his central precept of *ahiṃsā,*[15] which he glossed as 'nonviolence', though he conceded that the *Gītā* was not basically a text on *ahiṃsā* (Gowda 2011, 183). However, Gandhi understood that the *Gītā*'s central message of non-attachment (*anāsakti*) would naturally culminate in *ahiṃsā* and 'truth' (Gowda 2011, 183). Developing a notion of nonviolence from the *Gītā* is not farfetched if one understands the *Gītā* to lead to a perfection of *yoga* with a constant reference to God. The *Bhg* bases itself quite clearly on a practice of *sāṅkhya* and *yoga* that resembles in its details the language and practices laid out in the *Yoga Sūtra* of Patañjali, with the 24 categories of *prakṛti*[16] and its relation with an eternal self or *puruṣa.* The *Yoga Sūtra,* in fact, requires the practice of *ahiṃsā*[17] (*Yoga Sūtra* II. 35). If one sets aside the war context in which the text is told[18] and if one were to develop the rigorous practice of mind that *Bhg* leads toward, it is easy enough to imagine that the perfected *yogin* would not and could not participate in violence.

Gandhi often quoted from the *Gītā* and referred to it often in his political life from 1890 to 1925, and he delivered a series of 218 lectures on the *Gītā* at Satyagraha Ashram, Ahmedabad, delivered in morning prayers over nine months in 1926 (Gandhi 1926–27). Later, he completed a Gujarati translation of the *Bhg* in 1929 (Gandhi 1929). It was titled *Anāsaktiyoga* (*The Yoga of Non-attachment*).[19] Here, Gandhi highlights the element of non-attachment of *Bhg* as a central principle. Now, Gandhi defined the notion of non-attachment loosely as renouncing only selfish ends, not all ends, and he defined it basically as the development of love and compassion toward others, which in turn produces a host of virtues (Gowda 2011, 196). But, here, above all, Gandhi must be seen as a *karmayogin* doing political action for the benefit of the world. Naturally, he did do his actions with his own kind of *bhakti* toward God, which or who meant for him 'Truth', as for M.K. Gandhi, God, in the end, was Truth alone, as he laid out clearly in his autobiography, *The Story of My Experiments with Truth.*

Among the three nationalist leaders discussed in this chapter, Gandhi from the beginning of his political life behaved, one could argue, with the simplicity and humility of an advanced *yogin.* While Sri Aurobindo became a great *yogin* in retirement from the world, Gandhi dressed and conducted himself publicly as a *karma yogin* always and earned the title of 'Great Soul' (*Mahātmā*) in the process. Gandhi may have understood at an intellectual level that the *Gītā* had three *yogas* that it brought forward, but his devotion was truly to the *karma-yoga* aimed at social change throughout his storied career. Of course, like the others, he believed that the nationalist project was a spiritual project as well and that is why he decried tendencies toward violence in the movement, because he believed that these would destroy India's spirit.

A survey of the views on the *Bhg* of the Indian nationalists Tilak, Aurobindo, and Gandhi would not be complete without reference to their interpretation of passages that deal with the traditional hierarchy of classes that it seems to endorse, which in modern terms reduces to the notion of castes and their ranking. The *Gītā*, of course, has *dharma*, or social law, as a central focus. The first word of the *Gītā* is in fact *dharma*. Kṛṣṇa too emphasizes in *Bhg* IV.13 that he created the four *varṇas* of society: brahmin, warrior, merchant, and servant. One of Arjuna's arguments against going into this internecine battle is that such strife can lead to the mixture of 'castes' and the destruction of the eternal social law (*Bhg* I.43–4).

It can safely be said that none of these leaders endorsed the traditional Indian notion that one's birth should determine one's status in society. But none of them reject the notion of such class stratification outright. They all adopt what might be called the 'soft' view on the traditional system that the division of labor is natural in societies and that this idea of four rungs of society is just a sensible way to talk about the division of labor. It is doubtful, however, that this was the original view of the *Gītā*. It should not surprise anyone that the *dalit* nationalist leader B.R. Ambedkar, who oversaw the writing of independent India's constitution, vehemently condemned such 'fudging' in regard to what he regarded as a violent and irredeemable system of traditional social ranking. Despite the good intentions of these nationalists, Ambedkar roundly condemned this aspect of their views, and the former untouchables he led were adamantly anti-Gandhian, despite all the efforts that the Mahātmā had made on the behalf of those whom he described as *harijan*.[20] It is no surprise perhaps that among the Indian nationalists, Ambedkar's was the most negative toward the *Gītā*. For all its purported glory, he saw *Bhg* as counterrevolutionary and reactionary, in part because of these views about social stratification enshrined in it (Kumar 2013, 127–54).

Notes

1 Hence *Mhb*.
2 1556–1605 CE.
3 For references, see Qasemi (2014). Abul Fazl (1551–1602) made two prose translation of *Bhg* (Qasemi 2014, 54–5); Dara Shikoh (1615–59) made a translation (Qasemi 2014, 56); there was a translation whose authorship is unknown (Qasemi 2014, 56–7); Chandra Sen made a translation (1684–5) (Qasemi 2014, 57); an abridged translation with Muslim comments was written by 'Abdur-Rahman Chishti, which was completed by 'Abdur Rasul 'Abbasi Alawi Chishti in 1655–6 (Qasemi 2014, 58); Anand Khan wrote a version of *Bhg* in verse (circa 1750) (Qasemi 2014, 58); Laksmi Narayan Suru wrote a version of *Gītā* (n.d.) (Qasemi 2014, 58); Shaikh 'Abdullah did a *Bhg* (n.d.) (Qasemi 2014, 59); Pandit Jeo did a version (n.d.) (Qasemi 2014, 59); also, Mushi Daya Ram Khushdil Kashmiri (n.d) (Qasemi 2014, 62); Bakshi Dena Nath (n.d.) (Qasemi 2014, 63); Gulab Rai (n.d.) (Qasemi 2014, 64); Bikram Sri Krishna wrote a verse summary (n.d.) (Qasemi 2014, 64); Anonymous (n.d.) (Qasemi 2014, 65); Anonymous (n.d.) (Qasemi 2014, 67); Anonymous versified translation (n.d.) (Qasemi 2014, 67); Anonymous in prose (n.d.) (Qasemi 2014, 67); Krishna Das (n.d.), (Qasemi 2014, 69); Anonymous, word by word translation (n.d.) (Qasemi 2014, 69); Sri Dhar Gosain (n.d.) (Qasemi 2014, 69); Wadi 'ul Bustami wrote an Arabic translation in verse (n.d.) (Qasemi 2014, 75); Anonymous commentary on *Gītā* (n.d.) (Qasemi 2014, 75); Anonymous in verse form (Qasemi 2014, 75); also there are some partial translations (n.d.) (Qasemi 2014, 57–76).
4 Aka Chatterji.

5 In the critical edition of the *MBh*, *Kṛṣṇa* is almost never depicted as an avatar outside of the *Bhg*. Some argue that this does not necessarily indicate that he was not an avatar elsewhere in *MBh*. There is an incident from Kṛṣṇa's childhood where his mother, Yaśodā, once opened baby Kṛṣṇa's mouth to get something that he had put in it that didn't belong, as a child will. When she opened his mouth, she saw the whole universe there and realized, in that moment, the divine nature of her child. But after a few moments, she was made by Kṛṣṇa to forget this completely. So an emic argument can be made that, in the *MBh*, Kṛṣna was always a concealed *avatāra*, his true nature revealed in the *Bhg*, alone, only to be forgotten again. Most Western scholars, however, see the *Bhg* as a text inserted into it at a later date, which makes Kṛṣṇa into an avatar of Viṣṇu, after the fact, as it were.

6 This, however, emphasizes that the *Bhg* is not at all a treatise that dwells on arguments for the 'just war'.

7 Interestingly, the text itself begins with the word '*dharma*' (*Bhg 1.1*).

8 Vyāsa himself the teller (or reteller) of the *MBh* and also participant in its action was a scruffy, unsightly 'orthodox' renunciant.

9 *Bhg* III. 4–5.

10 Whose title echoes of the nationalist message of the *Gītā* in *karma yoga*.

11 *Sthitaprajña* and its equivalent *sthitadhī*, along with the phrase that describes this 'steadied wisdom' *prajñā pratiṣṭhitā*, are found describing the karma *yogin* in *Bhg*, chapter II. *Sthitaprajña, Bhg* II. 54–5; *sthitadhī, Bhg* II.56 and 61; *prajñā pratiṣṭhitā, Bhg* II.54, 57–8, 69.

12 With the exception of Aurobindo, who was the only major dissenter in regard to this understanding.

13 The first series of *Essays on the Gītā* appeared in the monthly review *Arya* between August 1916 and July 1918. It was revised by Sri Aurobindo and published as a book in 1922. The second series appeared in the *Arya* between August 1918 and July 1920. In 1928, Sri Aurobindo brought out an extensively revised edition in book form of his complete series.

14 A testimony to his own merging of nationalism and religion.

15 Lit. non-killing.

16 Nature.

17 There, taken to be non-killing and nonviolence.

18 Which all traditional commentators understand to outline, in essence, a spiritual war for the self's perfection.

19 Mahadev Desai eventually rendered this book in English and published it in 1946.

20 Those born of God.

Bibliography

Aurobindo, Sri. 1996. *Essays on the Gītā*. 9th ed. Pondicherry: Sri Aurobindo Ashram.

Aurobindo, Sri. 2003a. *The Complete Works of Sri Aurobindo*. Vol. 1. Pondicherry: Sri Aurobindo Publication Department. (https://www.sriaurobindoashram.org/sriaurobindo/writings.php. Accessed online Mar. 2019).

Aurobindo, Sri. 2003b. *The Complete Works of Sri Aurobindo*. Vol. 6–7. Pondicherry: Sri Aurobindo Publication Department. (https://www.sriaurobindoashram.org/sriaurobindo/writings.php. Accessed online Mar. 2019).

Aurobindo, Sri. 2003c. *The Complete Works of Sri Aurobindo*. Vol. 8. Pondicherry: Sri Aurobindo Publication Department. (https://www.sriaurobindoashram.org/sriaurobindo/writings.php. Accessed online Mar. 2019).

Bilimoria, Purshottama. "Muhammad Iqbāl and the *Bhagavd-gītā Part One*." *Sutra Journal*. May 2016 (www.sutrajournal.com. Accessed online Feb. 2019).

Chakraborty, Dipesh and Rochona Majumdar. 2013. "Gandhi's *Gītā* and Politics and Such." In *Political Thought in Action: The Bhagavad-gītā and Modern India*. Edited by Shruti Kapila and Faisal Devji. Cambridge: Cambridge University Press.

Frasca, Richard A. 1990. *Theatre of the Mahābhārata*. Honolulu: University of Hawaii Press.

Gandhi, Mohandas Karamchand. 1926–27. *The Collected Works of Mahatma Gandhi*. Vol. XXXII. Ahmedabad: The Publication Division Ministry of Information and Broadcasting Government of India.

Gandhi, Mohandas Karamchand. 1929. *The Collected Works of Mahatma Gandhi*. Vol. XLI. Ahmedabad: The Publication Division Ministry of Information and Broadcasting Government of India.

Gowda, K. Nagappa. 2011. *The Bhagavad-gītā in the Nationalist Discourse*. Oxford: Oxford University Press.

Kapila, Shruti and Faisal Devji (eds.). 2013. *Political Thought in Action: The Bhagavad-gītā and Modern India*. Cambridge: Cambridge University Press.

Kumar, Aishwary. 2013. "Ambedkar's Inheritances." In *Political Thought in Action: The Bhagavad-gītā and Modern India*. Edited by Shruti Kapila and Faisal Devji. Cambridge: Cambridge University Press.

Minor, Robert (ed.). 1986. *Modern Indian Interpreters of the Bhagavad-gītā*. Albany: State University of New York Press.

Pollock, Sheldon. 2006. *The Language of the Gods in the World of Men: Sanskrit Culture and Power in Premodern India*. Berkely: University of California Press.

Qasemi, Sharif Husain (ed.). 2014. *A Descriptive Catalogue of Persian Translations of Indian Works*. New Delhi: National Mission for Manuscripts.

Sartori, Andrew. 2013. "The Transfiguration of Duty on Aurobindo's Essays on the *Gītā*." In *Political Thought in Action*. Edited by Sruti Kapila and Faisal Devji. Cambridge: Cambridge University Press.

Thomas, P.M. 1987. *20th Century Indian Interpretations of the Bhagavad-gītā: Tilak, Gandhi and Aurobindo*. Bangalore: The Christian Institute for the Study of Religion and Society.

Tilak, Bal Gangadhar. 1971. *Gītā Rahasya*. Poona: Tilak Brothers.

Truschke, Audrey. 2012. *Cosmopolitan Encounters: Sanskrit and Persian at the Mughal Court*. Dissertation, Columbia University.

9

THE *GĪTĀ* OF THE GURUS

The *Bhagavad-gītā* since Indian independence

J.E. Llewellyn

The Bhagavad-gītā was a frequent subject of commentary in the first half of the 20th century, and this has continued since India became independent of British rule in 1947. This chapter is dedicated to a survey of commentaries on the *Gītā* by some of the most influential thinkers of that later period. Specifically, the reader will encounter five religious teachers. Taking them in chronological order on the basis of when their works on the *Gītā* were published, we begin with the founder of the transcendental meditation movement, Maharishi Mahesh Yogi, whose commentary on the *Gītā* (limited to the first six chapters) was published in 1967. An abridged version of A.C. Bhaktivedanta Swami Prabhupada's *Gītā* commentary was published in 1968, with the complete text appearing in 1972. Prabhupada was the founder of the International Society of Kṛṣṇa Consciousness. In that same year, 1972, Swami Chinmayananda's commentary was published, and his organization the Chinmaya Mission has kept it in print since. Swami Rama, the founder of the Himalayan International Institute of *Yoga* Science and Philosophy, published his commentary on the *Gītā* in 1984. And, finally, the *Gītā* commentary of Anandamurti Gurumaa, of the Rishi Chaitanya Ashram, came out in English in 2016. Among the many works on the *Gītā* that might have been included in this chapter, these were chosen to represent a range of teachers and perspectives.

Increasingly over the course of the 20th century, attracting Western followers was seen as an important validation of Hindu religious teachers (Llewellyn 2004). It is significant that three of our five *Gītā* commentators are primarily remembered for their popularity outside India; they are Maharishi, Prabhupada, and Swami Rama. This is a substantial change from the first half of the 20th century, reflecting a certain globalization of Hinduism. However, none of these *Gītā* commentators is remembered as a major political figure. In the first half of the 20th century, it is remarkable that some of the towering giants of the nationalist movement also wrote extensively about the *Bhagavad-gītā*, but that tradition has not continued in independent India. No major political figure has composed an important work on the *Gītā* since 1947, as political leadership has become less a religious vocation. That is why this is a chapter about the *Gītā* of the gurus, because the authors who are its subject were the heads of Hindu religious organizations. Contrasts between our commentators will be noted occasionally throughout this chapter, with a conclusion at the end drawing some more substantial comparisons.

Maharishi

Our first commentator, Maharishi Mahesh Yogi (1918–2008), born Mahesh Prasad Varma, is best known for his role in founding and promoting the transcendental meditation movement. According to Cynthia Ann Humes, Maharishi devoted himself to the spiritual path at age 24 after first encountering his would-be guru, Swami Brahmananda Saraswati, in 1940. At this time, Brahmananda encouraged Maharishi to finish his schooling before joining him on the spiritual path. Maharishi did as he was instructed and earned his bachelor's degree in physics from Allahabad University in 1942 (Humes 2013, 508). Following the death of his guru, in 1955 Maharishi began teaching transcendental meditation in South India, and soon he was traveling outside India as well. Over time, Maharishi founded many other programs and organizations like the Global Country of World Peace and claimed that with transcendental meditation, he could in fact create world peace. Maharishi is also well known for his role as spiritual advisor to the Beatles, the Beach Boys, and other celebrities who visited his ashram in the late 1960s and early 1970s, after his movement had begun picking up momentum.

Maharishi asserted that he had rediscovered transcendental meditation and credits his guru with teaching this form of 'deep meditation' to him during their 13 years together. Once Maharishi began to teach transcendental meditation to a Western audience, as Humes puts it, he 'sought to strip away those aspects that Americans felt uncomfortable with'. Humes further explains that 'Uttering specially selected *mantras* for twenty minutes twice a day, Maharishi promised that the individual could experience Absolute Being in Cosmic Consciousness without all the cultural baggage' (Humes 2005, 57). Later in his career, Maharishi began reinserting more of the Hindu/*Vedic* religion into his teachings, which alienated some of his followers (ibid., 73).

Maharishi Mahesh Yogi's commentary on the *Bhagavad-gītā*, which spans only the first six chapters, presents itself as an advertisement for transcendental meditation. Not only is this practice central to his understanding of the *Gītā*, but Maharishi also asserts that his commentary, with its emphasis on transcendental meditation, provides the practical application that other commentaries lack. In explaining the process of transcendental meditation while commenting on verse 4.38, he states,

> We meditate for about half an hour and follow this by coming out to act in practical life for about ten hours, by which time we begin to feel that we are out of the influence of the morning meditation. We meditate again

> in the same way and again let the influence fade by coming into practical life; we keep repeating the process of gaining the state of Universal Being in transcendence (*samādhi*) during meditation and of coming out to regain individuality in the field of relative existence. This allows for more infusion of being into the nature of the mind even when it is engaged in activity through the senses.
>
> *(Maharishi 1990, 313)*

At the beginning of his commentary on the *Gītā*, Maharishi acknowledges his debt to Śaṅkara (ibid., 21). This should come as no surprise given that Maharishi's guru Brahmananda was himself a Śaṅkarācārya, a teacher in the medieval philosopher's lineage. Yet Maharishi also admits that Śaṅkara became misunderstood over time. The *saṁnyāsins*, or renouncers, who have been the main exponents of his teaching, have wrongly claimed that his religion is 'completely closed to householders, who form the main section of society, and open only to themselves' (ibid., 257). Maharishi's religion applied to both renouncers and householders, to both the path of action and the path of knowledge, and for him, the bridge between them was the practice of transcendental meditation.

In his introduction and elsewhere, Maharishi formulates his interpretation of the *Gītā* according to four levels of consciousness: the waking state, transcendental consciousness, cosmic consciousness, and God consciousness (Maharishi 1990, 20). Waking consciousness is the typical state of an individual who has not practiced meditation or undergone any process of self-transformation. This is to be considered the average state of human existence. Transcendental consciousness is achieved through meditation (specifically transcendental meditation) and stays in meditation. Cosmic consciousness, in Maharishi's discussion, enables one to retain the insight gained in transcendental consciousness and return to the world of activity. Once cosmic consciousness has been achieved, the next step is attaining the state of God consciousness. At one point in this commentary, Maharishi adds two other levels to this system, inserting dreaming and sleeping consciousness between the waking and transcendental states (ibid., 276).[1]

Since the highest stage is called God consciousness, it might seem as if the culmination of Maharishi's teaching is the path of devotion. Early on in his commentary, Maharishi argues that Śaṅkara's disciples did get their teacher wrong in emphasizing renunciation at the expense of devotion (Maharishi 1990, 13). Yet there is little of the path of devotion here – nothing about Kṛṣṇa's mythology, for example. Maharishi does affirm that Kṛṣṇa is an 'Incarnation of God' (ibid., 259). But then he expands on this by writing that 'The Incarnation of Lord Kṛṣṇa is such a special manifestation of *Brahman*, the eternal immutable being' (ibid., 262), moving from a personal to an impersonal conception of the highest truth. At one point in the commentary, Maharishi commends devotion, but only as a stepping stone to final fulfillment. Commenting on verse 6.32, he explains that

> The present verse dissolves the bond of devotion, for this can no longer exist when intimacy becomes complete. While devotion served as a link to

> maintain Union, this remained in some degree on the level of formality. . . . As the Union grows more complete, the link of worship, of adoration and devotion, finds fulfillment in its own extinction, leaving worshipper and worshipped together in perfect oneness, in the oneness of absolute Unity.
>
> *(Maharishi 1990, 447–8)*

Taking the traditional *Advaita Vedānta* stance here, Maharishi understands the final state to be absorption into unity, leaving no separation between the worshiper and the worshiped. Devotion, while necessary to reach that final stage, in the end falls away.

As a teacher situated between India and the West, Maharishi's comments on caste in this book are significant. Following the lamentation by Arjuna in *Bhagavad-gītā* 1.45, of the social destruction that would be caused by a war between two factions of the same family, Maharishi admits that 'The loss of family and caste *dharmas* is a calamity for the social order, a destruction of righteousness; it is a sin against God' (Maharishi 1990, 70). When the *Gītā* says that Arjuna must do his 'allotted duty', Maharishi explains that

> In those parts of the world where natural divisions of society still exist, a man's duty is apparent by virtue of his birth in a particular family. Thus, Arjuna is born a *kṣatriya* and it is natural for him to fight.
>
> *(ibid., 191)*

As 'natural divisions of society exist' in India's caste system, people there must do what that system dictates. Perhaps in this Maharishi was just following the teaching of his guru Brahmananda. Humes says that he could become a Śaṅkarācārya only by meeting the requirements of that office, including that he 'respected the caste system' (Humes 2005, 59). This would have put Maharishi in conflict with many early-20th-century *Gītā* commentators and with all the others surveyed in this chapter, who rejected caste that was based on birth. However, this embrace of caste is not prominent in Maharishi's commentary. It would have been largely irrelevant to Maharishi's Western disciples, as they lived in parts of the world without these 'natural divisions'.

Prabhupada

Next we consider a commentary unique in this chapter for its emphasis on devotion. When A.C. Bhaktivedanta Swami Prabhupada arrived in the United States in 1965, this elderly renouncer would have seemed an unlikely candidate to found a global religious movement. He was born in what is now the Indian state of West Bengal in 1896 to a prosperous family from a trading caste. Having married while still at Scottish Churches' College in Kolkata, he would go on to have five children and a career in pharmaceuticals. When he was 26, Prabhupada first met the man who was to become his guru, Bhaktisiddhanta Sarasvati, a devotee of Kṛṣṇa in the *Gauḍīya Vaiṣṇava* tradition that was founded by Kṛṣṇa Caitanya in the 16th century. Prabhupada finally became a renouncer in 1959, to dedicate his life to the propagation of Kṛṣṇa devotion (Tamal Krishna Goswami 2012, 32–4).

Prabhupada reported that Bhaktisiddhanta had commissioned him to use his knowledge of English to spread the *Gauḍīya* message. When he came to the United States for this purpose, his approach was radically different from other Indian teachers in the United States, who adapted their preaching to their audience. His followers 'practiced an altogether foreign way of life, rising by 4:30 in the morning, wearing flowing saffron robes, and adhering to a diet of vegetarian food ritually offered first to Kṛṣṇa' (Tamal Krishna and Gupta 2005, 82). Prabhupada arrived with copies of his three-volume translation of the first canto of the great classic of Kṛṣṇa devotion, the *Bhāgavata Purāṇa*. However, in the United States, he turned his attention first to the *Bhagavad-gītā*, producing an English translation and commentary, published in an abridged version in 1968 and then in full in 1972. Prabhupada was also active as the leader of a growing institution. Incorporated in 1966, the International Society of Kṛṣṇa Consciousness managed more than a hundred temples by the time of Prabhupada's death in 1977 (ibid., 82). Although Prabhupada prided himself on maintaining the *Gauḍīya* tradition in the United States, Tamal Krishna Goswami and Ravi M. Gupta do admit that he made some innovations as well. Chief among these was that 'Prabhupada gave women a vital role in his mission' (ibid., 89). Another example of what Goswami and Gupta call acceptance-in-rejection of tradition concerned caste. On the one hand, Prabhupada respected 'the ministerial role of *brāhmaṇas*', but he also offered initiation to his Western disciples, and even invested them with the sacred thread (ibid., 91). '*Vaiṣṇava bhakti* affords one *brāhmaṇical* status automatically', he insisted (Tamal Kṛṣṇa 2012, 110).

The distinctive emphasis in A.C. Bhaktivedanta Swami Prabhupada's commentary on the *Gītā* is devotion to Kṛṣṇa as 'the Supreme Personality of Godhead'. In fact, Robert D. Baird has argued that the commentator even finds this in places in the *Bhagavad-gītā* where it doesn't seem to be present (Baird 1986, 201–3). Prabhupada says that the ultimate is expressed in three forms (and this formulation is found elsewhere in *Gauḍīya Vaiṣṇavism*): 'Absolute truth is realized in three phases of understanding, namely *Brahman* or the impersonal all-pervasive spirit; *Paramātmā*, or the localized aspect of the Supreme within the heart of all living entities; and *Bhagavān*, or the Supreme Personality of Godhead, Lord Kṛṣṇa' (Prabhupada 1972, 76). But the greatest devotees are those who concentrate on the third, on Kṛṣṇa. Prabhupada exalts Kṛṣṇa to such a great extent that he even eclipses Viṣṇu. Although the Kṛṣṇa who speaks in the *Bhagavad-gītā* is sometimes understood to be an incarnation of Viṣṇu, that is not Prabhupada's theology. At the beginning of the eleventh chapter of the *Gītā*, the commentator explains, 'This chapter reveals Kṛṣṇa as the cause of all causes; he is even the cause of Mahā-Visnu, and from him the material universes emanate. Kṛṣṇa is not an incarnation; he is the source of all the incarnations' (ibid., 563). This theological inversion has the ironic effect of reducing the power of the experience that Arjuna has in chapter 11. This is not a climactic vision of Kṛṣṇa's true cosmic nature as God, because for Prabhupada, Kṛṣṇa's highest form was the human that Arjuna had been seeing all along.

In this description of Kṛṣṇa's three forms, *Brahman* is *not* the ultimate. Throughout this book, Prabhupada takes issue with those whom he calls impersonalists, who think that the ultimate is an impersonal philosophical principle. Disagreeing with the *Advaita* view that the material world is just an illusion, Prabhupada insists that the world is real, and he maintains that the soul and God remain eternally distinct, rejecting the '*Māyāvādī* theory that after liberation the individual soul, separated by the covering of *māyā* or illusion, will merge into the impersonal *Brahman* and lose its individual existence' (Prabhupada 1972, 92).

Prabhupada understood himself to be a disciple of the founder of the *Gauḍīya* school, Caitanya, and this gave him particular authority to pen this commentary. Others have written about using the *Gītā* 'to fulfill someone's personal ambition' or to 'make a good business' (Prabhupada 1972, xii, 224). However, Prabhupada claimed that his right to interpret the *Gītā* came from a chain of 'disciplic succession' that went back to Kṛṣṇa himself (ibid., 36). Essentially, he argues that he writes about the teaching of the *Gītā* as he learned it from the teacher himself – that is, from Kṛṣṇa. This is why Prabhupada titled his commentary *The Bhagavad-gītā As It Is* (on this, see Davis 2015, 165). Prabhupada accepts the common *Gauḍīya* doctrine that Caitanya was himself an incarnation of Kṛṣṇa, so there is a sense in which this commentary is based on Kṛṣṇa's teaching twice over, originating in Kṛṣṇa and mediated through Caitanya (Prabhupada 1972, 236).

The complex view about caste noted earlier in this chapter is evident in Prabhupada's commentary on the *Bhagavad-gītā*. In some contexts, he seems to largely uphold the caste system, and at one point, he writes,

> therefore, according to the *Vedic* system, there are instituted the four orders of life and the four statuses of life, called the caste system and the spiritual order system. There are different rules and regulations for different castes or divisions of society, and if a person is able to follow them, he will automatically be raised to the highest platform of spiritual realization.
>
> *(Prabhupada 1972, 780)*

However, caste duty is not advocated by Prabhupada as an end in itself, but it is subordinated to devotion.

> Everyone should think that he is engaged in a particular type of occupation by Hṛṣīkeśa, the master of the senses [this is an epithet of Kṛṣṇa in the *Bhagavad-gītā*]. And, by the result of the work in which he is engaged, the Supreme Personality of Godhead, Śrī Kṛṣṇa, should be worshiped.
>
> *(ibid., 844)*

From the earliest extant, complete commentary on the *Bhagavad-gītā* by Śaṅkara, a significant conflict has developed over what that text teaches about renunciation as opposed to action in the world. Prabhupada affirms that a devotee does not have to become a renouncer:

> If one can mold his family life in this way to develop Kṛṣṇa consciousness, following these four principles [chanting the Hare Kṛṣṇa *mantra*, eating only food offered to Kṛṣṇa, reading devotional literature, and worshipping Him], then there is no need to change from family life to renounced life.

Yet he acknowledges that this may not be possible for all devotees. 'But if it is not congenial, not favorable for spiritual advancement, then family life should be abandoned' (Prabhupada 1972, 663). Prabhupada even warns that there is some danger for an immature devotee who takes to renunciation just to gain 'cheap adoration from the innocent public' (ibid., 169). Overall, Prabhupada embraces *varṇāśrama-dharma*, the religion in which there are not only four castes but also four stages of life, all the while affirming that devotion is what is really important in any of the stages.

Chinmayananda

Our third commentator, Swami Chinmayananda (1916–1993), was born in Ernakulam in the Indian state of Kerala; his name before becoming a renouncer was Poothampalli Balakrishna Menon. He attended Lucknow University beginning in 1940, studying English literature. He supported the nationalist movement burgeoning at that time and was arrested in 1942. He became a journalist, but his life took a different path when he visited the Ashram of Swami Sivananda, the founder of the Divine Life Society. In 1949, Chinmayananda was initiated as a renouncer by Sivananda.

Chinmayananda began in 1951 to give public lectures, which he called *jñāna-yajñas*, literally 'knowledge sacrifices'. Early on, he preached on the *Upanisads* but soon also spoke on the *Bhagavad-gītā*. Like his *guru* Sivananda, Chinmayananda generally lectured in English. And like Sivananda, Chinmayananda's religious teaching was based on *Advaita Vedānta*. However, Jacobsen suggests that '[h]e presented himself as nonsectarian and claimed to speak for all Hindus, a characteristic that is typical of the modern, English-speaking Hindu *gurus* who serve the educated middle class' (Jacobsen 2013, 445). The Chinmaya Mission was founded in 1953 to propagate Chinmayananda's teaching. From 1965, Chinmayananda conducted preaching tours overseas, beginning in places with a significant Indian diaspora population. Jacobsen reports that by 2011 there were 307 Chinmaya Mission centers around the world (ibid., 450). In 1963, Chinmayananda 'suggested that a "world Hindu conference" be organized to achieve the goal of unifying Hinduism' (ibid., 451). Then his center in Mumbai played host to the founding meeting of the Vishva Hindu Parishad (VHP, also known as the World Hindu Council) in the following year. The VHP played a prominent role in the rise of Hindu nationalist politics in later decades, but by that time, Chinmayananda does not seem to have remained active. For example, Jacobsen notes that 'The biography published by Chinmaya Mission, *He Did It, Swami Chinmayananda: A Legacy*, hardly mentions his involvement with the VHP' (ibid., 451). *The Holy Geeta*, Swami Chinmayananda's commentary on *The Bhagavad-gītā*, was published first in 1976.

At one point in *The Holy Geeta*, Chinmayananda says, 'for self-development, each type of seeker, according to the vehicle available, chooses either the path-of-Devotion or the path-of-Action or the path-of-Knowledge. To each one of them, his "Path" is easiest' (Chinmayananda 2016, 836). Here he seems to affirm the tolerant position that there are different kinds of religion suited for different kinds of people. But this tolerance has an edge to it, as *The Holy Geeta* also argues that religion of knowledge is highest, with the religion of action only allowed as a preparation for it:

> To consider the path-of-Action (*karma-yoga*) and the path-of-Knowledge (*Jñāna-yoga*) as competitive is to understand neither of them. They, being complementary, are to be practised SERIALLY one after the other. Selfless activity gives a chance to the mind to exhaust many of its existing mental impressions.
>
> *(ibid., 194, original capitalization)*

The swami also insists that knowledge is the direct means to liberation from rebirth, whereas action leads to this only indirectly (ibid., 196). On this point, Chinmayananda seems to be following closely Śaṅkara's commentary on the *Gītā*. This should come as no surprise given that that medieval philosopher is cited frequently by Chinmayananda, and his guru, Swami Sivananda, himself wrote a commentary on the *Gītā* heavily indebted to Śaṅkara (Miller 1986).

Consistent with this emphasis on knowledge over action, Chinmayananda characterizes Arjuna as 'intellectually an average man' and later as 'a confused average man', unprepared for 'the highest methods of subtle meditation' (Chinmayananda 2016, 193, 396). In some commentaries on the *Gītā*, such as Prabhupada's, Arjuna is taken as the most exalted example of a devotee, but not by Chinmayananda. Introducing verses in the eighteenth chapter of the *Gītā* about caste, *The Holy Geeta* reads,

> In the following stanzas, by the discussions contained in them, in the immediate context of the Kṛṣṇa-Arjuna summit talks, the Lord is only trying to make Arjuna understand that his inner equipment is such that he can be classified only as a *kṣatriya*. Being a *kṣatriya*, his duty is to fight, championing the cause of the good, and thus establish righteousness. He cannot, with profit, retire to the jungle and meditate for self-unfoldment, since he will have to grow, first of all, into the status of the *sattvic* personality (*brāhmaṇa*) before he can successfully strive on the path of total retirement and a life of rewarding contemplation.
>
> *(Chinmayananda 2016, 1189–90)*

In other words, people such as *brāhmaṇas*, who have the quality of *sattva* (translated by Chinmayananda as 'purity' but also as 'unactivity'), are qualified for renunciation. But Arjuna is a *kṣatriya*, for whom such a discipline is not appropriate. For Chinmayananda, as for Śaṅkara, if the *Gītā* seems to emphasize the religion of action, that is only because this is the proper teaching for the warrior Arjuna.

Although Chinmayananda talks about caste in the preceding quote, this does not mean that he embraces caste based on birth as it is practiced in contemporary India. In the 18th chapter and elsewhere, the *Gītā* does seem to indicate that people must do their caste duty. Chinmayananda affirms this, yet assignment to one of these castes should be based on the temperament of the individual and not 'a sheer accident of birth' (Chinmayananda 2016, 245). In the ideal harmonious society, 'all "castes" should not be competitive but co-operative units'. But that is not what Chinmayananda found in contemporary India, because

> later on, in the power politics of the early middle-ages in India, this communal feeling cropped up in its present ugliness, and in the general ignorance among the ordinary people at that time, the cheap *paṇḍit*s could parade their assumed knowledge by quoting, IN BITS, stanzas like this one.
>
> *(ibid., 281)*

Thus, the so-called learned have taken advantage of their position to set different caste groups against each other, even using the *Gītā* itself for that purpose. About the contemporary *brāhmaṇa*, Chinmayananda laments that 'alas! he gets no reverence', but that is because he claims 'his distinction by birth alone' and 'has not striven to deserve it' (ibid., 1191–2). For example, Arjuna must act as warrior, according to this logic, not because he was born in the warrior caste but because he has a warrior's nature.

It was noted earlier that the religion of action is subordinated to the religion of knowledge in *The Holy Geeta.* The same could be said for the religion of devotion as well. In a couple of passages, quoting Śaṅkara is a powerful tool used by Chinmayananda to accomplish this subordination. For example, our modern commentator embraces *bhakti* but rejects the 'cheap connotation' that it has come to have when translated as 'devotion'. For himself, Chinmayananda defines *bhakti* as 'selfless love, seeking a fulfilment in itself, when directed towards the divine with firm faith and an all-out belief'. This love leads to a union in which 'the lovers become one with their beloveds'. At this point in its argument, *The Holy Geeta* adds, 'Therefore, Śaṅkara describes *Bhakti* as "the identification of the ego with its Real Nature"' (Chinmayananda 2016, 561–2). Here we are no longer talking about the passion of the lover for the beloved or even of the devotee for God but rather of the realization of the *ātman* by the individual. In other words, we have shifted from devotion to knowledge. Consistent with this turn from devotion, in his commentary, Chinmayananda repeatedly transforms Kṛṣṇa himself. In *Gītā* 3.3, for instance, Kṛṣṇa speaks not as the 'Blue Boy of Vṛndāvana, not as the Beloved of the *gopīs*' but as 'the Eternal substratum for the entire PLURALISTIC world, as the Cause of all Creation, as the Might in all substances' (ibid., 196). Just as loving devotion becomes dispassionate contemplation in *The Holy Geeta*, so too is the God who is the object of devotion transformed into the absolute that is the proper object of contemplation.

Swami Rama

There is something of this emphasis on knowledge in our fourth commentator as well. Swami Rama (1925–96) came to the West in 1969 at the behest of his guru Bengali Baba of the Himalayas. In the United States, Swami Rama founded the Himalayan International Institute of *Yoga* Science and Philosophy in Honesdale, Pennsylvania, and began sharing his teachings on *yoga* and *tantra* with his contemporary Western audience (Tigunait 2001, 300). Among the many books that Swami Rama wrote, *Perennial Psychology of the Bhagavad-gītā* combines his South Asian roots with his modern aspirations and desire to make *yoga* accessible to all. Based on the teachings he pulled from the conversation between Kṛṣṇa and Arjuna, in *Perennial Psychology of the Bhagavad-gītā*, Swami Rama offers advice to modern psychologists and aspiring students of *yoga* while also critiquing the methods of contemporary gurus.

To Swami Rama, understanding the psychological aspects of *yogic* teaching, notably the *Gītā*'s presentation of *yoga*, is key to accomplishing the goals of life. Because of this understanding, psychology became the primary focus of his *Gītā* commentary. In the introduction to his commentary, Swami Rama states,

> The *Bhagavad-gītā* is the fountainhead of Eastern psychology, and this commentary is designed to draw out its psychological concepts and make them accessible to all students. These profound psychological insights are intertwined in the *Bhagavad-gītā* with philosophical concepts, so the task undertaken here is to separate the psychological principles and to explain their practical application.
>
> *(Swami Rama 1984, 1)*

In working to offer his students a practical path based on the *Gītā*'s teachings, Swami Rama adds to the common framework of *Gītā* commentary by including modern psychology and instruction for practicing various *yoga* techniques.

Swami Rama, like most other commentators, has his own idea of which path offered in the *Gītā* is best. While he is not as bold as Śaṅkara in asserting that the path of knowledge is superior to the other paths, Swami Rama does make passing remarks that betray its loftier status. He explains that the religion of knowledge, which he often calls the path of renunciation, cannot be practiced by everyone. He says, 'The student should understand that renunciation is not a path to be followed by just anyone; following the path of renunciation is like walking on the edge of a razor' (Swami Rama 1984, 207). He also explains that for the majority of society, and this includes Arjuna, action is the only path suited to them: 'We have already explained that the path of renunciation is only for the fortunate few;

the masses are more inclined toward action. The path of action is thus the only path for the people of the world' (ibid., 206–7).

Though Swami Rama talks about action and knowledge, the path of devotion is not so prominent in his commentary. At one point, he understands Kṛṣṇa to be offering four *yogic* paths in the *Gītā*, of which devotion is the fourth (Swami Rama 1984, 298). He explains that 'The fourth group of aspirants is not learned. They depend on the teachings imparted to them by the sages, and they strictly follow that knowledge with full faith and devotion. Their path is the path of devotion and faith' (ibid., 382). Swami Rama is assigning the four paths to individuals of certain abilities in this statement, with those who follow devotion having limited intellectual capacity.

Elsewhere, Swami Rama divides people into four groups, which mirror the four main castes that some Hindu texts describe:

> The first category, those who are mentally brilliant and have profound control over their senses and minds, should devote more time to unfolding their awareness and should use their brilliance to serve society. Their *dharma* (duty) is to serve others through their brilliance and intelligence, to teach and to impart knowledge. The second category, those who are less inclined toward the path of *jñāna* but are physically strong, should learn to use their physical powers in performing their duties. Third is that category of people who have practical knowledge for living in the world. They can earn and gain and at the same time share their earnings with others generously. Fourth are those who can attend to the needs of others and perform services for others and thus make their livelihood.
>
> *(Swami Rama 1984, 131)*

However, this division of society is not the same as caste as it is currently practiced in India. It was initially established 'for the welfare of society and for the distribution of labor' (Swami Rama 1984, 131). It was 'not meant to create disparity, caste, or rigid categories based on birth in a particular family' (ibid., 456). Thus, like Chinmayananda, Swami Rama condemns contemporary caste practice as divisive.

Swami Rama determines the relationship of Kṛṣṇa and Arjuna to be that of a guru and his disciple, deeming Kṛṣṇa the perfect *yogi*, who is able to lead the perfect student, Arjuna (and this is in spite of what we noted earlier about Arjuna's being competent only for the religion of action), down the path to understanding the self. He states,

> Arjuna is the embodiment of a good *sadhaka*, and Sri Kṛṣṇa a competent teacher. The dialogue [between Kṛṣṇa and Arjuna] helps one to confront and analyze his weaknesses. Sri Kṛṣṇa, a perfect *yogi*, is aware of Arjuna's inner turmoil and allows him to express himself.
>
> *(Swami Rama 1984, 27–8)*

Although Swami Rama in passing mentions Kṛṣṇa as an incarnation, he clearly predominately interprets Kṛṣṇa as the supreme guru, as opposed to Lord of all, and the intended object of devotion, unlike Prabhupada. As the ideal guide, Kṛṣṇa is contrasted with the 'fake teachers', whom Swami Rama refers to often:

> Many fake teachers perform so-called miracles that are never referred to in the scriptures. They perform those tricks to acquire a large following just to satisfy their egos. The seeker should be careful and should not follow a modern teacher without knowing him well and comparing his teaching with those of authentic scriptures.
>
> *(ibid., 418)*

Swami Rama understands therapists' practicing contemporary psychology to be spiritual guides. He does not, however, think that they are equipped to deal with the issues that their clients bring them:

> Modern therapists have theoretical knowledge to a certain extent, but they are still caught up in the unresolved issues emanating from their own unconscious. They have not gone through an adequate training program to reach a genuine state of equanimity and tranquility, though they may pose as though they are peaceful and content. Many therapists suffer from the same conflicts as their clients.
>
> *(Swami Rama 1984, 52–3)*

Through this explanation, Swami Rama alludes to modern psychologists' generally having the knowledge but often not the personal experience needed to be able to adequately help their clients. This statement reinforces Swami Rama's continual assertion that *sādhanā* (personal practice) must be a key component of the modern student's pursuits. Swami Rama also states that psychological therapy addresses only the surface of a client's issues and does not fix the root of the problem. He contrasts this description of modern therapy with the psychology of *yoga* that he finds in the *Gītā*:

> The therapy applied by Sri Kṛṣṇa includes knowledge of the Self, the organization of internal states, the explanation of various methods of *sādhana*, and the way to perform one's duties skillfully and selflessly. Sri Kṛṣṇa does not merely deal with the surface problems or the symptoms presented by Arjuna but with Arjuna's whole being from the beginning to its final destiny.
>
> *(Swami Rama 1984, 53)*

This demonstrates that, according to Swami Rama, while modern psychology is incomplete, *yoga* psychology is both broader and deeper, reaching to the realization of the highest self.

Consistent with his emphasis on *sādhana*, Swami Rama offers instruction for various *yogic* practices that the *Gītā* is not so explicit in addressing. Commenting on *Gītā* 5.27–9, Swami Rama says,

> This passage explains a practical method of *sādhana* that helps one to attain a concentrated mind and then leads him to a higher step of one-pointedness. When the aspirant learns to be still, keeping his head, neck, and trunk straight in a comfortable and steady pose such as *sukhāsana* (the easy pose) or *siddhāsana* (the accomplished pose), and when he practices the same posture every day, the disturbances that arise from the body, such as tremors, twitches, shaking, and jerking, are tamed and brought under control.
>
> *(Swami Rama 1984, 225)*

Here two specific *yoga* postures are recommended. We will encounter some specifics about *yoga* in Anandamurti's commentary as well.

Anandamurti

Our fifth and final commentator, Anandamurti Gurumaa was born Gurpreet Grover in Amritsar, in the Indian province of Punjab, in 1966. Her parents were Sikhs, but they sent their daughter to an English medium convent school. She became a disciple of the Nirmala Sikh Sant Dalel Singh, although Anandamurti later admitted that 'she probably spent less than six hours total in his presence' (Rudert 2017, 113). She was initiated as a renouncer by Dalel Singh, but apparently rather informally, as she simply brought a renouncer's clothing to a meeting with the *sant*, who blessed them. The young woman developed a reputation as a religious teacher, not only in India but also in the Indian diaspora, and she has made regular speaking tours to the US and the UK, which she started doing in 1998. Her fame was greatly enhanced when she started to preach regularly on cable television channels in India around the year 2000. Presently, Anandamurti resides with her disciples at an ashram that she built in Gannaur, Haryana. Preaching mostly in Hindi but sometimes in English as well, Anandamurti's followers are mostly Indians who are educated and well off. Unlike Maharishi, Prabhupada, and Swami Rama, she has a relatively limited following among non-Indians.

At the conclusion of her book-length study of Anandamurti and her movement, Angela Rudert spells out three ways that her teaching is new in comparison with that of other gurus. First is 'her pluralism and her syncretic identity', drawing on various religious sources in her teaching. A second new feature of Anandamurti's work is her commitment to 'gender activism', which includes not only speaking out strongly against sexism but also founding a nongovernmental organization, called Shakti, to provide financial support for girls' education. Finally, there is Anandamurti's 'embrace of new media' (ibid., 186). This chapter will address the first two items of Rudert's list, but not the third, since it is not evident in the content of her commentary on the *Gītā*. However, Anandamurti's book is a reflection of her use of new media; it was published in 2016 by Anandamurti's press, Gurumaa Vani, an English translation of her Hindi commentary on the *Bhagavad-gītā*, which was in turn based on a 71-DVD series of sermons on the *Gītā*.

About Rudert's first novelty, Anandamurti's 'pluralism and her syncretic identity', it is certainly the case that her taste is eclectic in the religious exemplars invoked in her commentary on the *Gītā*. From the Hindu tradition, she celebrates the medieval philosopher Śaṅkara (Anandmurti 2016, 2, 371–2) and devotees from north India (such as Mirabai and Ravidas, 2, 132), Maharashtra (Jñāndev on 2, 49; Tukaram on 1, 39–40), and Bengal (Ramakrishna, 1, 212–14). Anandamurti also tells stories from Sikhism (Guru Nanak on 1, 400–2; Guru Gobind Singh on 1, 443–4), Buddhism (the Buddha, 2, 421–2), Islam (Muhammad on 2, 128; and the Sufis Baba Bulleh Shah and Baba Farid on 2, 156), and Christianity (Jesus, 1, 91). And she mentions the 20th-century gurus J. Krishnamurti (1, 301), B.K.S. Iyengar (1, 437), and George Gurdjieff (1, 423–4). Anandamurti provides a principled justification for this eclecticism when she writes, 'A scripture is a compilation of the words spoken by enlightened, awakened beings. Thus to me the words of Kabir, Rehdas, Buddha, Sufis, the *Gurbani* are as much scriptures as are the *Upaniṣad*s and the *Bhagavad-gītā*' (ibid., 2, 383). Those who do not realize the basic common truth behind this variety make the mistake of arguing against each other: 'So the Hindu zealot brandishes the *Gītā*, the Muslim fanatic venerates the Quran, the devout Christian holds the Bible in the highest esteem and the diehard Sikh passionately cherishes the Gurbani' (ibid., 2, 171–2). That Anandamurti would have the authority to comment on any of this implies that she is among these 'enlightened, awakened beings'. And she does say at one point that

> Knowledge of the substratum i.e. the *Brahman* makes the illusion of this tree-of-*saṁsāra* disappear. I can say that for me the illusion of this gigantic tree of life has ended. And this is every *gyani*'s [a *gyani* or *jñāni* is a 'knower'] reality.
>
> *(ibid., 2, 339)*

About Rudert's second novelty, concerning Anandamurti's 'gender activism', there is criticism of sexism in her commentary and of casteism, too. The guru consistently argues against caste based on birth. About the priest caste, she writes, 'Who is a *brāhmaṇa*? It is not someone who is born in a *brāhmaṇa* family. Our sages have said that the one who has realized *Brahman* is a *brāhmaṇa*' (Anandamurti 2016, 1, 32). Anandamurti goes so far as to argue that some verses in the *Gītā* that appear to praise *brāhmaṇas* are interpolations by self-interested members of that caste. About her discernment of this, she explains that

> The *Bhagavad-gītā* is a very ancient scripture and which supplementary verse was appended in which era – this is an issue for Historians to decide, and I don't claim to be one! Thus it is not in my purview to

> gather substantiating evidence. I can but speak from my own inner inspiration that says Sri Kṛṣṇa cannot put forth anything which is illogical or irrational
>
> *(ibid., 2, 410)*

Even though the commentator admits that she doesn't have the qualifications to undertake a critical study of the development of the *Gītā*, her 'inner inspiration' has convinced her that the *Gītā* cannot contain anything that is 'illogical or irrational'; she implicitly arrogates to herself the authority to determine which verses do not meet that test, including any that appear casteist.

As for sexism, when the *Gītā* (in 9.32) implicitly disparages women (as well as lower-caste men) by affirming that salvation is open *even to them*, Anandamurti excises this verse as, once again, an interpolation (Anandamurti 2016, 2, 125). She does admit ruefully that men have used the *Gītā* to advance their own interests:

> There is no dearth of men who quote the *Gītā* as an endorsement of their superiority – arguing that God is said to be male, in effect, they assert that women should treat men as God and be subservient to them. It is seen world over that men cite their scriptures as a justification for regarding women as inferior to them.
>
> *(ibid., 2, 203–4)*

Anandamurti's critique of sexism is unique among the commentators in this chapter.

About the religious teaching of the *Gītā*, Anandamurti at one point affirms that the text allows for different kinds of religion for different kinds of people:

> In the question put by Arjuna viz. which path is superior – path of *jñāna* [knowledge], path of devotion or path of *karma* [action] *yoga* – the Lord replies that superior or inferior is not the issue, for it is a matter of individual perspective and aptitude.
>
> *(Anandamurti 2016, 1, 423)*

Yet the commentary leans in the direction of the religion of knowledge over that of devotion. One indication of this is that Anandamurti repeatedly argues that when the *Gītā* urges devotion to God, it is not talking about 'the form of Sri Kṛṣṇa' but rather 'the formless cosmic Self' (ibid., 1, 550; but also see 1, 158; 1, 339; 1, 343; 1, 570; 2, 17–18; 2, 13; 2, 196). And in no fewer than three places, Anandamurti stigmatizes devotional verses as interpolated. 'This was done in an attempt to dilute the original pure *Vedānta* knowledge so that it would be more appealing and palatable to those following the path of devotion, the *bhakta*s (devotees) of Lord Kṛṣṇa and Lord Viṣṇu' (ibid., 1, 336; but also 2,131; and 2,196). So apparently her position is that the 'original, pure' *Gītā* is about knowledge, but its devotionalism is derivative and inauthentic. This is definitely not the position of Prabhupada, as we saw earlier in this chapter.

Yoga practice is mandatory at Anandamurti's ashram, and the commentary occasionally includes references to *haṭha yoga*, even in contexts where the original text of the *Gītā* does not appear to be about *yoga*. According to Anandamurti, the benefits of *yoga* are not only spiritual but also physical. Mentioning specific practices, the author writes, '*Sūrya Namaskāra* enhances the functioning of the adrenal, thyroid and parathyroid glands. *Sarvāṇgāsana*, on the other hand, directly improves the functioning of the pineal and pituitary glands' (Anandamurti 2016, 1, 68). The commentator mentions health in other contexts as well, urging her followers to adopt a moderate diet, for example, and reduce stress. There is a certain New Age blending of traditional Indian and modern scientific ideas in other contexts, too. At one point, Anandamurti argues that contemporary scientific techniques were known in ancient India, such as cloning (ibid., 1, 112); also, she insists that Indian 'astrology is not some humbug but an advanced science' (ibid., 2,48). In the conclusion, we will see that a certain mixing of the modern and the traditional is characteristic of all these commentaries.

Some concluding comparisons

What do all these commentaries have to say about the *Bhagavad-gītā*? Taken together, a certain monism is dominant in these works, including an emphasis on the path of knowledge and a tendency to describe the ultimate experience as merging in an impersonal absolute. For some of our commentators, this is tied to an explicit allegiance to the *Advaita Vedānta* of 8th-century philosopher Śaṅkara. We have seen this tie most clearly in the case of Maharishi Mahesh Yogi, whose own guru was a Śaṅkarācārya, the head of a major monastic institution said to have been founded by Śaṅkara. Swami Chinmayananda also regarded himself as a renouncer in the *Advaita* tradition; the commentary of his guru, Sivananda, on the *Gītā* was itself heavily indebted to Śaṅkara. Swami Rama is remembered by his followers as in the Śrī Vidyā Tantric school, but his commentary tends to monism as well. As noted earlier, Anandamurti Gurumaa's guru was not a Hindu at all but a Nirmala Sikh, and yet her commentary runs in the same direction. The clear exception to this monistic trend is A.C. Bhaktivedanta Swami Prabhupada, who attacks the impersonalists, opting instead for devotion to Kṛṣṇa as 'the Supreme Personality of Godhead'. Scholars have noted the predominance of a kind of '*Neo-Vedānta*' in modern India, and in general, these commentaries are evidence of that, Prabhupada excepted (King 1999, 135–42 and passim).

If adherence to *Advaita* could be taken as a kind of traditionalism, there is some modernism in these commentaries on the *Gītā* as well. In a different article, I noted that the modern emphasis on social reform is common in works on the *Gītā* from the first half of the 20th century in their condemnation of the way that caste is practiced in contemporary India (Llewellyn 2019). This trend continues in independent India in most of these commentaries. Chinmayananda, Swami Rama and Anandamurti condemn caste as socially divisive – in spite of what the *Gītā* has to say in favor of caste. Prabhupada commended reverence for *brāhmaṇas* but then initiated his Western disciples as if they were *brāhmaṇas*, since for him devotion trumped caste based on birth. The one exception to this trend is Maharishi, who does not take advantage of references to caste in the *Gītā* to criticize contemporary practice.

Of course, there are other ways that Maharishi's commentary on the *Bhagavad-gītā* is quite modern. This is particularly evident in his contention that the secret to the spiritual realization the *Gītā* describes is transcendental meditation. Since this need be practiced only for a brief period each morning and evening, it is the perfect regimen for the seeker on the go in the busy modern world. Perhaps the most modern commentary here is Swami Rama's, in that it engages with psychotherapy. However, he largely condemns it in favor of psychological insights that he regards as deeper, which are derived in part from the *yoga* tradition. Swami Rama is best known as a *yoga* teacher, and *yoga* is a part of the daily routine at Anandamurti's ashram as well; both of these teachers find opportunities to introduce discussion of *yoga* practices into their commentaries on the *Gītā*. Even though it is rooted in a tradition that is centuries old in South Asia, *yoga* has certainly flourished in the modern era. So there is something that is at once traditional and modern in the relative prominence of *yoga* in some of our commentaries.

Although there is a certain emphasis on monism and of the path of knowledge in these commentaries, they all assume that a follower of the *Bhagavad-gītā* need not be a renouncer but may well be a householder. This arguably reflects the *Gītā*'s own emphasis on righteous action in the world. It also reflects the audience to which our commentators sought to appeal. Although all five were themselves renouncers, their teaching was certainly not limited to renouncers but was intended for a much broader public. One of Chinmayananda's teachers, Swami Tapovan, 'maintained that *Vedānta* should be taught only to a few *sadhu*s [or renouncers] who were qualified and who had left the world'. Disagreeing with him, Chinmayananda concluded that this wisdom 'should be taught to everyone and not to just a select few' (Jacobsen 2013, 447); all of our other four *Gītā* commentators had similar ambitions.

In the first half of the 20th century, the *Bhagavad-gītā* was a subject of commentary by some of the leading religious and political thinkers of that era. Political leaders have not continued to produce substantial works on the *Gītā* in independent India, but we have seen in this chapter that interest in that book has been sustained among major religious figures. The commentaries that we have studied in this chapter show not only continuity but also change. They are by authors whose following is largely Indian, such as Chinmayananda and Anandamurti but also by those who have enjoyed great success in the West, such as Maharishi, Prabhupada, and Swami Rama. Although most of these religious leaders are men, one, Anandamurti, is a woman who has been active on women's issues. Some of our commentators have particularly promoted *yoga* or other specific meditation practices in a way that is at once traditional and new. Even in the 21st century, religious leaders work to ground their teaching, however new, in a book that is two thousand years old, the *Bhagavad-gītā*.

Acknowledgment

I am grateful to my student Lindsey Argo, who wrote the first draft of the sections of this chapter about Maharishi and Swami Rama and who made other suggestions throughout.

Note

1 A reviewer familiar with his thought pointed out to me that Maharishi in his later work added a seventh stage of consciousness, which he called unitary consciousness.

References

Anandmurti, Gurumaa. 2016. *Śrimad Bhagavad-gītā*. 2 vols. Delhi: Guramaa Vani.

Baird, Robert D. 1986. "Swami Bhaktivedanta and the *Bhagavad-gītā* 'As It Is'." In *Modern Indian Interpreters of the Bhagavad-gītā*. Edited by Robert N. Minor, pp. 200–21. Albany: State University of New York Press.

Chinmayananda, Swami. 2016. *The Holy Geeta*. Reprint of the second edition. Mumbai: Central Chinmaya Mission Trust.

Davis, Richard H. 2015. *The Bhagavad-gītā: A Biography*. Princeton: Princeton University Press.

Humes, Cynthia Ann. 2005. "Maharishi Mahesh Yogi: Beyond the TM Technique." In *Gurus in America*. Edited by Thomas A. Forsthoefel and Cynthia Ann Humes, pp. 55–79. Albany: State University of New York Press.

Humes, Cynthia Ann. 2013. "Maharishi Mahesh Yogi and Transcendental Meditation." In *Brill's Encyclopedia of Hinduism*. Edited by Knut A. Jacobsen. Vol. V, pp. 508–14. Leiden: Brill.

Jacobsen, Knut A. 2013. "Chinmayananda and the Chinmaya Mission." In *Brill's Encyclopedia of Hinduism*. Edited by Knut A. Jacobsen. Vol. V, pp. 446–52. Leiden: Brill.

King, Richard. 1999. *Orientalism and Religion: Postcolonial Theory, India and 'the Mystic East'*. London: Routledge.

Llewellyn, J.E. 2004. "Groups and Gurus." In *Contemporary Hinduism: Ritual, Culture, and Practice*. Edited by Robin Rinehart, pp. 213–41. Santa Barbara, CA: ABC-CLIO.

Llewellyn, J.E. 2019. "The Modern *Bhagavad-Gītā*: Caste in Twentieth-Century Commentaries." *International Journal of Hindu Studies*, 23(3) (December): 309–23.

Maharishi, Mahesh Yogi. 1990. *Maharishi Mahesh Yogi on the Bhagavad-gītā: A New Translation and Commentary with Sanskrit Text: Chapters 1 to 6*. London: Arkana. Reprint of the 1967 original.

Miller, David M. 1986. "Swami Sivananda and the *Bhagavad-gītā*." In *Modern Indian Interpreters of the Bhagavad-gītā*. Edited by Robert N. Minor, pp. 173–99. Albany: State University of New York Press.

Prabhupada, A.C. Bhaktivedanta Swami. 1972. *The Bhagavad-gītā as It Is*. Mumbai: Bhaktivedanta Book Trust.

Rama, Swami. 1984. *Perennial Psychology of the Bhagavad-gītā*. Honesdale, PA: Himalayan Institute.

Rudert, Angela. 2017. *Shakti's New Voice: Guru Devotion in a Woman-Led Spiritual Movement*. Lanham, MD: Lexington Books.

Tamal, Krishna Goswami. 2012. *A Living Theology of Kṛṣṇa Bhakti: Essential Teachings of A. C. Bhaktivedanta Swami Prabhupada.* Edited with introduction and conclusion by Graham M. Schweig. New York: Oxford University Press.

Tamal, Krishna Goswami and Ravi M. Gupta. 2005. "Kṛṣṇa and Culture: What Happens When the Lord of Vrindavana Moves to New York City." In *Gurus in America.* Edited by Thomas A. Forsthoefel and Cynthia Ann Humes, pp. 81–95. Albany: State University of New York Press.

Tigunait, Rajmani. 2001. *At the Eleventh Hour: The Biography of Swami Rama.* Honesdale, PA: Himalayan Institute Press.

10

ARJUNA AND ACYUTA

The import of epithets in the *Bhagavad-gītā*

Raj Balkaran

The inaugural verse of the *Bhagavad-gītā* (*Bhg*) has Dhṛtarāṣṭra asking Sañjaya about events on the battlefield, the field of Kuru.[1] Sañjaya had been granted the supernatural gift of remote viewing, empowered to perceive the Kurukṣetra events at great distances, through his mind's eye. The fact that the *Bhg* is relayed *to* one who lacks visual sight (Dhṛtarāṣṭhra) *by* one who is physically absent from the scene he describes is a most clever thematic frame, serving to launch the listener of the *Bhg* into the imagined space of ideals. The *Bhg* is a superlatively structured text, heavily drawing on the chiastic practices innate to Sanskrit frame narratives. It even goes so far as to strategically deploy the epithets of Kṛṣṇa for the sake of this chiastic structure. This chapter engages Bhargava's "Names and Epithets of Kṛṣṇa in the *Bhagavad-gītā*" as a launchpad to demonstrate the *Gītā*'s structural sophistication, focusing on the clever tripartite placement of Kṛṣṇa's epithet Acyuta.

The synergy of the question being asked, the career of the questioner, and the career of the respondent necessarily colour an unfolding Sanskrit narrative. The fact that Arjuna is the son of Indra, for example, will surely come to bear on his role as warrior and his *dharma* to fight in so formidable a fashion. Also, that Kṛṣṇa was sent as an envoy for peace to the Kaurava court is certainly relevant – he knows firsthand that all efforts have been exhausted and that the time for deliberation is behind them. Warfare is their last resort. The natures and careers of each of these characters communicate volumes even before they open their mouths. While exegetical import might be generally drawn from the entire known career of an expositor, an author might opt to emphasize an aspect of that career through use of a specific epithet. An epithet generally refers to a descriptor implemented in the place of a proper name, invoking or conferring a specific attribute to its subject. Harkening to the semantic and thematic meaningfulness of Sanskrit names, I posit that epithets are purposefully deployed. An epithet is able to emphasize the aspect of a character's nature or career which best resonates with the juncture at which it is implemented.

A multitude of appellations for Kṛṣṇa are implemented throughout the *Gītā*.[2] Bhargava informs us during his study of Kṛṣna's appellations that the "name" Kṛṣṇa itself occurs on 12 occasions and that his other common names, Keśava and Govinda, occur on seven and on two occasions respectively. He then proceeds to address Kṛṣṇa's epithets. Bhargava divides Kṛṣṇa's epithets into three categories: first, his patronymics, i.e. Mādhava (descendent of Madhu), Vārṣṇeya (descendent of Vṛṣṇi), and Vāsudeva (descendent of Vasudeva), occurring twice each; second, epithets invoking his martial prowess, i.e. Keśiṇisūdana (slayer of Keśin) occurring once, Janārdarna (destroyer of evil people) occurring on six occasions, and Madhusūdana (slayer of Madhu) occurring on five occasions; and, third, epithets referring to his "moral qualities," i.e. Hṛṣīkeśa (controller of the senses) occurring seven times and Acyuta (which according to Bhargava means "one not deviating from righteousness or not yielding to passions" [Bhargava 1979, 94]), occurring on three occasions.

Through his analysis of Kṛṣṇa's epithets, Bhargava engages the *Gītā* through a diachronic lens, pursuing an epithet import which is *historically* telling. I address his process not necessarily for the sake of challenging the veracity of his conclusions but for the sake of re-examining how he arrives at them. I in fact find his conclusions unfounded, but it is more his methodology which I problematize here: in proceeding to diachronically dissect the *Gītā*, he fails to register the synchronic mastery with which it orchestrates the epithets of Kṛṣṇa. Bhargava notes that it is only in chapters 7–12 that Kṛṣṇa declares his divine supremacy, and it is therefore only in these chapters that Arjuna addresses Kṛṣṇa with divine appellations, such as Puruṣottama, Śāśvata Divya Puruṣa, Sanātana Puruṣa, Purāṇa Puruṣa, Parameśvara, Ādi-deva, Aja, and Ananta. He soundly reasons that these epithets are conspicuously confined to the middle third of the text, as follows:

> Even if it is said that Arjuna was not fully aware of the divine nature of Kṛṣṇa until the latter dwelt upon it at some length in Chapter VII, it does not solve the problem, for in that case he should have addressed Kṛṣṇa as God at least in the last six chapters. On the other hand, having expressed regret in verse 41 of Chapter XI for addressing by his mere name one whose divine nature he did not know before, Arjuna does not feel any compunction in again addressing him as Kṛṣṇa in verse 1 of Chapter XVII.
>
> *(Bhargava 1979)*

I agree with him in that "metrical considerations, of course, do not stand in the way of such a use, for Puruṣottama or Parameśvara could well have been used in place of Madhusūdana which occurs as many as four times in the earlier chapters" (Bhargava 1979). Based on this observation of the distribution of epithets in the text, he makes the hazardous leap that "the only inevitable conclusion" (Bhargava 1979) to be made is that the middle six chapters of the *Gītā* are interpolations from a later time, when Kṛṣṇa was deified, and that the first and last thirds comprise the more authentic strata of the text, wherein Kṛṣṇa was a "human teacher" (Bhargava 1979). He elsewhere notes that "because of his reverence for

Kṛṣṇa as a great teacher, Arjuna has also addressed him twice as prabhu, Master or Lord (XI.4; XIV.21)" (Bhargava 1979, 94). Yet, of course, Prabhu carries with it divine association, perhaps no less than with *Īśvara*, both of which are common appellations of God. But it is understandable why Barghava would opt to de-emphasize the divine aspect of this appellation given that is straddles the middle and the third (and final) parts of the *Gītā*, occurring in chapters 11 and 14.

The misguided notion that older, "more-original" versions of texts such as the *Gītā* were necessarily markedly less "sectarian" (in contrast to their fallen-from-grace extant corruption, which is all we have to work with) is not only corrosive to the final work we have in hand but also intellectually perilous. At what point during the process of churning from the *Gītā*'s "original form" to its present from did the non-sectarian milk become sectarian butter? In which portions of the *Gītā* are Kṛṣṇa sufficiently bereft of divine stature as to be said to assuredly comprise the original, human character before succumbing to sectarian divinization? The milk did not become butter instantly; nor could the butter have been produced from anything absent within the "original" milk. Might we actually envisage such a one capable of the sagacious profundity elucidated in the chapter 2 as not inspiring awe, and commanding reverence, as a god among men as it were? From the outset, Kṛṣṇa speaks from the perspective of one who has realized the infinite beyond the finite fluctuations of phenomenal experience, and such a one can scarcely be accurately described as strictly a human. From the genesis of his exposition,[3] Kṛṣṇa conveys depths of experience which arguably a mere mortal could not possess, and despite our anachronistic deliberation over whether the status of God incarnate can be rightly applied to him throughout the work, it is clear whenever he opens his mouth that the *Gītā* presents us with a figure who is nothing short of titanic in his range and depth of insight. Theological appropriation notwithstanding, as one might aptly refer to as 'divine' a powerful piece of music, a transformative landscape, or the ways of a small child, never was there a time when the *Gītā*'s Kṛṣṇa was not divine.

Let us return to Bhargava's quandary: "why *is* it that Arjuna addresses Kṛṣṇa by words signifying God, such as *Puruṣottama* or *Parameśvara*, only in the intervening six chapters of the *Bhagavad-gītā* and not in the preceding or succeeding ones?"[4] The question is not whether the epithets used are intentionally arranged but rather what the intention behind their arrangement was. Or perhaps put in terms more appropriate to the study at hand (for who can know the intentions of the author of a single contemporary work, much less those of the inter-generational armada of authors who produced the *Gītā*), how do these epithets structurally function within the synchronic chambers of the text? The conspicuity of the clustering of divinized epithets in the middle third of the text is not telling of an absence of awareness but rather of a deliberate decision.

To establish third-portions of the text, one must *begin* with 18 chapters rather than end up there. Arjuna refers to Kṛṣṇa as God only in the middle of the *Gītā*: if we take the chapters of the *Gītā* to be representative of the parvans of *Mahābhārata* as a whole (since both the *Gītā*'s chapter and the *Mahābhārata*'s parvans both number 18), then it is the middle third of the *Gītā* which mimics the war itself (occurring in the middle third of the *Mahābhātata*'s parvans), during the course of which Kṛṣṇa and Arjuna move in the same chariot as one being and during which time Kṛṣṇa reveals his divinity to Arjuna. It is perhaps part of the design of the authors to have Kṛṣṇa do so during the middle third of the *Gītā*, whereas one might opt to save this climax for its conclusion.[5] It is also in the same third, in proximity with the revelation of his divine form, that the authors address Kṛṣṇa as Yogin, Yogeśvara, and Mahāyogeśvara – and these epithets are again echoed in the final chapter (10.17, 11.4, 11.9, 18.75, and 18.78). It is specifically so that they might be showcased through chiastic enframement that the most 'divine' portions of Kṛṣṇa's exposition find themselves squarely in the heart of the text. The first and last third of the *Mahābhārata* might be viewed as preceding and succeeding narrative associates which frame the middle third, highlighting the war itself, and the same might be said of Kṛṣṇa's overt divinity with respect to the *Gītā*.

It is doubtful that the authors of the *Gītā* responsible for the verses of the "middle intervening chapters" would not have been cognizant of Bhargava's observation. Had they intended to introduce a new identity to Kṛṣṇa's character in the form of a brand-new series of epithets (e.g. Parameśvara), would they have conspicuously and unconvincingly clustered that introduction into a specific space rather than spread it around in a more organic fashion? This would have been easily accomplished since Parameśvara is metrically interchangeable with Madhusūdana, used so often throughout the *Gītā*. Even if we wish to view these authors as forgers, Trojan-horsing theology into an innately non-sectarian text, let us not underestimate their literary prowess. Based on the verses they have produced, they would be capable of a far more seamless forgery, if that were indeed their intent.

The epithets employed throughout the *Gītā* are certainly not whimsical, and careful analysis of which ones are used in which contexts will necessarily prove illumining. The *Gītā* itself draws our attention to the importance of appellations. During the revelation of Kṛṣṇa's cosmic form (the climax of the material conveying his divine nature), the bedazzled Arjuna actually expresses regret for the familiarity with which he has this far addressed the Lord. Having just beheld Kṛṣṇa's terrifying cosmic form and declaring aloud that Kṛṣṇa is one with everything, the remorseful Arjuna also declares,

> For whatever I uttered rashly, imagining you my equal, calling "Hey Kṛṣṇa! Hey Yadava! Hey friend!" ignorant of your greatness, through familiarity, or out of affection – And as if in joke I treated you improperly when it came to sport, rest, sitting, or eating, alone or even in public, Achyuta – I ask you, the Immeasurable, forgiveness.[6]

He repents for addressing Kṛṣṇa in a mundane manner, exhibiting ignorance of his divine identity. While commenting on the ineptitude of his previous appellations, Arjuna addresses the Lord as Acyuta. While during his analysis, Bhargava deems it a designation of moral fortitude, glossing it as "one not deviating from righteousness or not yielding to passions" (Bhargava 1979, 94), clearly the appellation Acyuta here carries with it the divine association of one who is imperishable and who is not merely unfallen but 'unfellable'. Given that this appellation occurs at the heart of Kṛṣṇa's revelation of divinity, one might be tempted to dismiss it as a 'later sectarian interpolation'. And while it may well in fact be so, it's far more than that with respect to the structure of the *Gītā* as a whole. Diachronically dismissing this appellation would thoughtlessly overlook the mechanics of authorship innate to the production of the *Gītā* as we have it, unravelling its mastery before even registering it. Not only is the epithet Acyuta not isolated to the "interpolated" heart of the text; it occurs at two other junctures, which hold tremendous import for its significance.

Of the numerous epithets by which Kṛṣṇa is addressed, Arjuna choses to address him as Acyuta the *first* time he opens his mouth in the text, saying, "Achyuta, draw up my chariot between the two armies."[7] The importance of this frame is dually significant: it is both the first time an epithet is used and the first line of the conversational exchange between Kṛṣṇa and Arjuna comprising the *Bhg.* Similarly, in the *last* line of their exchange, Arjuna again addresses Kṛṣṇa as Acyuta, declaring, "My delusion has been obliterated, and through your grace, Achyuta, I have remembered myself. I stand, my doubt dispelled. I shall do as you say."[8] The *only* three times that this epithet appears in the *Gītā* are directly after the cosmic form (when Arjuna realizes Kṛṣṇa's divinity) where epithets themselves are the topic of conversation, at the beginning of Arjuna's and Kṛṣṇa's *saṃvāda*, and at the end of their *saṃvāda*. Therefore, not only are all of Kṛṣṇa's numerous epithets used in the *Gītā* framed by this one (which is first and last among them), but also Arjuna's entire interlocution is framed by this one insofar as he addresses Kṛṣṇa as Acyuta in the last verse of his discourse. Acyuta is not only the first and the last of the Kṛṣṇa's epithets but also the foremost, since Arjuna uses it (and only it) while admonishing the use of inappropriate epithets. Given the hermeneutic principles established in this chapter, the authors of the *Gītā* clearly wish to make known the significance of this epithet. Consequently, that the thematic airbrushing innate to the Acyuta placement ever occurred suggests that the latest of the *Gītā*'s authors surveyed the text as a whole. We've established based on placement *that* the appellation Acyuta is meaningful. Now, *what* does it mean? To do justice to this question, let us turn to the narrative impetus of the *Gītā*,[9] paying special attention to the problem it purports to address.

Chapter 1 presents us with the primary problem to be resolved: upon beholding the loved ones who populate the enemy forces, the mighty Arjuna, having just partaken in an electrifying sounding of conchs to announce the onset of war, laments:

> Kṛṣṇa, when I see my own people, eager to fight, on the brink, my limbs grow heavy, and my mouth is parched, my body trembles, and my hair bristles, my bow, Gandiva, falls from my hand, my skin's on fire, I can no longer stand – my mind is reeling. . . . It would be better for me if Dhṛtarāṣṭra's armed men were to kill me in battle, unresisting and unarmed.
>
> (Bhg *1.28–46) (Johnson 1994, 5–6)*

Arjuna is rendered impotent, unable to physically perform as a warrior. His inability to do so compromises the welfare of society, which requires protection from its current state of imperilment. *Dharma*, already crippled with old age, shall surely suffer destruction if Arjuna refuses to stand up and fight: without his might, the forces of righteousness personified by the *Pāṇḍavas* cannot prevail. On the gross, outer, immediate level, the problem presented is that Arjuna flaccidly sinks into his chariot, unable to physically perform, just moments after partaking in the ritual consecration of the sacrifice of war.

Chapter 2 highlights the subtler dimension of this primary problem, detailing a second, interrelated, inner layer of Arjuna's conundrum. The narrative takes us from the physical-social realm into the emotional-mental realm. Thus, the chapter's initial frame consists of Kṛṣṇa addressing an Arjuna whose eyes brim with tears (2.1). Kṛṣṇa lovingly chastises him, in hopes of rousing him out of his despondency (2.2–3), because at this point, the despondency is the main problem. In response, Arjuna conveys his anguished confusion as to what he ought to do. He is bewildered, and deeply suffering, and it is this state of suffering which brings him to his knees before Kṛṣṇa, in search of peace of mind (2.4–8). He reiterates the problem of the impetus in declaring that he will not fight (2.9); however, in seeking clarity and guidance, he gives Kṛṣṇa licence to address the underlying issue: it is not such that he is unwilling to fight, but rather, he cannot bring himself to fight, being 'down and out' emotionally. It is at this point that Kṛṣṇa peers out from beneath his cousin cap and reveals his guru persona, offering a lengthy discourse from the perspective of the wise (2.10).

The problem presented in chapter 1 is an outer one – Arjuna is unable to fight, unable to protect the righteous and punish the wicked, unable to stand beside his brothers when they need him most, and indeed unable to stand at all. In chapter 2, however, we are given access to the extent to which that outer social problem is instigated by an inner, ethical, emotional, psychospiritual one. Viewed through these lenses, the ethical and spiritual discourses in the *Gītā*, then, promise on one level to address the social problem, enabling the warrior to fight. But to do so, they must first assuage Arjuna's anguish. This dimension details great suffering and occasions a vulnerable and despairing Arjuna to seek refuge in the supportive wisdom of Kṛṣṇa. It is therefore Arjuna's turmoil which directly occasions Kṛṣṇa's exposition.

At the conclusion of his exposition, Kṛṣṇa asks, "Pārtha, have you listened to this, single-mindedly? Dhanañjaya, has your delusion born of ignorance been dispelled?" (18.72). In so doing, he refers to Arjuna's suffering, which frames the discourse. However, Arjuna's disheartenment is only the shadow of the *Gītā*'s impetus: the primary narrative problem is Arjuna's despondency. Arjuna's response is therefore telling. The densely packed verse[10] concludes the exchange between Kṛṣṇa and Arjuna and efficiently serves as the *Gītā*'s terminal frame. Over the course of this single verse, Arjuna does the following:

1 Resolves the inner exposition of the *Gītā*, saying
"through your grace, I have remembered myself" (*smṛtir labdhā . . . mayā*), which is probably a double-entendre on *smṛti*, connoting that he has attained the *smṛti* literature of the *Gītā*'s teachings

2 Resolves the emotional impetus in declaring
"my delusion has been obliterated; my doubt dispelled"
(*naṣṭo mohaḥ . . . gata-saṁdehaḥ*)

3 Regains his physical ability and resolves the social problem, declaring
"I stand [and] shall act in accordance to your counsel"
(*sthito 'asmi . . . kariṣye vacanaṁ tava*).

All of the words in this rich Sanskrit verse have been accounted for but one: the vocative, Acyuta. Which dimension of the narrative does this epithet best invoke – Arjuna's physical and social dilemma, his emotional one, or his ethical one?

The problem presented in the *Gītā* is a warrior sinking in his chariot at the onset of battle. In his lament in chapter 2, Arjuna mentions "my limbs grow heavy, and my mouth is parched, my body trembles, and my hair bristles, my bow, Gāṇḍīva, falls from my hand, my skin's on fire, I can no longer stand" (2.28–46). He is unable to physically fight, and so great is his grief that he is unable to even physically stand. Therefore, chapter 1 concludes with a summary of the dilemma: Saṃjaya informs us that "Having spoken thus on the field of conflict, Arjuna sank down into the chariot, letting slip his bow and arrow, his mind distracted with grief" (2.47). It is therefore Kṛṣṇa's mission to get Arjuna to physically stand and engage in combat. In chapter 2, where Kṛṣṇa addresses Arjuna's grief, his first advice reads: "Abandon this base, inner weakness. Get up, Incinerator of the Foe!" (2.2–3). Similarly, even in the midst of chapter 2, he returns to this thesis to say "So, rise, son of Kunti, determined to fight" (2.37). Although two entire chapters of abstract philosophy have elapsed, Kṛṣṇa ends chapter 4 by again imploring Arjuna to fight. However, this time, he explicitly ties the call to arms to a call to emotional and spiritual awareness: "therefore, having severed with the blade of knowledge this doubt of yours, which stems from ignorance, and is fixed in the heart, act with discipline, Bharata – arise!" (uttiṣṭha; 4.42). Also, during chapter 11, Kṛṣṇa again demands Arjuna "therefore arise!" (11.33 *tasmād uttiṣṭha*) immediately following the revelation of his cosmic form. Kṛṣṇa's call to rise therefore cleverly transcends all dimensions of the *Gītā*'s narrative, in that Arjuna has fallen in all senses yet Kṛṣṇa as Acyuta most certainly has not.

The symbolism of the epithet Acyuta is most elegant: not only is Kṛṣṇa unfallen in a spiritual sense (in being undisturbed, permanently unshaken and unshakable, and indeed imperishable), but he also reveals his imperishable nature to compel Arjuna to become physically unfallen, commanding him throughout to stand and fight. The dilemma which frames the *Gītā* consists of an Arjuna who, upon standing erect and summoning the onset of war by blowing his conch alongside his brethren, falls hopelessly into despair, sinking into his chariot. Only his unfallen charioteer, Acyuta, can succeed in inspiring him to stand up and fight – in short, to return to his own upstanding, unfallen state. Kṛṣṇa calls Arjuna to return to his original nature in a spiritual sense but also, and more importantly for the protection of *dharma*, to return to his original, unfallen nature in a physical sense. Arjuna first uses the appellation Acyuta while the scene is being set, and he and Kṛṣṇa have just ritually consecrated the war through the sounding of their mighty conchs. Arjuna next uses it immediately after the divine vision of Kṛṣṇa's cosmic form. And Arjuna finally uses it once he is again ready to stand and fight, having returned to the state he was in at the beginning of the *Gītā*. For this reason, both their entire discourse (and consequently all of Kṛṣṇa's epithets occurring in it) are framed by Arjuna's first and final address to Kṛṣṇa, honouring him as Acyuta. Supported by the unfallen Kṛṣṇa, Arjuna is empowered to again become physically, emotionally, and spiritually upstanding.

Notes

1 Dharma-kṣetre kuru-kṣetre samavetā yuyutsavaḥ | māmakāḥ pāṇḍavāś caiva kim akurvata Sañjaya ||

2 For an exhaustive list of epithets, see (Bhargava 1979).

3 1.11–12:

> You utter wise words, yet you have been mourning those who should not be mourned; the truly wise do not grieve for the living or the dead. There was never a time when I was not, or you. Or these rulers of men. Nor will there ever be a time when we shall cease to be, all of us hereafter.

4 (Bhargava 1979, 95), italics my own.

5 For a full treatment on the significance of the middle section in chiastic composition, see Mary Douglas's *Thinking in Circles* (Douglas 2007).

6 *Bhg* 11.41–2 (Johnson 1994, 52).

7 1.21 *senayor ubhayor madhye rathaṁ sthāpaya me 'cyuta*. See (Johnson 1994, 4).

8 18.73 *naṣṭo mohaḥ smṛtir labdhā tvat-prasādān mayācyuta | sthito 'smi gatasandehaḥ kariṣye vacanaṁ tava*. See (Johnson 1994, 81). As an important aside, let us not mistake here that Arjuna is blindly acting according to Kṛṣṇa's dictates – a few verses earlier, Kṛṣṇa specifically tells him to act as he desires. He does what Kṛṣṇa says *presumably because* he sees the wisdom in it.

9 The impetus touched on here is actually the tip of the iceberg of a chiastic design proper to the *Bhg*. For a more detailed treatment of this, see (Balkaran 2019, 88–101).

10

> *naṣṭo mohaḥ smṛtir labdhā tvatprasādān mayācyuta |*
> *sthito 'asmi gata-samdehaḥ kariṣye vacanam tava ||*
> *(Bhg 18.73).*

Works Cited

Balkaran, Raj. 2019. *The Goddess and The King in Indian Myth: Ring Composition, Royal Power, and the Dharmic Double Helix*. London: Routledge.

Bhargava, P.L. 1979. "Names and Epithets of Kṛṣṇa in the *Bhagavadgītā*." *Indologica Taurinensia*, VII(7): 93–6.

Douglas, Mary. 2007. *Thinking in Circles: An Essay on Ring Composition*. New Haven: Yale University Press.

Johnson, W.J. (trans.). 1994. *The Bhagavad-gītā*. New York: Oxford University Press.

INDEX

Printed in Australia
AUHW021650260922
369422AU00012B/61